Rebel Without a Clue
- The Jester's Tale

Roger Crawford

 New Generation Publishing

For Heather, wherever I may find her

Where are you this moment?
Only in my dreams.
You're missing, but you're always
A heartbeat from me.
I'm lost now without you,
I don't know where you are.
I keep watching, I keep hoping,
But time keeps us apart.

Is there a way I can find you,
Is there a sign I should know,
Is there a road I could follow
To bring you back home?

Excerpt from *'If I could be where you are'*
By Enya, from her album 'Amarantine'

DEDICATIONS

To my mother and father, who made me
To my adopted mother and father, who made me what I am
To my wife Rosa, who has stood by me through some very difficult
times

*Dorothy Banting, my birth mother,
taken around 2005*

*Elizabeth Williamson and dog Ginger,
in 1930. She became my Adoptive Mum*

*Charles Crawford in the 1930's,
who married Elizabeth just
before the War and was my
adoptive Dad.*

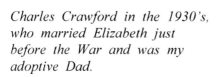

ACKNOWLEDGMENTS

To Ray Barry, who persuaded me to stand for election in 2010, and to my friend George Standen who acted as my agent in the campaign.

To Nigel Ace, who supported and encouraged me to campaign on all fronts.

To everyone who has supported and helped me over ten years.

And to Judge Janet Case of Chester, who restored some of my faith in the British Justice system.

NOT EVER FORGETTING

Judge Michael Payne of Oxford combined Court, who proved to me beyond any shadow of doubt that the Family Court needs reform, and inspired me to join the Father's movement. . . . .

...and also Pamela Hodgkins of the charity NORCAP, who showed me that even though someone may say that they work for 'truth, reconciliation and hope', they do not necessarily believe in it or think any individual worthy of it.

I am only one man
I can only do what one man can do
But what one man can do, I will.
I would rather be criticised for doing something wrong
Than criticised for not doing anything at all.

Anon.

IN MEMORY OF W. GEORGE STANDEN

George, my election agent and friend, passed away shortly before Christmas 2014. I knew him only in the latter years of his life. I first met him at a Fathers 4 Justice meeting in Reading; he was still able to walk a little then but within eighteen months was completely housebound. At the meeting in Reading he asked if anyone might help him in his campaign for justice for his son and I had a quiet word with him afterwards, agreeing to help if I could. George actually helped me far more than I could ever help him. His indomitable spirit overcame all the worst that his failing physical powers could throw at him, and in this he was helped in no small measure by his main carer, Sarah. Sarah the carer certainly lived up to her title. George helped prepare my election leaflets and did most of the background work associated with standing for election, and was also my main contact when I needed publicity for the rooftop demos. Unfailingly courteous and considerate, with many a wise word for me; I miss him.

REBEL WITHOUT A CLUE

PREFACE

This book was originally going to be about my experiences in the Oxford Family Court, which led me to go protesting on various roofs and campaign for the 'Equal Parenting Alliance' Party in the 2010 General Election, in Oxford East. I had been encouraged to write it by several people, but it seemed churlish of me to only write about the worst experience of my life (in that Court) when I have had such a charmed life and had such good fortune. I wanted to acknowledge this, and the many good people who have enhanced my years of life. So it gradually became more autobiographical. I trust it is humorous and interesting enough; I have enjoyed writing it. I hope that you enjoy reading it.

I would like to take the opportunity of thanking everyone who has contributed to this book, especially Baroness Agnes von Mehren who has proof-read it and offered sage advice; Vicky Haigh; Pam Wilson of the Grandparent's Action Group; Rosy Stanesby of Children 4 Justice; Hilary Lawson; and Natasha Phillips of the 'Researching Reform' website. I would like to put on record my appreciation of the help, support and friendship I have received from these and so many others over many a long year.

PRELUDE PART 1

I'm sixty-four as I write this. I was born in the early autumn of 1948, which, according to one survey, was the best year of all in which to be born. I don't dispute it; compared with children today, we had enormous freedoms despite our very strict parents (by today's standards). And compared with many children brought up in earlier years, we were well-fed and well-clothed. We were of a generation who experienced life climbing trees, messing about in streams, making catapults, riding bikes on the pavements, standing on the ends of platforms train-spotting and getting covered in smuts, talking to the bargees on the Grand Union Canal, imagining travelling to far-off lands whilst sat in a dustbin lid in the back yard. We even thought of jetting off into Space on a contraption made out of old bicycles and other rubbish.

We felt very naughty playing 'doctors and nurses', having midnight feasts which included drinking lots of 'Cydrax', and then having farting competitions. One or two of us even tried to set light to them, until someone suffered a backfire. We never had a car, so we didn't miss one; no TV so we didn't miss that; no mobiles, I-pads, computers, etc. etc. But we had books, the radio, (or wireless as we called it) and our vivid imaginations. To illustrate this, I developed the theme of flying off into space in something resembling a dustbin, and, inspired by reading an early Patrick Moore book on astronomy, wrote my own 'Space Travel Book' in 1957. It is amusing (well, to me anyway!) to read in childish writing the various rules I devised for the spacecraft. Under the heading 'Fights in the Spaceship' I've written: 'Fights in the Spaceship are Prohibited. Fights may cause damage, or even set a room on fire; or they may disturb the driver and the spaceship will crash into a meteor, or a planet, a moon, perhaps even into a star and then we will probably get frizzled up. Fights, also, will probably disturb the Captain. So please don't fight.' There's even a rule about taking snuff. 'Please don't use snuff, either, because it makes you sneeze, and will distract the driver and Captain from their attention.' And 'Vacume [sic] Cleaners'. 'In a spaceship, vacuum cleaners are wind-up, because there is no electricity in Space. Of course, they do the job more slowly, but we can't help that'.

For our parents, life was hard. There was still rationing, right into the early fifties on some items, and for men in particular the working day was a long one. Most women were more-or-less tied to the house and especially, to the kitchen. There were still plenty of slum properties, though I wasn't brought up in one.

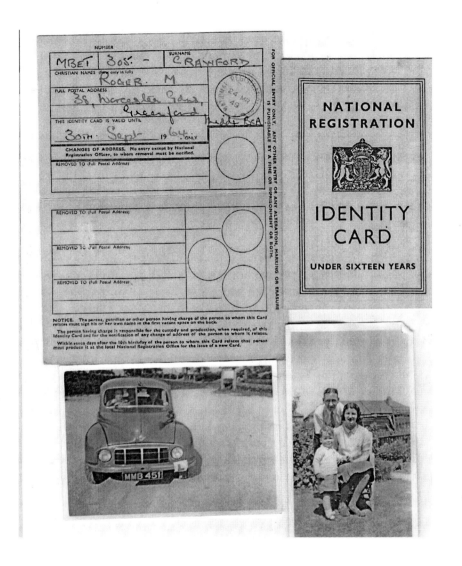

Pictures from childhood: my Identity Card, Auntie Muriel's Morris Minor, Dad, Mum and me in 1951. The car's number plate would be worth a few bob now!

Coal fires in every room led to a lot of work and a lot of dust. So, adults had far less 'freedom' than now, but we kids had a lot more. It was a great time to be a kid.

I was adopted as a baby. My birth parents (unusually in those days, they weren't married) already had one boy when I was conceived and they were extremely poor. It was decided that I would have a better chance in life if I were adopted. Having me adopted was a totally selfless act on behalf of my mother (in particular), but it upset her so much that she determined that if there were any more children, no matter how poor they were, she'd keep them. I later heard that she had tried to get me back, but failed. There were more; four more. And she kept her resolve, so I was the only one of her children to be adopted.

My new parents were unable to have children themselves. I believe that the tables were turned a little; it was my adopted Dad I think who really wanted children, my mother not so keen. She did a great job of raising me though, and there is no doubt I had a privileged childhood compared to my birth siblings.

My 'new' Mum came from a very respectable, upright, uptight, Victorian family. Her father was an area manager for W.H. Smith & Sons in Newcastle-upon-Tyne. 'New' Dad had come from a hard-working, lower-middle-class background and had been brought up in Chester. He had worked his way up from the factory floor in the Iron and Steel industry, working at Shotton in Flint, and by the time I appeared on the scene, had moved with Mum to London and worked for the British Iron and Steel Research Association. Later, he moved on to become an editor of Steel Times, with his offices in John Adam Street in the centre of London.

As a result of all this, I was brought up in a typical nineteen-thirties 'semi' in Worcester Gardens, Greenford, West London. You could see the J. Lyons factory from my bedroom window, and wake up to smell the coffee! You could just glimpse the steam trains on the line from Paddington to Birmingham, too.

I spent quite a lot of time looking out of this window as I was always getting into (minor) trouble and being sent to my room. One summer's day I had the window wide open and a sparrow alighted on the bars across the window (I believe they were put there to stop me falling out) with something caught in its foot. The bird displayed no fear of me, and I shouted down to Dad that there was a bird in my room. He came up, and couldn't believe his eyes to see this little sparrow sitting, bold as brass, on the window bars. 'He wants me to help him' said Dad and gently offered his arm to the bird.

I watched spellbound as the bird fluttered on to his arm and lifted its foot. Dad was quite often rather clumsy with animals (and children!) but on this occasion he was extremely careful and very gently removed the offending sticky bit of gravel that was lodged in the bird's foot before placing the bird back on the window bar. The bird chirruped its thanks and flew off - I've never forgotten that. Later we learned it had visited other houses but had been ushered out.

It was a neighbourly street. Desperately dull to look at, just a narrow, straight road, flanked with these semis, yet as friendly - at least for us kids - as any back-to-back street up north. I can just remember the street party we had to celebrate the Coronation of Elizabeth in 1953, and also crowding round our neighbour's television set to watch the ceremony - one of two T.V.s in the whole street. Everyone, it seemed, left their doors open in the summer and neighbours would pop in and out, usually to borrow something. The doors were never locked, except at night. People looked out for each other; no-one was worried about burglaries as there was nothing much to steal!

People go on today about 'The Gay Community' or the 'Black Community' or 'the Travelling Community'. We just were a community. We were often told to 'get out of the house and don't come back until tea-time'. Someone would always see us and know where we were and what we were up to. Today we have 'neighbourhood watch', where if anyone sees a few kids playing in the street it results in a call to the police and probably a visit from social services. Compare and contrast. When my little friend, Jennifer, died of leukaemia at around the age of seven, the whole street rallied round and packed St. Barnabus' Church for her funeral. In my opinion, far better than any 'counselling' that seems compulsory today. When Mum heard the news, she came up to tell me (I think I was in bed with a chest infection) and very gently gave me the news. I remember this vividly for two reasons - one, Mum never spoke to me gently. And two, I hadn't known Jennifer was so ill. I don't remember crying, and I think I just accepted it, though I did miss her.

We walked to school, of course. I went to Wood End Infants on Whitton Avenue. This was on the other side of a main road to us, so there was a zebra crossing and a lollipop lady; initially Mum came with me but then trusted me to walk on my own or with my friends.

Our teacher was Mrs. Oliver, who seemed to take a shine to me and sometimes came home with me at lunchtime. I had described the flowers in our garden to her and she came to see them and talk to Mum. She probably expressed her concern about my lack of academic ability but I was oblivious to that.

I acquired the nickname 'Dreamy Daniel' as I was always in a world of my own. Mum and Dad wanted me to be academically bright, so tried to instil into me the need to learn, usually involving The Beacon Book of Arithmetic as maths was my very worst subject. It didn't work, but I learned reading at an early age and the first book I read without help was one called 'Michael Drives the Car' - anyone remember it?

Class of '56. My class at Wood End Infants School, I'm Second in from top left. Note how happy we all seem to be - except for the teacher!

There was a lot of corporal punishment in those days. Mum was very tall and couldn't be bothered to bend down to slap the back of my legs, so she picked me up by my hair with one hand and slapped the back of my legs with the other. At school, board rubbers were thrown at us, sticks of chalk, slippers - almost anything. We got pretty adept at dodging these missiles, which often hit the child behind instead. I don't think I, or any of the others, have been 'mentally scarred' or 'traumatised' by all this, but I leave it to others to judge. Perhaps the kids behind me were!

Mum and Dad adopted another baby when I was three. My first memories of him are of him wailing, kicking and screaming as he was handed over and I was thinking 'I don't like this!'. They called him Antony and almost from the word go we scrapped like cat and dog. In later life we were as good as estranged, but when he fell on hard times a few years ago I'm pleased to say we were reconciled, and it is with great sadness that I have to relate he died in February 2012. When Mum died a few years earlier, we had come across his adoption details. Compared with adopting today, it was so simple. Mum received a letter from the relevant authority saying that they'd just received this baby and would she like to come and see him. 'If you like the look of him, you can take him home with you'. And that was it. She did.

Portrait photo of Antony and me done by Sopers of Harrow (a department store) approx. 1954.

Mum was very religious. Dad wasn't, particularly, but Mum was the forceful one in their marriage and we had to attend the 'Gospel Hall' in Oldfield Lane, right by the little old hump-backed bridge over the canal, every Sunday afternoon.

Both my brother and I were united in our loathing of this, and bunked-off it once. We were missed, and reported; we'd forgotten that Dad came to collect us afterwards! He always took us for a walk along the canal and over Horsenden Hill if the weather was fine, which I absolutely loved, but on this occasion we were marched straight home and sent to bed with no tea. Dad and I often picked armfuls of wild flowers (common ones like cow-parsley) and he showed me how to dry and press them and put them in a book. He was a bit over-zealous with his maths tuition I think but he instilled in me a deep love of nature, which has been a constant source of joy throughout my life and a comfort even in my darkest moments.

In the winter of 1952 there was the infamous great smog of London, caused by a high pressure system with cold, still air and the mist thereby created mingled with the smoke of thousands of coal fires, factory chimneys and steam trains to form a gassy-smelling yellow blanket of fog. You could hardly see your hand in front of your face.

Being prone to chest infections, mum kept me indoors but you could still taste the evil sooty smog inside.

It went on for days and I have heard it said that it was responsible for more deaths than the Blitz. As a result of this, the Government quickly passed the Clean Air Act which compelled people to burn only smokeless fuels. I was lucky to escape with a mere chesty cough.

No account of my early life would be complete without mentioning the magic of steam trains. Mum quite often used to shop at Ealing Broadway (there was a department store called Bentalls there, where she liked to shop) and we walked down to Greenford Station on the Central Line to get the little push-pull train which ran to Ealing. Greenford Station is quite elevated and you could see the plume of steam and smoke making its way towards the station from quite a distance.

As the fussy little tank engine brought in its one or two-coach train I always jumped up and down with excitement and was enthralled with every minute of the journey. When we got to Ealing Broadway station I raced along to see the engine take water. One day I had just got alongside the engine when it suddenly let off steam, which terrified me, and Mum eventually found me, shaking with fear and crying, at the top of the steps leading to the exit. I got a wallop for 'running away'. When I was a little older, she left me to look after Antony (my brother) in the park overlooking the railway lines whilst she went shopping. There was a constant procession of gleaming green locomotives with copper-capped fittings and long passenger or freight trains, many of the engines with names, 'Grange' 'Hall' 'Manor' 'County' 'Castle' or 'King' - total magic. It was lucky Antony didn't wander off because I would never have missed him. In fact I probably would have encouraged him to.

Mum's parents still lived in Tynemouth and we occasionally went by train to visit them. They lived in a large Victorian house not far from the sea-front. My first sight of the sea was on my first visit there, and I couldn't wait to go down to it. Racing into the water I suddenly froze (literally) - God, it was cold! This must have been my very first serious taste of disillusionment. I refused to go in ever again. But my memories of Tyneside are warm ones; the bustle of the fish markets; watching the huge ships sailing down the coaly River Tyne towards the sea, piloted by little tug-boats; the cranes loading and unloading goods from ship to rail and vice-versa; and above all, the friendliness of the people. All the buses had the simple advertisement 'Shop at Binns' on them, and Mum seemed so happy to be back 'home'. I got walloped less often in Newcastle.

Later, Grandpa and Grandma moved to a bungalow in Cullercoats, just up the coast from Tynemouth. And as Grandma became more frail, she always seemed to be falling and injuring herself, needing Mum and us boys to visit and look after her. I missed so much school! And, best of all, we travelled up to Newcastle on the 10 a.m. departure from King's Cross - the 'Flying Scotsman'. This was invariably headed by what I now know was an 'A4' class loco - a 'streak'. These were streamlined locomotives, and they had a gorgeous chime whistle. They were fast and glamorous. We were served coffee in our compartment, and then ate in the restaurant car. I felt very grown-up drinking my tonic water, complete with ice and lemon, with my meal.

We were met by Mum's brother, my Uncle John, at Newcastle station. I loved him. I always took a 'Dinky Toy' with me and as he talked to my mother he would examine it constantly, whilst smoking his pipe. I've loved the smell of pipe-smoke ever since. When we went home, he always gave Antony and me a half-crown each, which was quite a bit for young boys at that time.

Later, I learned he'd been the chairman of the Ports of Tyne Authority, and received an OBE for his work, but my memory of him is of a benign and very gentle Uncle, a completely self-effacing man of unfailing courtesy. Typically of him, he declined the offer of going to receive his OBE from the Palace as his wife, Mary, was not well. I have the letters pleading with him to come, but no, he received his medal by post with no ceremony. 'Don't forget to thank the engine driver when you get to King's Cross' he said. I never forgot. And once was rewarded by an invitation into the cab. No boy could have ever asked for more.

PRELUDE PART II

At the very end of the fifties, it was decided that Grandma and Grandpa could no longer live on their own and should come and live with us. This would mean a move to a larger house. I didn't want to leave Greenford and all my friends there, and these included our adult neighbours, and I'm sure I played-up a bit. I also didn't want to stop travelling on the 'Flying Scotsman'!

I remember going to look at various houses with Mum, before she settled on a large semi-detached thirties house in Kenton, near Harrow-on-the-Hill. I think the price being asked for it in 1958 was £5,000 which seemed a hell of a lot of money. But it was big enough for Grandpa and Grandma to live downstairs and it had a big garden, which I had to admit was great. It meant a change of school of course. I haven't mentioned that my grandparents owned a car, which they had bought new in 1949. It was a Vauxhall Velox, with a six-cylinder engine; Mum had to go up to Cullercoats by train and then drive back with it. This was no mean feat in those days, as the A1 still threaded its way through all the towns such as Doncaster, Grantham, Stamford, Peterborough etc. My Grandfather refused to drive, but Grandma did and my mother had also learned. Dad hadn't. The house had a garage for the car. It was in this car that I was first taken so see the countryside, which has since been such an inspiration for me. Whilst still living at Cullercoats, Grandma drove us out to see The Cheviot Hills, and the favourite destination was Rothbury. We went out through Monkseaton and the coalfields there, then through Morpeth, into the wild hills and I was told that Scotland wasn't far away. I begged them to take us further, into Scotland, but it was deemed just too far for a day trip.

With my grandparents came a piano, a good metal-framed one with excellent tone and pitch. Mum had learned to play and I now keep her various badges relating to her prowess. She inspired me to play too, and I did quite well and loved it, but only got to Grade VI as I could never master the Theory exam which you had to pass to go any further. Mum was at least pleased that her love of music was echoed in me, and sent me to the Harrow School of Music whose head, Mr. Bloye Gilbert, was the finest teacher of the piano that anyone could have had.

He had recently married his wife 'Mac'; when I first met her I asked her if she was the new 'char' (charwoman). She collapsed in a fit of laughter and said that she supposed so. She never forgot this, and never let me forget either!

There was one child, a daughter, Sarah. I remember quite clearly being presented with her for my admiration by her very proud mother. Bloye tragically died young but 'Mac' lived until 2013. I was privileged to be invited to the celebration of her long life, held in the beautiful church at Westbury-on-Trym in Bristol in December 2013.

As we were due to move in the autumn, it was agreed that I should start attending the new school immediately after the summer holidays that year. The new school, Mount Stewart, was around five miles away from Greenford so we had to take a taxi every morning and evening. Not any old taxi - this was a private one, a Daimler, and we felt very grand. I'm sure my grandparents must have paid for it.

I never liked Kenton much. The residents were far less friendly than those in Greenford. It was awfully respectable, most people had cars and other expensive possessions; they all locked themselves away and I felt like a fish out of water.

I missed everything terribly - the hens that many people kept in their gardens at Greenford, the Canal, my friends, Horsenden Hill, the lovely Philadelphus (we called it Syringa) tree with its beautiful scented flowers in the summer, the road-sweeper and the dustmen I had always talked to, the milkman and his friendly horse, the paraffin man with his unfriendly one, the ice-cream man - oh, everything. The loss felt like a huge hole in my heart and there were many, many nights I cried myself to sleep.
I didn't like the school much either, and was frightened of the headmaster, Mr. Rudge, widely known as Mr. Grudge. But of course, we made friends and eventually you have to come to terms with things and make the best of them. Mr. Rudge was a swimming fanatic, and I think Mount Stewart was one of the very first State schools to have its own swimming-pool. And it wasn't heated. Swimming was compulsory.

Remembering my baptism of ice in the North Sea, I dreaded every lesson and by God that water was often bloody cold. I was regularly pushed in by Mr. Rudge - common practice with wimps like me in those days - and once he held my head under until I thought I was going to drown. Coughing and spluttering, gasping for air, I emerged to his sneering disdain and the laughter of my class teacher who shouted 'We'll make half a man of you yet, Crawford!'.

Which reminds me of some of the expressions used in those days which now don't seem to make any sense at all. 'You'll be laughing on the other

11

side of your face in a minute!' 'You're as daft as a brush!'. And after being walloped, 'Do you want some more?' There were plenty of others, but I can't remember them now.

At least we were able to go out in the car every so often, and this included trips to Ruislip Lido and Harrow Weald Common, which reminded me of the countryside. But my parents found it hard. My Grandfather died within a year of the move and Grandma became ever more demanding, a martinet really. I will never forget that every day, on the stroke of midday, she would thump the floor with her walking-stick and shout 'BETTY! BETTY!' (Mum's name was Elizabeth) demanding her Babycham, brought in a fine glass on a silver tray. Dad, I think, felt somewhat beholden, as it was my Grandparents money that had at least partly bought the house. Grandma died about three years later.

With my grandparents had also come a television set. A Ferguson Black & White effort, with a tiny screen. We were only allowed to watch certain programmes. 'Watch with Mother' was obviously one, though we didn't watch with mother because she was always too busy. We were allowed to watch 'Dixon of Dock Green', 'Blue Peter', and the News. Whenever boxing came on, Grandma would cover the screen with the Radio Times. After she had died, we could watch 'The Lone Ranger' and other cowboy films, and later I remember the first episode of Dr. Who with William Hartnell. I loved 'Whirlybirds' and the Adventures of Tintin, Captain Pugwash, Noggin the Nog, and Tales from the Riverbank narrated by Johnny Morris. All these will bring back memories to those who watched T.V. in those years. Around 1963 Dad started watching 'That was the Week that Was' and he let me see it. I thought it shocking that they were lampooning politicians and even the Queen, but Dad said it was OK as we were entering a new era. How right he was. One programme we were never allowed to see, even in the seventies, was the Dave Allen Show. Mum saw to that.

Despite being a much grander house than the little one in Greenford, this one was still very cold in the winter. All the windows were single-glazed of course and I often woke up to find the 'frost flowers' decorating the inside of my bedroom window. Around 1962 Dad installed a form of central heating which he described as 'background' heating. It wasn't deemed healthy to be totally warm. I remember it as being almost totally useless!

We had a little coal-fired stove in the 'breakfast room' (originally a servant-girl's room I think) called an 'Ideal boiler'. It, too, was virtually useless and never kept in overnight. All the main rooms, incidentally, had bell-pushes in them which flagged up on a display board when pushed, in the 'breakfast room'. The main rooms had carpets, the breakfast room had lino which Mum kept - she was, after all, from the North.

Almost as soon as Grandma was buried, my father's mother was taken very ill with shingles. I loved 'Grandma Crawford' as she was called. She was a Welsh lady and spoke the language fluently, and lived with my father's unmarried sister, Muriel, in Chester. Dad's father had died when I was very young - I scarcely remember him. Anyway, we again had to make a train journey, this time from Euston and behind a 'Duchess' class locomotive. Oh the joy! A fortnight off school and another long-ish train journey on a different railway. We changed at Crewe and as a schoolboy, it seemed like a piece of Heaven with an intensive service of steam trains to all points of the Kingdom. Then being in awe of the beautiful station at Chester General, and being met by Auntie Muriel in her early split-screen Morris Minor car - just perfect for a district nurse, which she was.

Grandma Crawford recovered from her shingles and went on to live to a great age. With Auntie Muriel having a car, we again had trips out; to Park Gate on the Wirral, and over the border into Wales where we climbed Moel Fammau one very windy day. Far, far better than sitting in a stuffy classroom! I must mention too Mr. and Mrs. Hoddinott, friends of my grandmother, who always made me very welcome if I called round. Their garden backed-on to the main railway line and he had constructed a superb model railway, so I often found an excuse to call. We also always called on 'Auntie Blodwyn' affectionately known as 'Blod' with her companion, simply known as 'Talbot'. These were two elderly ladies (at least they seemed elderly to me), and I think Blodwyn was an old flame of my father. He'd been very ill with meningitis before the war, and Blodwyn I think had nursed him. Where 'Talbot' had come from I have no idea, but I loved them both and sometimes was allowed to visit them on my own. I just loved sitting in front of their coal fire in an evening, their cat Binky on my lap, and 'Talbot' being despatched into the kitchen to make the best cocoa I've ever tasted.

One of the less-pleasant aspects of being a kid in the fifties and early sixties was the six-monthly visits to the dentist. I don't remember the dentist at Greenford, but the one mum went to in Kenton was not pleasant. He only had the old-fashioned drill, which struck fear into my very bones. Once he was drilling a tooth when I held up my hand to indicate it was beginning to hurt but he just kept on. Tears were running down my face with the pain but still he wouldn't stop. After this, Mum found another dentist close by, Mr. Ritchie, who had modern equipment and injections to make your gums go numb and vastly reduce any pain. Ian Ritchie was a most amenable, jokey, young man then and he continued to see to my teeth until I was nearly fifty. I almost looked forward to going to the dentist now. We still keep in touch and he is just as amenable to this day. How many dentists keep in touch with their ex-patients after they retire?

Kenton, Middlesex, around 1960, from a Frith's Series Postcard. Wish you were here?

In 1960 I spectacularly failed my 11-plus exam and was destined for the local secondary modern, Claremont. This caused my parents considerable anxiety. Dad was a Socialist and did not believe in Private schooling, yet wanted desperately for me to be a success and to give me the best possible education even if it meant betraying his own beliefs, and costing him a packet. Me, I wanted to go with all my other friends to Claremont. I didn't want to be a 'posh kid'.

Nevertheless, and despite all the aforementioned, I was driven to a very small private school in Wembley, on the top of a hill right in front of the famous Stadium, to take their entrance exam. I remember one of the questions being 'What is M1?'. I failed abysmally in Maths (at least) but shone in English, so passed the exam - they must have needed the money, so, in due course, I was kitted-out with the most hideous stripy uniform and started my secondary education at Wembley Independent Grammar School. I soon found it was actually quite OK.

The Headmaster, in total contrast to Mr. Rudge, was a kindly, very intelligent and sensitive man called Mr. Avery. We had small classes - around 20 in each class - and it was a mixed school, though the proportion of girls was about 2%! The teachers were mostly fresh out of university and pretty naive; I spent a lot of the time I should have been listening, gazing out of the window looking over the houses towards Harrow-on-the-Hill and listening instead to the clanking and whistling of the steam trains on the main line in between. I made some very good friends and had an inordinate amount of fun. I have never known anyone else get away with not doing homework (hurriedly copying friend's work when necessary).

In my later years there, we got up to all sorts of escapades which would seem very mild today but then were regarded as daring. Once we took the classroom door off its hinges so when our maths. tutor entered in his usual brisk fashion, he took the door with him, crashing into the hapless pupils nearest the door and showering them with glass.

Once, for some forgotten reason, a teacher had to eat his spotted dick and custard lunchtime dessert whilst supervising us. One of my classmates took careful aim with an improvised catapult and scored a direct hit on the custard jug, sending it flying to the floor where it landed upside-down of course, the custard finding its way through a hole to dribble on to the headmaster's desk below, whilst he was interviewing a prospective pupil. The cane was used sparingly, but we got it that time. I got three strokes for 'aiding and abetting' (I had supplied the rubber band) and my friend got six. He caned our hands - no bottom - beating at this school! I got the cane about three times, once for breaking wind 'unnecessarily loudly' in a maths lesson, which I still think was a bit harsh. The other time was for playing truant.

Nineteen-sixty-one was a year of liberation for me. Before then, every other weekend I went with Dad to ice-skate at Queen's Ice Club in Bayswater, London. I'd gone there with him at an early age and as soon as I saw people skating on the ice I wanted to join them. I loved it, and Dad paid for me to have lessons so that in the end I'd become quite a competent skater. I had two instructors, the first one was Mr. Barnett who asked if I would do a copy of my aforementioned 'Space Book' specially for him. I did, and it took me three months! It seems unbelievable now, but the chap who ran the skate hire department and the cloakroom constantly hawked and spat, so the floor was peppered with quivering globules of phlegm which we studiously avoided. In the end, Dad asked him to refrain and the mild-mannered man apologised.

These days Dad would have been sworn at, or worse. Buses still had 'no spitting' signs affixed to the back of the seats, so it was obviously quite a common problem.

But in 1961 all this changed. It was the start of my becoming an adult, and I was given enormous personal freedoms. Knowing how much I loved the countryside (mainly due to enjoying our holidays which deserve a separate chapter), Mum and Dad encouraged me to purchase a One Inch Ordnance Survey Map (Sheet 159, The Chilterns) and plan a walk, including how to get to and from, and take a friend. For some reason we elected to go to Woburn, which meant a train journey into London and then out again on a different line to Flitwick. This wasn't even covered by the OS map! Odd, though, that the area is the one in which I now live. Perhaps it was because we'd heard of Woburn somewhere, but Mum suggested it would be easier, quicker, and cheaper to go to somewhere on the Metropolitan Line, which ran through Harrow.

In March 1961, aged twelve, Roger Tappin and I boarded a Metropolitan Line train from our local stations and met up on the platform at Harrow-on-the-Hill to take an Aylesbury-bound train to the station at Chalfont & Latimer, the start of our carefully-planned walk. We were both full of enthusiasm and excitement as we boarded the 'fast' train, headed by one of those electric locomotives we called 'bugs', first stop Moor Park.

All these loco's had names, our one I remember was 'Sir Ralph Verney'. At the following station, Rickmansworth, the electric loco was swapped for a steam one for the rest of the journey. We got off to watch this fascinating operation, which was achieved in under four minutes and involved the fireman jumping down between loco and train to disconnect and reconnect couplings and hoses. 'Elf 'n' safety would have apoplectic fits these days but it was normal, essential practice then. Now, we felt, we were entering the 'real' countryside. The line from Rickmansworth climbs steeply and we hung our heads out of the window to hear and smell the loco working very hard up the gradient. Alighting at Chalfont, we were covered in smuts and deliriously happy, and we went up to the engine to thank the driver and to watch the departure. In the 'bay' platform opposite was the shuttle train to Chesham, and although it was electric by then, we watched that go, too.

With rucksacks on our backs and heavy 'Tuf' boots on our feet, it was obvious we were out for a hike and the ticket-collector wished us well in our adventure and we felt very grown-up indeed. The walk took us to Chenies, then down a tiny lane to the crystal-clear River Chess where we had our lunch. It was a gloriously sunny day and I think both of us thought we had discovered paradise. Certainly I will never forget that discovery of the beautiful Chess Valley, which is just as beautiful today (away from where the M25 crosses it and makes it hideous with noise). No motorway then, so we walked all the way to Rickmansworth to catch the train, headed by 'John Hampden', home.

That day began a love-affair with the Chiltern countryside that has never really left me. We only had one more walk that year, in August, but again it was a revelation and the start for me of a friendship which lasted twenty years. This time we went further out, feeling really adventurous, and started the walk at Great Missenden. We walked up Frith Hill and then across the fields to a little village called Ballinger Common, which consisted of a few pretty cottages strung out along a quiet road, two pubs, a village hall, and a tiny chapel.

There was also The Village Post Office and Stores (and Library), where I met for the first time the genial postmistress, Miss Gray and her cat, Tom, who always slept in the shop window.

It was a hot day, so Miss Gray plied us with cold lemonade (4d. a glass) and as I looked around, quite fascinated by the place, I saw that she didn't have electric light. Instead, a fine Victorian paraffin lamp hung over the counter and smaller ones were placed around on the many surfaces.
It was as if we had entered another, enchanting, earlier age. I absolutely loved it, and I grew to love her, too. She was quite elderly, and full of enthusiasm for our walk, naming places I had only yet seen on the map, and describing them, so I was agog to visit them.

I dislike being as old as I am (64 as I write) but I would not wish to be a day younger if it meant I missed-out on knowing people such as Miss Gray. From time to time that morning, various villagers came and went, all of them being introduced to us by name and many also becoming friends over the years. The one I remember best was a Major Gurney, who had been gassed in the first world war and retired to a little cottage with his wife, just opposite the post office. They had a mynah bird which we found hilarious, and he proudly showed us his allotment where he grew wonderful vegetables. When Miss Gray retired from the post office in 1966 I 'inherited' that wonderful hanging oil-lamp, and today it hangs in my kitchen, a poignant reminder to me of those halcyon days.
When we finally left this haven of warmth and friendliness, we walked on past the little village of The Lee (more recently often depicted in 'Midsomer Murders') and on over the hills, finishing at Wendover. Our day was made complete by securing a compartment very close to the engine, and the driver and fireman throwing lumps of coal at our outstretched heads as the

train rattled its way to Rickmansworth. None of the lumps hit us. The next month, the changeover at Rickmansworth was stopped, the Metropolitan Line truncated to finish at Amersham, and characterless electric trains made the journey faster, but far less interesting. My friend Andrew and I travelled the line on the last day of steam passenger operations, not really believing that it was all coming to an end. It wasn't all bad, though - British Railways still operated steam over the line for another five years afterwards, albeit with increasing irregularity and unreliability.

Later I became involved with the campaign to save the ex-Great Central Line, which shared the Metropolitan Line tracks to Amersham and Aylesbury and then went north to Leicester, Nottingham and Sheffield. Dr. Beeching was wielding his famous 'axe' on the railway network and this finely-engineered main line, built to the continental loading-gauge, was for the chop. It seemed ludicrous to me at the time and it still seems ludicrous to me now, but the line finally shut in 1966 after only just over a half-century in operation. It wasn't really Beeching's fault of course - people were just not using the railways, and he was given the job of rationalising them; but he became very much a hate figure, along with Ernest Marples the Minister for Transport.

Last Day of steam on the Underground, 9th. September 1961. The locomotive has been spruced-up specially for the occasion, and is seen taking water prior to heading its train northwards from Rickmansworth.

I had a sticker saying 'Beeching Must Go!' which I attached to my school bag and flaunted it at every opportunity. The line north of Aylesbury became more and more run-down as the closure neared, and I travelled on one of the last regular trains to Woodford Halse. That place had been a major junction and locomotive works but in 1966 it had become almost totally derelict, a very sad sight indeed.

Train spotter's 'bible': Cover of Ian Allen's ABC of the Midland Region, price 2/6d. in 1962.

I thought that Woodford should have become the new city rather than Milton Keynes, which would have saved both the line and the place, but the die was cast by then.

From 1962 I walked, with friends or on my own, almost every Saturday except for a couple of months during the incredibly hard winter of 1962/3. My love for the Chiltern Hills became a passion. I read many books about them including the County Book Series on Buckinghamshire, written by Alison Uttley who was well-known for her 'Little Grey Rabbit' and other children's books, and who I felt excelled in describing her adopted County. She lived at Beaconsfield and we corresponded for some years, though I never met her. I did meet J.H.B. Peel who wrote a regular column for the Telegraph newspaper entitled 'Country Talk', and who lived at Prestwood near Great Missenden. His love for the Chilterns particularly was very strong, but he was uneasy talking to youngsters - very diffident and awkward. He was becoming increasingly unhappy about the suburbanisation of South Bucks and moved to Devon in the late sixties.

I founded the 'Chiltern Conservation Society' at school. In my youthful naivety I thought a bunch of schoolkids could influence the powers-that-be to stop despoiling the Chiltern countryside! But I hope we did at least do some good, by helping on the nature reserves of the Berks., Bucks., and Oxon. Naturalist's Trust (BBONT) under the kindly guidance of Mrs. Cowdy, who lived in a big house at The Lee. She was secretary of BBONT, if I remember rightly. One of the reserves was at Dancers End, near Tring. One day we arrived to do some clearance work, only to meet a group of travelling women emerging carrying armfuls of wild orchids and other precious flowers. 'Did you pick those here?', I asked, astounded. 'Oh, it's no good you looking for any' one woman replied, 'we've picked the lot!'.

There's no doubt I quickly took my freedoms for granted. My mother always invited those friends I walked with to stay for supper, if I brought them home. From 1963 we took to cycling in the Hills as well as walking, and it was almost always that we came back to 'my place'. My friends knew they'd be welcome and get well-fed. It was only very occasionally that I was invited to their homes!

Sundays, though, remained a day of confinement and religious observance. Mum had been brought up in the non-conformist tradition, and there was a Congregational Church at Hindes Road, Harrow, which she took us to every Sunday. We weren't keen. But we were very lucky. The Minister was the Rev. Owen Butler until 1962, then he left to go to Minehead in Somerset and we welcomed the Rev. Ronald Bocking to the position.

Both Ministers were true Christians in the very best sense, their influence (and that of their wives) beneficial to all who came into contact with them. Their leadership and guidance filtered down to the various Sunday schools (Beginners, Primary, Junior, Junior Church, Seniors, and Young People's Fellowship) and we were taught not only the teachings of Christ, but experienced the values, tolerance and openness of those teachings in practice. It turned my reluctance around, and in the seventies I became a Sunday school teacher for a while, and a Church Member. Almost every memory of that place is positive, and we will return to it a little later in this book.

Meanwhile, back at school, the mayhem continued. Don't get me wrong - there were some fine teachers and I think I generally received a far better education than I would have had if I'd not gone there. They didn't just teach us the three R's but they tried to instil worthwhile values in us, too. My 'passion for the Chilterns' was applauded and never, once, derided.

My exam. results, though, were consistently abysmal. But how about this for a generous comment in one of my reports? On Latin, I'd got 4% in one exam. The tutor, known as 'Mr. Mac', could have been utterly scathing - and he probably should have been, because that piss-poor mark was due to complete apathy on my part - but he wrote 'This boy is nobody's fool, but Latin is just not his subject'. My maths. results were just as bad, at my Geometry mock O-level paper I got 3% - 'I found difficulty in giving you any marks at all, Crawford!' said the Head. I always partly redeemed myself by getting consistently good results in English and Geography and, to a lesser extent, Biology.

My friend, who I sat next to at our old-fashioned desk (with inkwell and pen) was far better than I academically, but was so naive it was hilarious. His name was Clive Cohen, and he became an orthodox Jew in later life. I often wonder if he is happy. An only child, he was short and had two protruding front teeth which made him the butt of many of our jokes. It would be called bullying today, but he seemed to thrive on all the attention.

Our class was told the 'Facts of Life' in 1963. Clive was a little younger than me, but would have been nearly fourteen at this stage. He knew absolutely nothing about these all-important (and all-consuming to us) facts and caused uproar in the class when he asked, in all seriousness, whether babies were born 'sunny side up'. He was one of the most untidy boys in the class, even surpassing me. His desk was a disgrace. Books were shoved in willy-nilly, and unfortunately for him were not securely contained, as the desks were open-fronted towards us as we were sat at them. We always had

21

to stand up when the master or mistress came in, and as we did so another friend of mine, John Kaucz, who sat behind us, and I pushed our desk forward slightly (Clive and I were sat at the front of the row). When we were permitted to sit, after the 'Good morning, Form IV' and our 'Good morning, Miss Parks', we caused the desk to shoot backwards and as it hit the desk behind, all of Clive's books cascaded out onto his lap and onto the floor. It worked every time. And every time, the class erupted into laughter and often the teacher was rendered helpless with mirth as well. It took at least five minutes off every lesson.

In my last year at the school, I wrote a spoof book about Clive and the 'Lisp Times' newspaper (Clive had a lisp) and both of these were illustrated by John Kaucz. He was a brilliant artist and cartoonist and went on to study architecture at Edinburgh University before landing a coveted job in Bahrain.

Previous literary efforts: The cover of my 'Space Book' approx. 1958. And. . .

Illustrations from Clive Cohen book, 1964.

We again had swimming lessons at this school, but we had to travel to Vale Farm Swimming Pool in Sudbury on a trolleybus, and only in the summer term. There were separate changing rooms and I almost always got away with staying in mine throughout the lesson time, so I didn't go in the water very often! When it was time to go home (lessons were always in the afternoon), I emerged nonchalantly from my cubicle with everyone else, pausing only to dip my trunks in the fountain so mum assumed I'd had the lesson. I never got found out. In the winter months we went to a gym on the Finchley Road, travelling by coach. I hated gym, and the bullying instructor, but enjoyed the journey which often took longer than scheduled due to heavy traffic. Neasden, Dollis Hill, Willesden and Kilburn looked very run-down in those days and I felt sorry for the people who had to live there.

I think my parents were very disappointed that I wanted to become a farm worker. Dad, in particular, said I should try journalism as my English was so good. All his efforts, and so much of his time and his money, had been spent in trying to 'make' me an academic of some sort. So the last year of my schooling was dominated by my father determined to improve my mathematics.

No such disappointment with my brother, who was quite outstanding in almost all school subjects and had effortlessly achieved a place at St. Nicholas Grammar School in Northwood once he'd left Mount Stewart. So he was allowed out to play in the evenings whilst I had to sit inside and do maths.

This was absolute purgatory for me and caused me great resentment. My father was determined - and I was just as stubborn. The irresistible force met with the immovable object. Inevitably, it caused clash after clash and there was a rift - an invisible wall - between us for many years. Not only was I as stubborn as a mule, but I was opinionated as well. By 1965, the thinking and values of young people were radically changing, and I embraced much of the new thinking wholeheartedly. I was never really a part of the hippie culture (in 1965 it hadn't started) but I was a 'free thinker'. I read 'The Fat of the Land' by John Seymour, written in 1961, which I found truly inspirational - and still do. He followed this in the seventies with a hugely successful book called 'Practical Self-Sufficiency' which by then resonated with the thousands and thousands of people who craved a simpler way of life. But 'The Fat of the Land' was truly radical, as the revolution had not started. . . .John was a pioneer in so many ways.

I also read another famous book 'The Farming Ladder' by George Henderson. So very different from John Seymour, and yet both stressed the importance of cultivating or farming the land with a reverence and respect; and leaving it better than you found it. I questioned all the values of my parents and of 'normal' society, and this questioning and doubting and debating and rebelling was encouraged and admired even by many of those who were irreversibly bound by the values gained in a previous age.

I hadn't a clue as to the hardships and deprivations suffered by so many in the thirties, let alone through two World Wars. No clue at all as to the grinding poverty they had endured, the hunger, the hopelessness and the fear many must have felt. I took the teachings of the New Testament very literally (when it suited) and thought those who strived for material comfort and security unenlightened. Of course, I was enjoying the fruits of that material comfort and security at the time.

Hypocrisy had nothing on me. What a little prig. Part of this priggishness was a reluctance to embrace the popular music scene, dismissing it all as shallow, it was classical and folk music for me. Some of this self-righteous veneer was rubbed off after a holiday with an elderly aunt, but I'll keep that for the chapter on holidays.

I was an avid reader of any books about traditional farming and of the countryside at this time. In 1964, a compilation of articles that had featured in 'The Farmer's Weekly' magazine was published as the 'Farmer's Bedside Book' and I asked my parents to purchase a copy for me as a Christmas present that year. The very first item in the book was a poem called 'Trip to the City' by an anonymous author. It made such an impression on me I have remembered it word for word ever since, and it was the inspiration for me to form the charity Earthshine, so it deserves a place here. I hope the reader gets as much pleasure from it as I still do, after all these years.

Could ambition plunder sorrow
Then would I weep to light the faces
Of the people in the streets.
For in their eyes has never been the wild world
Where a bird sings or the wind sweeps.
They've never seen the lacy damsons
Etched against December skies
Nor plucked at breath against a gale.
They've never seen the thin blue hummocks
Drift through Autumn woods,
Nor seen the cloud-dropped shadows
Slide along the hills.

They've never heard the almost silent sea
That whispers through the bracken on the cliffs,
Nor ever been so silent,
Nor ever been so still
To hear the gorse-pods popping
To the quiet clouds.
Perhaps, when I am old,
I shall no longer care
From where the wind is blowing,
But be like them
With eyesight shortened,
Straightened by the city street.

25

Oh, let the warm, soft mother wind blow from the hills,
And curl the jaws of lambs with yawns!
Turn up your collar, man in the street,
As you slipshod by with your aimless feet.
Turn up your collar, man in the street,
But listen to the wind.
And I? am less than a noise of twittering stars,
Or the shadows cast by the fluttering grass.

I took my 'O' levels in 1965. I passed two - English Language and Geography. I failed two, biology and to my surprise, English Literature. One of the books we had to study was 'Far from the Madding Crowd' by Thomas Hardy, which I loved and wrote about with enthusiasm. The others I can't remember, but obviously my lack of interest in them dragged a pass result below the surface.

I had never won anything at school, was useless at sports, but I won the School Prize for English Language in 1965. My mother was thrilled. It was to be presented at Speech Day in Wembley Town Hall the following year, and was the first school prize I had ever won. That particular evening I was cleaning up the oil lamp I'd just acquired from Ballinger Common Post Office and completely forgot the presentation. At around ten o'clock that night I suddenly remembered. Mum was in bed, but awake and I said 'You know what we've forgotten, don't you?' She looked blank. 'Speech Day'. She burst into tears; it was the first time I'd seen her cry. She was as angry with herself as with me for forgetting, and the sight of her crying - this inflexible, strong, 'iron lady' - left an impression on me never forgotten.

It was the beginning of a realisation in me that what I did or didn't do actually had an effect on others. Better late than never, I suppose.

Dad was insistent that I was not to become a farm labourer. I had to have some formal training, an apprenticeship perhaps or a go with the YMCA's 'British Boys for British Farms' scheme. In the end we settled on an apprenticeship. Right to the last moment he tried to persuade me to enter a journalistic career or at least Forestry (where there was a more formal approach to training) - anything but agriculture. So agriculture it was.

HOLIDAY FELLOWSHIP

One of the very best things for a child born in 1948 was the fact that our parents were entitled to two whole week's holiday each year, plus Bank Holidays and Christmas of course. The first holiday I can remember was in the glorious summer of 1955, in a hotel at Blackgang on the Isle of Wight. I remember a little of the journey; the bustling, smoky platforms at Waterloo with a streamlined locomotive at the front of our train, arriving at the station at Southampton and seeing the ferry we were to board; most clearly of all, the platform and trains on Ryde Pier and the journey across the Island to Ventnor.

Mum told me, years later, that I was a pain in the backside on that journey, not because I misbehaved, but because I was excited all the time and kept asking endless questions. I remember us catching a green double-decker 'Southdown' bus to Blackgang, the driver double-declutching on every gear-change, and seeing the hotel for the first time, an enticing green hill rising up behind it. Dad and I walked up that hill to see the view every morning before breakfast. There was a dog - Dennis the Dachshund (after the Toytown series on the radio) resident at the hotel, whom I loved, and also lots of butterflies kept in jam-jars in the rear grounds. One day I let them all go. I don't remember getting into trouble for it.

We went to Alum Bay to see the coloured sands, Blackgang Chine (which wasn't the commercial horror it is now but a beautiful valley filled with wild flowers), St. Catherine's lighthouse and lots of other wonders. When we went home we saw the 'Queen Mary' docked at Southampton, and I carried little fragments of the Island home with me which I kept for years.

The next year we went to Burnham-on-Sea in Somerset but the year after that, 1957, we started to have our holidays with the Holiday Fellowship, an organisation which had centres all over the country and promoted walking and the fellowship of all different people together on holiday. In those days 'H.F. Holidays' as it is now called, had special 'Family Centres' especially tailored to the needs of parents with young children. They were brilliant. We went to their centre at Milford-on-Sea in Hampshire, looking across the Solent to the Isle of Wight, and it was so good, we went there twice (in 1958 as well). Again we travelled by steam train, alighting at New Milton Station and getting a pre-war Austin Heavy Twelve taxi to Milford.

The holidays were very organised then. We were woken by a 'rising bell' and then summoned to the breakfast table by the 'breakfast bell'. Before the evening meal, again preceded by the 'dinner bell', we said or sang Grace, (and I cannot remember anyone being 'offended' by this); after dinner there were set activities each evening. I can't remember the Family Centre ones in particular, except there was a Concert every Thursday evening in which everyone was encouraged to take part. There was a single sitting at breakfast; and on Mondays, Tuesdays, Thursdays and Fridays there were organised walks of varying degrees of difficulty. 'A' the most difficult, 'B' of medium difficulty and length, 'C' easy and short. As kids we wanted to do the 'A' walks all the time.

Typical Holiday Fellowship Group photograph from 1961.

There was one walk which we took on the Isle of Wight. The Host, Harry, impressed on us all that we must not miss the bus back to the Ferry. (The walk had taken us over Tennyson Down and ended at the H.F. centre at Freshwater Bay).

Time and time again he stressed the importance of this. When we got back to the Ferry, there was no Harry. He'd missed the bus. The walks were led by the Secretary (usually on 'A' walks) who resided at the Centre all the summer, and the 'Host' ('B' walks) and the 'Hostess' ('C' walks) who were long-time members of the Holiday Fellowship and were usually married to each other. I think they got their holiday for free in return for their duties, which included all sorts of help and advice to the other holidaymakers. I enjoyed the holiday at Milford so much, when we got home I cried and cried because I knew it would be a whole year before we had another.

In 1959 (another lovely summer) and in 1960 we went to Towyn (as it was then spelt) on the Cambrian coast but by then we went by car. I wanted so much to travel by train, especially as my brother was always car-sick, but Mum explained that it cost a lot less to go by car. I quickly found that you saw a lot more of the countryside by car - the roads were generally narrower and the cars themselves slower then, and we travelled across country. We did it in one day, but by the end we were heartily sick of it. The AA used to do recommended routes to places, and their suggestion was to take the A40 to Oxford, then the A44 to Moreton-in-Marsh and Evesham, then on to Pershore and Worcester, then Kidderminster to Ludlow, and then across into Wales to Newtown and Machynlleth and to Towyn. It took hours and hours. But it was worth it - for there were mountains to climb!

How I relished the cool, sweet air of the Welsh mountains! The walks took us up them, sometimes climbing into the clouds which were a huge disappointment.

I thought the clouds would be fluffy and warm, but they were soggy and cold and you couldn't see anything in them. But climbing up above them, on to the top of Cader Idris, was absolutely magical, like being in Heaven I thought. The hosts at Towyn were a couple called Harry and Sue Southern, with their children Gillian and Peter. They had been at Milford the years before, and struck up a long-lasting friendship with Mum and Dad. It's a pleasure for me to report that we're still in touch and they are hale and hearty after all these years. I loved Harry's car - a pre-war Riley he called 'Betsy'. I have recently learned from him that it had a pre-selector gearbox, where you selected the next ratio at your leisure and then pressed the clutch for it to engage. The old RT London Transport buses featured this arrangement.

The special plus of a holiday at Towyn was - you've guessed it - the Tallyllyn Railway, the first narrow-gauge railway to be operated by volunteers in Britain. We used the little train to start one of the walks at Dolgoch Falls. On another day we ended a long walk at the little Halt at Garth, near Aberdovey, on the Cambrian Coast line. To stop the train, one had to signal to the driver as the train burst out of a nearby tunnel, and recognising my passion for the railway the walk leader allowed me to do this. I was thrilled when the large locomotive emerged from the tunnel, all green and shining with copper fittings and a headboard proclaiming that it was 'The Cambrian Coast Express'. And I had the power to stop it!

With squealing brakes and rushes of steam, the train shuddered to a stop at the tiny wooden platform and I spent the journey back to Towyn with my head hanging out of the door window, transfixed and in absolute delight at the sounds and smells of the train and of the beautiful scenery slipping by. It's something I've never forgotten.

Another walk started from Barmouth in the other direction, and again we travelled by train. This included the famous bridge over the Mawddch estuary and watching a long train depart from Barmouth Junction (as it was then known) towards Llangollen and Chester. We also rode on the little Fairbourne Railway, but I am anxious to get on now to our first holiday at an adult-orientated centre; Selworthy near Minehead in Somerset.

It was 1961, my year of 'liberation' and burgeoning appreciation of the countryside. I was absolutely thrilled and moved by the combination of the high moorlands of Exmoor and the rich red soil and green crops of the small fields in the valleys; the incredibly picturesque villages; the deep-sunk lanes and tracks; and the views from the cliffs and hills across the Bristol Channel to Wales. Miraculously, it looks much the same today.

The guest house was (and is) a pleasant, rambling building on the Holnicote Estate, most of which was (and is) owned by the National Trust. The holidays were always geared towards walking and the fellowship of the guests, and I enjoyed talking with the adults actually more than with youngsters of my own age.

This was appreciated by the adults, but not particularly by Mum and Dad whom I tended to ignore. I joined in with the evening activities fully, including Beetle-drives, country dancing, and sketches and piano-performances in the Concerts on Thursdays. There were no organised walks on Wednesdays so we went to the beach at Minehead, but I spent most of the afternoon on the platform at Minehead Station, underlining engine numbers in my Ian Allan 'Locospotters' Western Region book. Never have I enjoyed a holiday more than the two weeks we had at Selworthy, it was a magical time for me. I try to get down that way every year, and travel on the West Somerset Railway, simply to re-live some of the magic of all those years ago.

The next year we went to Coniston in the Lake District. It rained almost every day. We still walked a lot, but the only mountain I remember we climbed in fine weather was Helvellyn. This was the last year we travelled in the old Vauxhall Velox. It had the old 'traffikators', little arms that stuck out of the central door-pillar when you indicated a turn. On the Preston by-pass on the return journey, now part of the M.6, in foul weather mum indicated to overtake something and the wind was so strong that when she cancelled the indicator, the force of the wind kept it stuck out for miles afterwards. The car also had windscreen wipers that operated off the camshaft, so the faster the engine went, the faster the wipers went. Fine in theory, but not very effective in practice. But better than Ford's vacuum operated offerings.

In 1963 we went to Lynmouth in Devon, not that far from Selworthy. By then we had a new (for us) Vauxhall Velox, an American-looking job which I then thought brash and vulgar (and I still do). It was not like Mum at all to have such an ostentatious car, but she felt loyal to the Vauxhall marque. She drew the line at having the even flashier Cresta model though, with its two-tone paint and (often) leopardskin seats. The car had a soft, wallowy ride which made my brother's car-sickness even worse. It had a wide, slippery bench front seat large enough to accommodate both Antony and me alongside Mum, so of course he usually chucked up at least partly over me.

How I longed for our train journeys! People used to dangle a chain from the rear bumper or exhaust in the belief that it cured travel sickness, but Mum didn't believe in it.

The route took us up Porlock Hill near the end of the journey, the steepest main road hill in Britain with fearsome hairpin bends. We got stuck behind a little upright Ford Popular struggling up the slope - backwards! We were later told that the reverse gear was lower than first, but of course very little breeze got to the radiator and as we followed it the car disappeared in a cloud of steam as the radiator boiled. Mum was a good driver and got us safely past.

Brake 'fade' was a concern on long descents, where the drum brakes fitted in those days overheated, causing potential failure. The steep hill down to Lynmouth, Countisbury Hill, was taken very cautiously in low gear. The holiday Centre was right on the beach, and although I didn't like it quite as much as Selworthy, I was enthralled at night, looking across the water to the many lighthouses signalling along the South Wales coastline. The scenery and the walks equalled those at Selworthy, and one of the walks took us to Holnicote House. It was another great holiday and by this time I was determined to explore this part of Britain more. For the first time ever in my experience, this centre had a T.V. set and whilst we were there, news came across of the Great Train Robbery back in my familiar stomping ground of Buckinghamshire.

In 1964 we went to Conway in North Wales, and in 1965 - the last holiday with the family - we went to Derwentwater in the Lakes and I took my friend Clive along as well. It wasn't a good summer, but better than 1962, and I remember 'doing' the Langdale Pikes, Great Gable, and Blencathra in sunshine. By then, I was feeling a little nervous about starting work on the farm, but it was great to have Clive with us and he kept us all amused throughout the two weeks.

These holidays were, in my opinion, the best possible holidays available at that time. Certainly they were to me. I don't think my brother quite shared my enthusiasm, but he was a chronically shy boy and didn't find it as easy to mix with adults as I did. But for me these holidays really opened my eyes to the beauty of the British landscape, to the value of friendship, and to the great pleasures of walking in the hills, good food, and conversation. It is rare that the pleasure of reality exceeds that of expectation, but these holidays did it, every time. I owe my parents a great deal of gratitude for introducing me to them.

After the holiday in Conway in 1964, I spent a week with my elderly Aunt Ellen in a remote part of Shropshire. We had corresponded for a couple of years and she applauded my sense of unworldliness and seriousness. Aunt Ellen was a devout Christian, a vegan, and hater of any form of modern technology.

She lived in a tiny cottage on around four acres of land at a place called Gravels Bank, which is approximately mid-way between Minsterley and Bishops Castle in the Marches, also known as 'Mary Webb country' after the novelist who lived in and described these parts. We drove directly from Conway to her home, or rather to the end of the long grassy track which led to her home.

I'd met her once before, after another aunt, Ethel, had died and we were clearing out her possessions. Dad described Ellen as a 'crank' - a term he used for anyone who lived an 'alternative' lifestyle. She was like a little bird, and took me under her wing as it were - Antony whispered 'Good luck, rather you than me' as they got into the car and drove off. I suddenly felt lost and lonely, and this was completely unexpected - I had expected to feel elated. This feeling intensified when we got to her sparse cottage and I was told I was to sleep in the 'annexe' - a former tool-shed lean-to. Aunt

Ellen made unleavened bread and cooked her simple meals on a very old range in the fireplace; there was no electricity, no water laid on, and the toilet was an earth closet outside.

Aunt Ellen,Mum, Antony and me when I stayed with her in 1964. The door to my 'annexe' is far right.

Water came from a crystal-clear spring a quarter-of-a-mile up the hill.

After the comparative luxury of home and the lively company and good food of the holiday at Conway, the dark little cottage and the dead quiet were unnerving. Aunt Ellen was of indeterminate old age, probably in her seventies then, and went to bed more-or-less when it got dark. When I got into my rudimentary bed, there was a mouse in it.
I actually didn't mind this, and mouse and I slept together - or at least in the same room - that first night. Aunt Ellen's cat then chose to keep me company on subsequent nights, so mouse disappeared. I was so glad of the cat's warmth and company though.

Aunt Ellen was a great walker, and old as she was, she walked me off my feet. We walked up and over Corndon Hill, collecting bilberries on the way, onto the Stiperstones ridge, up to the Devil's Chair, and one day all the way to Bishops Castle. We visited some of her acquaintances some days and if they offered me coffee I gratefully accepted; Aunt Ellen would not touch coffee or tea but she didn't seem to object to me having it. She didn't drink milk either, but let me collect half a pint for my own use from a local farmer at Bromlow.

Much as I enjoyed walking over the Shropshire hills, (and loved the little town of Bishops Castle) I couldn't warm to the countryside in the immediate vicinity of Gravels Bank. It seemed hostile, bleak, and had a disturbing, haunted feel. Old lead-mines and gravel workings spoilt it for me. Living the life of rustic simplicity even for a few days bored me and at the same time, disturbed me.
Wasn't this what I had dreamed was the right way to live? Wasn't it what I wanted? Obviously not, but I couldn't quite work out why. It SHOULD have been! But I actually looked forward to returning home to Harrow.

The experience rather took the wind out of my sails, no bad thing at all since I had been so confident and dogmatic about everything. Aunt Ellen and I kept in regular contact, and I visited her again several times over the next few years, never for more than one night though. She died in the late seventies, and she is buried in the churchyard at Shelve, just down the road from her cottage. I tried to find her resting-place recently and regret I couldn't, but I did pass her cottage and was delighted to find it occupied by a young family living the 'good life'. Children played outside, washing billowed on the line, and outwardly it was not much changed - I think my aunt Ellen would approve.

In 1963 my friend Andrew and I joined the Youth Hostels Association so we could cycle and visit different parts of the country in one trip. You could only stay at Youth Hostels in England and Wales if you arrived on foot or by bicycle but people had already got round this by parking their cars nearby and walking in to the Hostel! We thought this disgusting; Youth Hostels were cheap with pretty basic facilities, designed for walkers and cyclists who did not have the money to travel around by car. We slept in dormitories, cooked in a communal kitchen and helped with the chores before leaving in the morning. Our longest trip was from Devon all the way back home.

Andrew had a holiday with his parents down at Bovey Tracey and at the end of it I travelled by train from Paddington, bicycle stored in the guard's compartment, and he met me at Newton Abbott. We stayed at Maypool Hostel for two nights, then off we went on a marathon ride (during which we got lost) to Bampton, and then on to Lynton Hostel where again we stayed for two nights.

We travelled the coast road to Minehead, descending Porlock Hill very gingerly, and I was able to show him Selworthy before overnighting at Holford in the Quantock Hills. I am proud that Andrew was so taken with Selworthy and the countryside around it that he chose it for his honeymoon years later, and lives nearby to this day. After Holford we cycled to Glastonbury and Wells before making our way via Marlborough and Goring back home.

Youth Hostels were a brilliant way for youngsters to discover their country, and indeed others, independently and inexpensively. They are now much more comfortable and family-friendly, and you can travel by car if you wish, but I can't help feeling that something has been lost along the way.

I am so glad we experienced them as they were originally conceived.

I now holiday, on my own or with my wife, in a camper van. The principle is the same; travelling independently and relatively inexpensively, staying where the fancy takes us, exploring remote parts of the countryside and not having to worry about accommodation and whether dogs are allowed or not. Campervans are incredibly expensive to buy now, I would say ridiculously so, so I converted an old school mini-coach myself with units from a caravan that had been dumped in a lay-by. Although I say it myself, the result is a comfortable and convenient 'van, built to our own design and the whole job cost less than £2,000 including the vehicle. For anyone inspired by this, a couple of tips. Minibuses and coaches that are used for schools are usually sold-off after ten years service; Councils don't like to have vehicles older than ten years operating services. The result is that they are available for ridiculously little money as they can't really be used in service anymore. Mine cost £350 cash. And a mini-bus or mini-coach is usually better trimmed and insulated than a delivery van would be, and already has side windows. And, coaches in Council services are well-looked-after and regularly serviced. We just pack up and go, whenever and wherever we can. Touch wood, I've had no trouble at all with mine. It's probably the nearest thing to freedom you can have, and you don't need to be rich. Just as well. . . .

TO BE A FARMER'S BOY?

August 11th., 1965, saw me cycle from Harrow to Dinton, near Aylesbury in Buckinghamshire, where I was to start my farming 'career'. Mum and Dad followed, carrying my clothes and stuff, in the car. We timed it perfectly; we arrived at Springhill Farm together.

In my usual dogmatic fashion I had insisted that any farm I worked on had to be 'organic' and a mixed farm. Such farms were pretty thin on the ground, then, as agribusiness was thought to be the way forward and 'muck and magic' was deemed retrograde by most, if not reactionary. The apprenticeship scheme was managed by the National Farmer's Union and I had written to their Buckinghamshire branch seeking an opening. They couldn't find one for me. This only placed the bit between my teeth, and I wrote off to numerous farms in the county explaining I wanted to learn as I worked.

One positive reply came back, from a Mr. Lance Coates who lived in Whitchurch, north of Aylesbury. He seemed to own a number of farms, one of which was Springhill Farm west of Aylesbury, and yes, the farm manager there wanted a pupil. They ran the farm along organic lines and although I really wanted to be nearer my friends in the Chilterns, I did at least realise I had very little choice. I duly met up with Mr. Case, the farm manager, in early July and was shown round the farm and offered the job. I could have the arranged holiday with my family (and Clive) in the Lake District before starting work in time for the Harvest. I was to live, initially, in the Farm House with the manager and his young wife, and their two-year-old son and new baby. Later I would move in with the sub-Manager, but at this time his wife was in hospital and he couldn't have coped with a young bloke around the place. My meals were to be had with the cowman and his wife in their little tied house.

When Mum and Dad departed, I again felt that peculiar sense of isolation, something like a fish out of water. Mr. and Mrs. Case, though, were kind to me and I loved playing hide-and-seek with their little boy. Again I was shown around, and my duties for the following day were described. We started at 7 a.m. and my job was to feed cattle and generally be on hand to usher cows into the milking parlour - not that they needed any ushering. They always have their own set order of going in, and indeed coming in to the yard from the fields. They know the time. I loved bringing in the cows. This farm had a large herd of pedigree Dairy Shorthorns, and the cows were such gentle, self-effacing beasts and were a pleasure to handle.

There were two bulls, Max and Revelex, who weren't quite as gentle! I kept my distance from them. I didn't like the rather off-hand way the cows were treated; I still had a rather idealised view of looking after them. This was to be rudely shattered over the next few weeks. After a couple of weeks, I was told I was to be lodged with Mr. and Mrs. Hoddinott who occupied Cowley Farmhouse, part of Springhill Farm. Springhill Farmhouse had every modern convenience for the time - centrally-heated, well carpeted, spacious, it was a most comfortable place, ideally set well off the road down its own drive flanked by tall elm trees. From its windows you looked over the farmland and across the valley of the River Thame to the green hills opposite. Cowley Farmhouse was the more picturesque; built of the local honey-coloured stone (very like Cotswold stone), it had crinkly rustic tiles on the roof and looked idyllic. But, by God, it was cold!

There was no central heating, no double-glazing of course, and precious little insulation and it was draughty. I had a cold little room at one end, with a bare bulb hanging from the ceiling and bare boards for the floor. The bedside table was just about big enough to place the all-important alarm clock.

The house was run by Mr. and Mrs. Hoddinott (no relation to my friends in Chester), who had a young son. There was also a resident lodger, the poultry-man called Arthur, about the most miserable individual I have ever met. Mrs. Hoddinott was Irish, and I think now, a manic-depressive. She always looked, to me, unhappy. Mr. Hoddinott was a swarthy, muscular man, dismissive of almost everything - especially me. I was a 'townie' and quite posh with it, I had no place on this farm and especially, should have no place in his house. I came to intensely dislike him. He always knew best; he would have no argument. And the way he treated the animals was, frankly, disgraceful. He would have no patience with them, walloping them, hard, for any trivial misdemeanour. I kept out of his way as much as I could, but this wasn't easy as we lived under the same roof. Mrs. Hoddinott didn't dare cross him. One day, she and I were talking and it happened that I mentioned that I had been adopted. She said I should be eternally grateful as I had been 'chosen'. At the time I thought this nonsense, but didn't say anything. Much later I learned that many of those who had been adopted actually felt they had 'missed out' in life as they had been rejected by their natural parents. I thought this nonsense, too. But it seems ironic, given what happened later in my life. However, I digress. . .

One day we were loading and stacking straw bales. I fed the elevator, which took the bales up from the tractor-trailer into the barn where they were to be stored. Mr. Hoddinott and Michael, the cowman, were taking the bales off the other end of the elevator and stacking them. I knew I had to carefully position the bales on the elevator as the machine was old and a wrongly-placed bale would jam up the whole contraption. Mr. Hoddinott became incandescent that I was taking such care, and bellowed at me to get a f*****g move on. Michael tried to explain to him that there were two of them and only one of me and I had been told to take care with the loading, but this just made him worse. So I started to throw the bales on as quick as I could, with the inevitable result that the machine jammed solid.

All work then had to come to a stop. Cursing and swearing at the machine and me, and shouting that I'd done this deliberately, he went off to get the boss. 'Don't worry' said Michael 'Mr. Case knows what he's like and I'll speak for you'. To his credit he did, and it was Hoddinott who got the blame. It was a hollow victory for me, though, because he had all sorts of ways of getting back at me. I got blamed for all sorts of things that he did; once he put rat-poison in with the pig food intending real harm to the pigs, he didn't care as long as I got the blame and preferably the sack. Fortunately I noticed the unusual pellets in the feed (though I didn't know what they were) and queried it. Of course he denied any involvement, but I knew. . . .

It was this incident that decided me to stop working at this farm. I wasn't happy with the work, anyway, by 1965 everything was mechanised and I really wanted to use my hands. I was disappointed, but any blame for my disappointment lay with me because I'd had an idealistic view of farming. People had tried to tell me, especially Dad, what farming was like, but I'd refused to listen. I did realise this, and felt disappointed with myself as well.

In my favour, all the staff on this farm, with the exception of Michael, didn't give a stuff about organic principles and only followed them because they had to. And the pupil who followed me lasted three weeks rather than my three months. With the apprenticeship scheme, you had to attend Agricultural College one day a week. I used to cycle to County Farm, as it was then known, (now called Hampden Hall) south of Aylesbury, on a Tuesday and it was there that a sympathetic tutor recommended I switched to horticulture. At that time, anyway, horticulture was a far more hands-on profession than agriculture; many jobs were done by hand, literally. It was the best piece of advice I could have been given, but unfortunately the first nursery I chose really wasn't very good at all.

I still was sticking to my organic principles. I wouldn't work anywhere that didn't embrace them. There was a little nursery at Butler's Cross, Ellesborough, right on the edge of the Chilterns that advertised itself as 'organic', so I went to see it. Yes, they could do with an apprentice. They grew vegetables and had a little shop that sold their own produce plus a range of goods such as the 'Heath and Heather' range of natural supplements and Allison's Compost-Grown Flour. And they found me Board and Lodging with a Mrs. Green, just up the road towards Wendover, who lived in one of those little wooden chalet-type bungalows that were put up in the 'thirties. I would be back in my beloved Chilterns again! So I jumped at the chance.

My time there was not a happy experience, again the ideals of an 'organic' approach to growing were not shared by those who actually did the job, so I will quickly pass over my time there but I should pay tribute to the redoubtable Mrs. Green, a lady well into her seventies who was unfailingly cheerful and made my little bedroom as homely as she could, and my life there more than just bearable. I was sad to leave her, but I left the nursery before I was pushed. This time I had managed six months.

I spent quite a lot of time searching for somewhere else, and was pragmatic enough to realise that perhaps I should not be as rigid in my approach as I had been. My mother had always believed that I had a 'guardian angel' watching over me, and when I discovered Hall's Nursery in Amersham, I believed it too. I started there in May 1966, and didn't look back. They weren't dogmatic about growing 'organically', but this was one of the last really traditional old-fashioned nurseries in Buckinghamshire. It was run by the Hall brothers, Charlie and Jim, helped by their wives, and it was there I learnt not only how to grow things and make things professionally, but to really live the life. The stuff was sold at their own little shop in Amersham New Town and we grew nearly all of it, all by hand. There was a rotovator but I wasn't allowed to use it - Jim had recently broken his leg as a result of this fearsome machine propelling him into a wall - and a modern oil-fired heating system in most of the greenhouses, but the methods used were those of the thirties and before.

The nursery was down at the end of a tiny little lane off Chestnut Lane on the borders of Amersham-on-the-Hill and Chesham Bois. Chestnut Lane was still semi-rural then, and the nursery was its own little enclave surrounded by trees, meadows and the odd large house. The brothers Hall lived next to each other in a large-ish house converted into two small-ish cottages. It was very peaceful. The brothers could not have been more different. Charlie was the eldest, a placid, pipe-smoking man who attended church every Sunday with his wife, Elsie. Jim was extrovert, often in trouble as a child, always cheerful and joking about something. He was married to a much younger lady called Barbara. They worked well together and shared one, devastating, thing in common - a heart condition. This was to end my time at the nursery, but not for five years, well after I had completed my apprenticeship.

I immediately felt at home at this place. A lot of time was spent teaching me how to do things, showing me how to bud and graft fruit trees, lay hedges, take cuttings, nurture seedlings, pot-up correctly (all clay pots), make wreaths and all the skills associated with a traditional nursery business. They knew I was interested even if I was often inept. I was told by the N.F.U. man that 'the ball was in my court' and if I didn't shape-up and keep this job, I would not be able to continue on the apprenticeship scheme. I needed no pushing, though - I flourished under the Hall's tutelage. I started a diary, and it is instructive and sometimes amusing now to look at it and read such snippets as :

'23rd. July 1969 - Weeded all the frames in morning, then started on the mower again. After running for a short while, a chain came off, nut fell off, and blades shook off! Much bad language. Then hoed wallflowers. Weather very hot, over 90, very still'. 'Thursday 14th. August - Sixteen rows of wallflowers planted. Most peculiar big insect found in fir-tree wood; took home, unidentified'. This is followed by an asterisk 'see Sept. 4th.' 'Sept. 4th. The insect. Woodwasp, the Lesser Horntail (Sirex noctilio), female. The first specimen recorded in Bucks.' I didn't say where it had been identified or who did it, but I believe it may been done at the Buckinghamshire museum at Aylesbury or possibly by someone at the Berks., Bucks and Oxon Naturalist's Trust.

I spent five very happy and fruitful years at Hall's Nursery, and by the time the nursery closed I had become quite proficient. I had served my apprenticeship and passed a number of City and Guilds exams. in horticulture and still proudly possess my 'Craftsman's Certificate', entitling me to 10% over the basic pay rate for an agricultural or horticultural labourer. The apprenticeship scheme was a damned good one, I cannot understand why such an obviously sound way of teaching non-academic pupils was dropped a few years later.

For most of the time at Hall's I had returned home to live, and travelled to Amersham each day on the train in the winter months or on my motor scooter in the better weather. I'd actually bought my first scooter, a Vespa 125, in 1966. It was a 1961 model and surprisingly reliable, but a pig to start when cold. The engine was a two-stroke and kept sooting-up the one plug. But I loved it. You could drive it on a provisional licence and, still then, with no helmet. I travelled hundreds of miles with the wind in my hair and resented having to buy and wear a helmet the following year, when the legislation was passed.

The day before the regulation came in, I took the day off just to experience for the last time the feeling of freedom and exhilaration of biking 'topless'. I scootered to Oxford and back. I got the bike serviced at Chesham Motorcycle Service, and Mr. Coppin who ran the business advised that really I should get a different scooter as mine was more-or-less worn-out. By then I'd passed my car test, but couldn't afford one of those, so Dad helped me purchase a brand-new 1968-model Vespa 150 Sprint, from Mr. Coppin of course. I never regretted it - Mr. and Mrs. Coppin were a very honest couple and took a great pride in selling me a brilliant little bike and in servicing it afterwards. It never, once, let me down. I explored a lot of Britain on that trusty machine, which I kept for over two years.

I once took my old school-chum, Clive, on it all the way from his house in Golder's Green to Winchcombe in the Cotswolds on a very clear, cold day in January. By the time we got back it was dark and we were both so cold that we couldn't get off the bike. We were, literally, frozen stiff. In 1968 I went on holiday on it and drove all the way down to Pembrokeshire to visit John Seymour, the author I mentioned earlier, and his family. It was a trip I'd repeat several times afterwards in the early seventies. I'll not forget the ride, in glorious weather, on the mountain road which leads from Llanwrtyd Wells to Tregaron, never thinking that in 1976 I'd be driving a COACH along it. . . .but I digress. Back to the nursery!

Once I'd passed my car driving test in 1967 I was asked to occasionally help out with the deliveries, using the firm's Ford Thames van. This had the engine between the front seats, a three-speed gearbox on the column, and the infamous vacuum wipers. It seemed very big at first but I enjoyed sitting right at the very front - there was no 'bonnet'. I enjoyed even more meeting the customers and poodling about the local by-ways. It made a great change from digging and hoeing.

In the summer of 1968 everything changed. Jim Hall suffered a massive heart attack, which he survived, but then another, which killed him. This was quite a shock, Jim was always the stronger physically of the two brothers and Charlie had already had a milder heart problem some years before. Jim's wife, Barbara, ran the shop but after Jim died she left; the two wives did not get on. So Elsie, Charlie's wife, now had to run the shop, Charlie had to spend more time there than before, and much of the nursery work was delegated to me. A girl, Linda, worked with me - in fact she was there before I started - but she soon fell in love with a builder who was working on building a school next door to the nursery, got pregnant, and left too. We had a succession of lads try their hand at helping us, but none of them lasted very long.

It definitely wasn't a 'trendy' place to work and the work was physically demanding and sometimes tedious and repetitive, and certainly not well-paid. I rather despised these 'youngsters' except one, who rejoiced in the name of 'Girth'. His girth was actually quite small, and he was an enthusiastic and capable lad. How he could want to start a career in banking I couldn't imagine, but that's what he did. I hope he's had as an enjoyable life as me.

The world around the nursery was changing very rapidly now. In addition to the hideous-looking school being built in the field next door, houses were being built further down Chestnut Lane and the character of the place began rapidly to alter. I had been very lucky seeing the area as it had been, virtually unchanged since the 'thirties. However, the nursery remained as it had been, an oasis of tradition and tranquillity in this fast-changing environment. I virtually ran the growing side of things at the nursery throughout 1969 and 1970 and it was a valuable and enlightening experience.

Then, just after Christmas 1970, Charlie Hall became ill, and then very ill, with pneumonia. He was admitted to Amersham Hospital and it was lucky he was, as a couple of days later he, too, suffered a heart attack. They saved his life, but the writing was on the wall for the nursery. The entry in my diary for Monday 11th. January states 'News Day. Shop closing at end of week, nursery ditto. I am staying on now only until the end of January, to help clear the stuff up. Emptied out chrysanths and cleaned Lizzy out'. 'Lizzy', by-the-way, was the oil-fired boiler which blew hot air through plastic pipes in the greenhouses!

'Emptying out the chrysanths' meant taking the plants which had flowered before Christmas out of their large pots, cutting them back almost to the roots, discarding the stems but keeping the roots and putting them in trays of earth. In the Spring, they would sprout and cuttings could be taken for next year's crop. Only this year, the roots were discarded as well, of course.

The day before this momentous news was told to me, I had attended the Wing Airport Resistance Association rally at Wing Equestrian Centre. I had forgotten all about this until I re-read my diary. In 1970 it had been proposed that there should be a third London Airport, and Wing (apt name) between Aylesbury and Leighton Buzzard had been selected as one of the possible sites. The others were Thurleigh in Bedfordshire and Foulness, off the coast of Essex near the Thames Estuary. Wing, apparently, was the favourite. Milton Keynes had begun to take shape so a huge airport at Wing would destroy almost all the countryside between London and Northampton, when all the necessary infrastructure had been put in place. There was an enormous outcry, and this rally was attended by 15,000 people, 2,000 of whom were still trying to get in at the end. I remember Cleo Lane singing and many others speaking; it was if Buckinghamshire had been singled out for ruination, as Milton Keynes had only recently been started, and the county has been much-loved by generations of Londoners as a green and healthy oasis. As I write, some of it is being threatened again with the new HS2 rail-link, rather ironic now as in 1970 the Great Central Railway line had been closed only four years previously. Joined-up thinking? Hardly. Anyway, the rally was a great success and in the end the airport plan was, thankfully, dropped.

During this time, I read in the 'Guardian' newspaper, which my parents had read since the days when it was the 'Manchester Guardian', that all the objectors to the project were 'middle class' - as if that were a crime. Shortly afterwards I heard about how much the proprietor of the paper got, and where he lived, along with several of the top reporters including the one who had written the offending article, and I thought how hypocritical that lot were. I've never read the 'Guardian' since.

My job was now to get-together all of the saleable stock and implements and try to sell them. We had numerous landscape gardeners as customers, and I started to ring round. The first week was really hectic as I had to help Mrs. Hall with the shop and, as she didn't drive, take her up to Amersham Hospital to visit Charlie. Fortunately their son and his fiancée came down from Solihull to help out that week, too. As word got round, many people came to the nursery to see if they could pick up a bargain and they often did. One elderly gentleman, a Mr. Worth, insisted on helping me out for nothing; he came every day to help load-up the van and often accompanied me on my deliveries; he said he thoroughly enjoyed working again! I do hope that I adequately expressed my appreciation, because his assistance was invaluable. I worked long hours during the four weeks, sometimes until eight in the evening (the greenhouses were lit).

Although I was due to leave at the end of January, I stayed on for a week or so after that to help clear some of the remaining stuff and procure for myself some of the items. So in February, with many expressions of goodwill and with much sadness on my part, I finally left the nursery for good. I had heard that the whole area was earmarked for 'development', and it was many, many years before I returned to see what had happened. I wish I could have bought it and kept it as it was!

Hollybush Lane and the nursery site is now 'Nursery Close'. I visited it in the late eighties and was astonished at how affected I was by the change. Not a trace of the nursery remains and there are just the ubiquitous 'executive homes' arranged in a circle. I've never gone back since.

Charlie Hall died of a further heart-attack later in 1971. For some reason I couldn't attend the funeral, so my mum very kindly did so for me.

UNIVERSITY CHALLENGE

Two of my friends, Andrew and Clive, had secured places at Leeds University. When I left Hall's, I decided I should have about a month off and visit them there. Andrew had 'digs' in a little street called Hawes Mount, whilst Clive had a room in a house for Jewish students called Hillel House. I decided to stay with Andrew.

I travelled up by train and found my own way to Hawes Mount, a typical Victorian back-to-back street in one of the many working-class areas of the city. It looked pretty grim and was scheduled to be demolished in one of those grandiose sixties/seventies plans which required everyone to live in a tower-block. I caught Hawes Mount and its environs right at the end of its life, just before the bulldozers moved in. Washing was still strung on lines over the street, a grubby little shop occupied almost every corner, toilets were still outside in the yards. I felt my spirits contract as I walked down the street but I sensed that what was going to replace them would be even worse.

The house Andrew shared was one of the larger ones with reasonably-sized rooms. It was bitterly cold and very basic. One of the other students who shared the house was ill and had gone home, so I was allocated his room. I was warned that he had the smelliest feet in Christendom and that the room might be a bit pongy. On the first night I got into bed and as it warmed up the smell became so overpowering I had to move out. That poor chap - I hope he got it sorted later in life. I spent the rest of my nights there on a put-you-up in the living room.

Andrew said that I should have no trouble in attending lectures if I was interested. Me, attending classes at University? He said that I could go with him and no-one would notice. I couldn't really see any point, as I wouldn't know what anything was about, and would prefer to explore Leeds or travel out into the surrounding countryside. But I was intrigued - I could say 'I've been to University' and be telling the truth! So I did one class, and I can't remember anything about it at all except meeting a Student Union rep. and getting a Union card. Was it Jack Straw? I think he was there at that time!

With my Union Card I could attend various Student functions including the 'hop' and I had a whale of a time. It was so different from life at the Nursery or at home, and I was surprised that I enjoyed every minute. I spent most days getting on the bus and going to Harrogate, Ilkley or York and then if there was time catching another bus to take me out into the

Yorkshire countryside. I distinctly remember getting on a half-cab single-decker bus to Grassington; it must have been one of the last still in service. According to my diary I walked over the moors via Mastiles Lane to Malham. Somehow I wangled a lift from Malham back to Headingly, being treated to tea and toast en route! This time at Leeds started me wondering whether I should consider doing something else. I returned home on the 17th. February, shortly after decimal day, and noted that I had lunch on the train. . .cost £1-18p.

Around the time I 'went to University', my brother suddenly 'dropped-out'. He had enjoyed a brilliant education at the Grammar School and had been recommended for a place at Cambridge University; but after leaving school he informed Mum and Dad he wouldn't go on to University. After my woeful academic achievements, they had been thrilled with my brother, but this news devastated them both. He started work sweeping floors in a factory before going on to sell kitchen furniture at M.F.I.

I wasn't around much at this time, but sensed the acute disappointment and bewilderment of my parents. In later years I asked Antony if he regretted his choice and he was adamant he didn't but I'm not entirely convinced. I don't think my mother ever really came to terms with what he did, but conceded 'it's his life'.

FAITH, HOPE, AND CHARITY

Despite my thoughts about doing something else, the very next day I went round to the Employment Exchange in search of a job. I expect I was nearly broke. They weren't much help, so the next day I got in my little Bond three-wheeler car and went looking myself.

I'd sold the scooter the previous autumn and invested in a second-hand 'Bond 875' three-wheeler, a much rarer vehicle than the Reliant which was made famous by the TV series 'Only Fools and Horses'. The Bond was much faster than the Reliant, it had a Hillman Imp power-unit at the back, over the two rear wheels. It was smaller than the Reliant but had four dinky seats. It was lethal, especially in snow as there was no weight over the single front wheel. In crosswinds it was a nightmare.

The previous Bonds had been the 'Minicar', which had a Villiers two-stroke engine mounted over the front wheel; slow, noisy and not very reliable but comparatively safe. I tried one for a week or so before buying the 875. It often wouldn't start on the battery, so you raised the bonnet and kick-started it; it was of course a motorcycle engine and retained the kick-start mechanism! It also had the odd characteristic that you could run the engine itself in reverse, so could (in theory at least) go backwards in top gear! The 875 model was at least a little more conventional, but it wasn't a nice vehicle to drive and by the time I started looking for my next job I had put it up for sale. I must have needed the money, because I got £240 for the Bond and spent £30 on an ex-Billingsgate Ford fish-van to replace it. Widely known as the 100E, these had a side valve engine, three-speed gearbox, vacuum wipers. . . .but four wheels at least. After collecting it, one of the first things I did at a stop for traffic lights was put it in reverse, as the slot for reverse was where every other make had first gear. Lights change, off I go. . . .backwards, into a Ford Zephyr waiting behind. 'First time driving this, mate?' asked the driver. Fortunately he was a Ford man, and knew exactly what I'd done and why I'd done it, and despite a dented front bumper found it hilarious. I still feel embarrassed, even now.

I found a couple of nurseries and the owner of the second said he could indeed do with a hand. This was only four miles from home, yet was in a lovely spot adjacent to Harrow Weald Common. It was then called the Kiln Nurseries and Garden Centre, the proprietor Mr. Smith. I was taken on at £12 a week as 'chief propagator' i.e. the chap who took the cuttings and nurtured the seedlings.

It was a far more modern and commercially-orientated business than Hall's. I found it took a bit of getting used to, plus the fact that about six others were working there. I was happy in my work but Mr. Smith was an irritable and anxious man, prone to losing his rag without warning and always worrying about the 'viability' of everything. Compared with Hall's, it was stressful. However, Mr. Smith must have thought I was OK because within a month he increased my wage to £14 a week - not at all bad at the time. I could fill my van with petrol for about £1-50.

One of the ladies working there, Mrs. Marks, befriended me and taught me quite a lot about how to avoid upsetting Mr. Smith. I'd agreed to work overtime for no pay in exchange for a long holiday in the summer, so in that summer I had about six weeks off and had a great time travelling round Wales and going as far as Pembrokeshire to visit John Seymour and his family.

The Ford van wouldn't have been up for this, so I looked around for something a bit better. One day in the Spring a very smart-looking red Hillman Minx convertible was driven into the nursery with a sign in the back window 'For Sale - £90'. Mr. Smith actually saw it first and took the trouble to inform me. I approached the owner, took it for a short drive, and clinched a deal at £85 cash. I loved that car. It was quiet, comfortable, reliable and you could have the hood fully closed, half-open in a 'Coupe-de-Ville' position or fully open. I had always felt a bit claustrophobic driving cars after my scooter, so this was fantastic. It started a love-affair with Rootes-built convertibles that lasted for years. By today's standards they are difficult to drive, with unassisted drum brakes, no power steering, slippery bench seats, etc. etc. but that was normal then. I drove with the hood either half-open or fully open whenever I could, and felt king of the road.

On one of the trips to Wales which I mention a little later, I was returning from staying with friends in the Cambrian Mountains in the Hillman when it suddenly cut out and stopped. It was pouring with rain and of course there were no mobile phones then. It was a quiet mountain road, too, miles from anywhere. I thought I'd have to walk many miles to the nearest farmhouse to ask if I could use their phone, but as I started leaving the car a Land Rover drew up. 'Trouble?' beamed the driver. I explained what had happened and he said he was no mechanic so he'd tow me into Llanybyther (the nearest garage open - it was a Sunday). I very gladly accepted. 'Keep the rope taught!' he instructed, and off we went. It was the first time I'd been towed so I kept the brakes lightly on, all the way. When we got to Llanybyther, they were red-hot! But the chap said I'd been brilliant at keeping the rope taught. I thanked him profusely and asked his name. 'Thurlow Craig' he said. 'The gentleman who writes for the Sunday Express?' I asked. 'The very same! I'm flattered such a young blade would have heard of me!' He wrote a regular column called 'Up Country' but I had no idea he lived in Wales. He seemed ever so pleased that a 'young person' knew it. 'Good luck' he said, and waved goodbye. A nice man. The garage was called 'Jack's Empire Motor Services' and they said they couldn't fix the car straight away, but to ring them during the next week.

Then I had to find out whether there was a bus to Carmarthen on this Sunday. There was - one - in four hours' time. I started walking, to keep warm and save a bit on the fare, through the pouring rain. Nowhere was open. When the bus finally got into Carmarthen it was too late to get a train to London, so I stayed in a 'Transport' House which was awful. I was soaked through, and no change of clothes. . . .

The car, whose distributor drive had sheared, was ready in a week. I took a newspaper train from Paddington back to Carmarthen one night and then got the bus back to Llanybyther where I collected the car. Half a mile down the road, it cut out again. I walked back to the garage, and after a bit of persuasion they came out and diagnosed water in the petrol. I had lost the cap and stuffed a rag in the filler, which of course had become soaked in the rain. . . .they drained and re-filled the tank, put a rubber cap on the filler, and I was away at last.

After this long holiday I began to think again about a change of direction, and started to look at smallholdings for sale in Wales. I wanted to be self-sufficient like John Seymour, but each time I saw a place that looked suitable I was assailed by those feelings of being out-of-my-depth and of loneliness, again. Throughout 1972 I looked at places, sometimes with a friend called Les who was thinking along similar lines but was actually more naïve about how to do it than me.

You could buy a four-acre smallholding with small farmhouse and outbuildings for around £4,000! But time and again, we pulled back from making any commitment.

I had friends who lived in the most remote part of the Cambrian mountains, up the longest, steepest stoniest track ever, and always enjoyed staying with them, and they were quite puzzled as to my hesitancy. Towards the end of 1972, after many more trips to Wales and talks with my friends, I decided I wanted to do more than just be self-sufficient, and with that decision came some serenity - it was the right decision for me. But what to do? It took about six months to arrive at what seemed to be the solution.

I have no recollection exactly when or how I came up with the idea of starting a children's charity, but it must have been late 1972 or early 1973. I had been thinking a lot about the holidays I had enjoyed as a child and after my trip to Leeds, had felt sorry for all those children who spent their holidays in such an urban environment. Somehow, the idea of buying a farm and using it as a farm but also to enable deprived city kids to enjoy holidays there and learn a bit about the countryside, developed in my head. I mentioned the idea to my friends and family and almost all were enthusiastic. 'This would be you' said one; 'you would never have been fulfilled just doing the farming'.

But how to get the idea out to the wider public? Well, the others at the nursery always insisted on having Radio 1 on all day and despite my dislike of it I noticed that Alan Freeman had a slot on his show called 'Youth Club Call'. It usually just name-tagged various youth clubs around the country with the briefest of details about what they did, but I thought it may be worth writing down my idea and sending it to him. I carefully composed my letter, making it as brief as possible yet giving a fairly full picture of the idea and I remember appealing to 'Happy and enthusiastic' young people.

To my surprise and delight, Alan read out the whole of my letter and added a few supportive comments of his own. This happened on the afternoon of Tuesday 27th. February 1973. He wanted to talk to me on the telephone but unfortunately for some reason I was in Yorkshire again on that day - I heard the broadcast on the car radio. I rang the BBC but they were unable to put me through to Alan after the show, and we never actually managed to talk until I made sure we did at one of the Radio 1 roadshows over a year later.

The reaction was overwhelming. On my return from Yorkshire there was a pile of letters for me, and this became a mountain over the next few days. I'm pleased to say I managed to reply to each one individually, though it took a while. Obviously there were a number of people who were just dreamers, but enough sounded interested and sincere enough to take the idea further. I cannot remember now how I managed to procure a room for a day in Guildford University, but it was done and the first meeting was held there on Saturday 12th. May. People came from all over, I think we had about fifty there, and a name was chosen - Earthshine. I had described it as 'The Farm & Community Project' but Earthshine was great. A chap named Mick Green thought of it, and he became a leading light for several years.

We agreed on a Treasurer, a chairman, and me as secretary. It all seemed very exciting, we were on a roll, and many had good ideas on how to raise money and keep people interested in the project. Most of us wanted to keep the organisation as informal as possible, including me, but we were told we had to have a committee if we were going to be recognised by the Charity Commissioners, so this was done, with some reluctance, in due course.

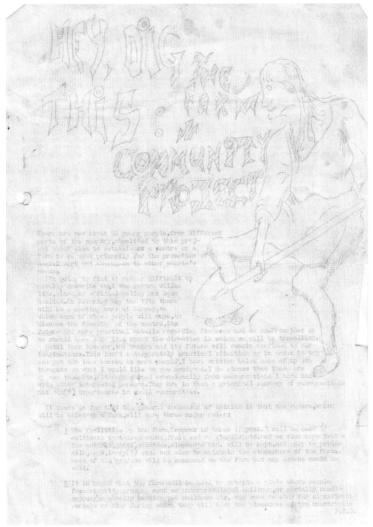

First Farm & Community Project leaflet, 1973.

We agreed that the farm idea might take some time, but we wanted to keep up the momentum and actually start doing some good as soon as possible. Step forward Paul Crouch who helped at a children's home in Sidcup,

51

Kent, and who had converted a 1950's Bedford coach into a big camper, suitable for transporting, and catering for, about twenty children at a time. As soon as we'd raised a little money, which we managed quite speedily, we purchased tents and other camping equipment and were able to offer 'country holidays for [deprived] city children'.

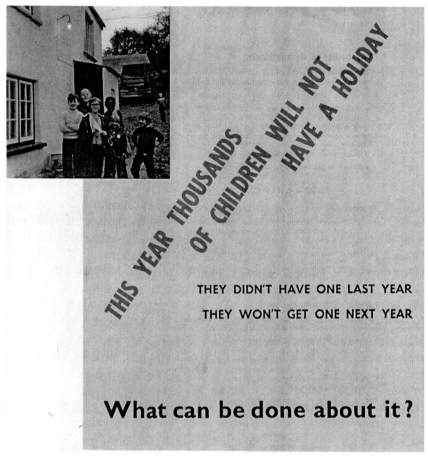

THIS YEAR THOUSANDS OF CHILDREN WILL NOT HAVE A HOLIDAY

THEY DIDN'T HAVE ONE LAST YEAR
THEY WON'T GET ONE NEXT YEAR

What can be done about it?

Earthshine leaflet, and picture of children on holiday.

Our first outing was the following Spring, but in the meantime Mick Green and I decided we should take our bus test (it wasn't compulsory then, if you were not driving for 'hire or reward'). Mick wanted to start his own coach company anyway, so it would be essential for him. I thought it would be sensible if I took the test, too. Paul gave Mick and I a practice run in the coach and I found driving such a long and wide vehicle quite scary, as well as extremely hard work. It seemed you more-or-less had to stand on the clutch and brake to make them work, the steering required the arms of

Charles Atlas to operate, and the gearlever ditto. You had to keep your fingers clear when putting it into first gear, for the lever struck the rear of the engine cover in this position, but after a few really painful experiences, you picked up the trick pretty fast! The engine was immediately next to the driver, and was a very noisy and underpowered diesel which meant a great deal of anticipation was required when pulling out into traffic. I needed a lot of practice before taking children on any trip at all. A proper training and test seemed wise.

In the winter of 1973/4 Mick and I travelled up to Nottingham for a week's intensive training with the Wallace School of Transport. They ran courses in London but were booked-up for weeks in advance, so after an initial assessment on their training ground at the White City, which confirmed we needed a week's training, we were booked into Nottingham. To get a full Public Service Vehicle licence you needed to take a test on a double-decker. Mick got an AEC vehicle, but I got a Leyland PD2 which was a pre-war design, complete with vacuum brakes, crash gearbox, and half-cab (like the Routemaster bus). It scared me!

The instructor had to bellow through the window behind me when the engine was running, and often he had to repeat his instructions as it was so difficult to hear him over the din. Over the week, we learned how to get the best out of the vehicle, look out for low trees and low bridges, reverse around corners and stop with the rear platform of the bus right by the bus stop. I was signed-off as being 'proficient' by the end of the week but Mick had to complete another week before they would put him in for test. (I felt pretty smug about this, as he had seemed the more confident of us two. I didn't mention it. Much).

The test had to be in Grantham as Nottingham was booked solid. On the morning of the test we motored over without incident and had time to go through the main street of the town to get the lie of the place. I had just reached the end of the High Street when the pin securing the driver's seat at the required height broke, and seat and I plummeted to the floor. To my instructor, it looked as if I'd gone through the floor as I'd become completely invisible to him. I managed to hold on to the wheel and brought the vehicle to a stand, perfectly (and by sheer chance) lined-up against the kerb. There was no time to lose as the Test was imminent, so we cobbled-together a repair, concealed our shock, and had a wry laugh before meeting the Tester. 'Not a word!' said my instructor.

Still shaking somewhat from this incident, I followed the tester's instructions except where he ordered me down a road where there was signed a low bridge. This was deliberate; if I'd gone down that road he would have failed me. Part of the test then involved hand-signals, which was farcical; I've short arms and the side window was a fair distance away, so only my hand showed. Anyone looking from outside would have thought I was waving at them. At the end of the test I had to answer several 'trick' questions, such as 'You're proceeding down a narrow road with cars either side; a child runs out and you know you cannot stop in time; what do you do?' The answer was to drive in to the parked cars. The same question, only this time it's a dog. You run over the dog.

I passed first time, and was shaking so much the instructor drove us back to Nottingham. But I was so pleased to have done it. I could drive a bus competently and had an 'all types of PSV' licence to prove it. My self-confidence went up a few notches that day, particularly when my instructor said 'I doubt whether anyone else would have taken the test after what happened this morning, never mind pass it. Well done!' Apparently the story was still being told at Wallace's years afterwards.

In due course, Mick passed his test too, but as it turned out he never again drove the 'Earthshine' bus. He was busy starting his own coach company in Southall, West London, which was to be called 'Untours'. The idea was to operate an alternative-type service which would take the adventurous to any remote part of the world, and be guide, courier and driver. To cut a long story short, none of this happened and he ended up doing school-runs in Southall and calling it Unity Coaches before going bust, giving up and emigrating to Australia. Before he did, though, he was very supportive of Earthshine and, indeed, myself.

In fact, I was made a director of Untours along with another of Mick's friends, Dave Lee, and Mick himself. I think this was due to a legal requirement, but I still have a card stating 'Roger Crawford - company director'! I did one or two jobs for Mick in the early days, and on one of them came closer to killing myself (not deliberately) than ever before or since. We picked up passengers who were using the 'Magic Bus' to go to India or Africa, from Holloway in London, and took them as far as Sheerness Docks where they boarded a boat for Europe.

In fact, in those days, I drove the coach onto the boat before they disembarked. On driving out of Sheerness, empty of course, I took a bend rather too fast and the old AEC coach I was driving skidded on the wet road on a left-hand bend approaching a bridge over a river, or some inlet. Everything seemed to happen in slow motion as I approached the low wall separating road from water. I really thought I was going to go right through it but had failed to notice a kerb immediately in front of it which deflected the coach back to the correct side of the road, and I managed to regain control. There was no damage to either bridge or coach so I rather nonchalantly drove on to Farthing Corner (now Medway) Services on the M2 and stopped there. As soon as I stopped I started shaking all over, delayed shock I suppose. I had been so lucky that there had been a kerb and that no-one had been coming the other way. I kept shaking for nearly an hour before feeling able to continue.

On a lighter note, I have been reminded of the occasion where I had to pick up the entire (and very large) O'Leary family who were distantly connected to Dave Lee. I was instructed to pick them up at one end of Regina Road in Southall but I mis-heard it as 'Vagina Road' and questioned it, much to the amusement of my fellow-directors.

Dave said he always knew it was a bit of a hole. . . .

I hesitated before including the following little nugget, but thought I should to indicate the vagaries of a coach operator's lot. Thank goodness this didn't have anything to do with me. Mick did manage to purchase a rather nice turbo-diesel Ford coach with a lovely interior, and he got some work doing touring work. His last assignment was to take a party of Japanese gentlemen on a day tour of London. When he got in the coach that morning, he thought there was a rather odd smell but couldn't quite place it, so used plenty of air-freshener before setting off. All went well until around midday when the sun came out and it became rather warm. Mick turned on the forced-air vents and immediately two poor gentlemen got showered with vomit from the two vents over their heads. Someone from the previous trip had been sick into a paper bag and left it on the parcel shelf, and the contents had leaked out and somehow got into the fresh-air system. It was this incident that made Mick decide to leave the U.K. for good. I presume it had the same effect on those two Japanese gentlemen!

He, some of his friends, and I all went on holiday to Ireland that summer. I had received some information about a 'Farm for Children' in Donegal and wanted to visit that, so one of the friends and I split from the rest after a few days near Rosslare and thumbed a lift northwards. No problem in those days, three different lifts got us to Dublin in a day. After enjoying the somewhat raucous nightlife for one evening, we then got the train to Belfast. This was at the height of the 'Troubles' of course. We had to change trains, and stations, to get to our destinations of Coleraine (the friend) and Londonderry (me) and the security was intense - oppressive even. On the train to Derry, everyone was sitting in the middle seats - to try to avoid the missiles that were often thrown at the train, I was told. I stayed one night in Derry in a room above a cache of petrol bombs, and then gratefully boarded a bus for Buncrana in Donegal. Derry seemed a very tense place; tanks and soldiers were everywhere, but I received nothing but courtesy and helpfulness. With my long, curly hair, dishevelled appearance and sloppy gait, I certainly did not look like a member of the armed forces. The bus seemed to take an age to get to Buncrana. Once there, it didn't seem to be worth the time and I remember it, perhaps unfairly, as being a totally uninteresting place. I got a fabulous breakfast, though, at the B&B I stayed at.

The 'Farm for Children' in Donegal. They had their work cut out! Note monkey just visible on the path.

The Farm lay some distance out of town and there were no buses, so I had to walk. The countryside seemed rather bleak but when the sun lit up the craggy hillsides it was magically transformed into a shining landscape. I don't know how I found the farm, but when I got there, no-one was about. There was, however, a monkey eyeing me suspiciously from a barn door. I had been expected, but after a couple of hours with no-one turning up, I decided to walk back to Buncrana. On entering the town, I was greeted by Angela who ran the farm. With disarming candour, she explained that she wondered if it was me she'd seen earlier but thought I wouldn't find the farm, and return 'in an hour or so'. She helped in a shop in the town and got paid, so this helped the finances. She didn't drive, so we walked back to the farm again.

The Farm for Children took in children, both Protestant and Catholic, who had been affected by the violence in Northern Ireland. Angela and her helpers hoped that the peace of the Donegal countryside would help heal the mental scars these children suffered, and give them a vision of something better. She had been brought up in Dublin and had always wanted to help kids. At first, she had been viewed with suspicion by the locals, particularly by the local Priest.

This part of Ireland was still very insular in the seventies, and each small community was more-or-less ruled by the Catholic Church. Indeed, the 'Magdalen Laundries' still operated at this time.

Angela worked hard to win over the Church, and one day had succeeded in persuading the Priest and a few of the more prominent members of the local Church to come and have tea and discuss what she was trying to do. Unfortunately the aforesaid monkey (rescued from somewhere) decided to play up on that day, throwing things about before sitting in front of the group and openly masturbating. Everything was tried in an effort to distract the creature, food, toys, but nothing worked.

Apparently the priest and his cohorts left quickly and hadn't been seen at the farm since. Angela and I talked long into the evening, and I admired her tenacity, but I vowed we would never have a monkey on our place! We lost touch after a few years and I wonder what became of the farm, and its ideals. I can't believe now that I thumbed a lift all the way from Buncrana to Larne, I must have been either brave or thoroughly foolhardy and naïve, but again I experienced no trouble. I got the ferry to Stranraer, then trains to Glasgow and on to Edinburgh, where a friend had left my car after borrowing it to tour Scotland whilst I was away.

Earthshine couldn't as yet afford to buy the bus from Paul, so he continued to stable, maintain and own it and as he was already in to giving holidays to children with it we worked together to agree dates etc. It was all so easy then. CRB checks were non-existent; I simply wrote to schools in inner-city areas asking if they would be interested in using it and they replied - usually, yes! The first group I took was from an 'Educationally sub-normal' school in Birmingham. I drove the bus up, stayed in it outside the school overnight, and they boarded it in the morning. For this first run, it was just a day trip to the Lickey Hills south of Birmingham but it was so successful word spread quickly and that first year - 1974 - we had to turn away more schools and groups than we could accept. The schools just paid for fuel and for the driver's food. Throughout the summers of 74, 75, and 76 I lived a bohemian kind of existence and they were the most carefree days of my life.

Because we'd started very quickly to offer holidays, and were seen to be doing things, support remained strong. People sent money but we needed a stronger monetary base and it was felt we should try and obtain charitable status.

After the summer of '74, I realised that I seemed to be able to communicate very well with young and disadvantaged people, whilst gaining the trust of teachers and group leaders. For some years, the Church in Harrow that I referred to earlier had put on pantomimes for the local children every winter, but for the '74 show they were short of participants. Some of the youngsters involved were asked to ask their friends if they could come along and help. I'd been involved in the pantos for some years, often as an ugly sister or a dame, so I was involved with this one as well; and noticed that some of the friends who'd been persuaded to come along were from poorer backgrounds. Although I had not flaunted what I was doing with Earthshine, word had obviously got around and in this new influx of young people I had found strong support for the project. They were really keen, and it seemed a logical progression to form a Youth Club for them. The Church agreed; and we had the use of two halls and the kitchen allocated to us every Thursday evening.

The Youth Club was by far the most successful venture I have ever undertaken, more than Earthshine even. We started to have discos, barn dances, there was badminton and many of the members became the backbone of the fund-raising for Earthshine. They were Earthshine's best envoys. Despite having quite a number of 'rough' kids, we had very little trouble.

There were complaints about noise (and occasionally, about graffiti) but nothing really serious. And the strength of support for Earthshine was such that we were able to organise a 23-mile-long sponsored walk from Henley-on-Thames to Princes Risborough in May '75 which raised enough money to buy the coach for Earthshine. Everyone on that walk was able to see the coach for themselves as it was positioned half-way along the route as a lunch stop. That day was a great success, and we repeated it for a further two years. I must pay tribute to the then landlord of the 'White Horse' pub on the Oxford road out of Henley, whom I had asked if he'd mind the car park being used for the start of our walk. Not only did he not mind, he opened the pub for us at an unfeasibly early hour so people could use the toilets and get a drink (of water!) each year we did it.

I walked the route the day before, putting up direction signs. At each major change of direction we had a marshal and along the route there were checkpoints where the walker's cards were stamped and anyone too tired to continue could stop and be given a lift to the destination. These became more frequent as the mileage increased, but an astonishingly high number of people completed the whole walk. Most of it was on footpaths, the latter following the Upper Icknield Way (now known as the Ridgeway Path). We treated many to a fish-and-chip supper at Princes Risborough - they richly deserved it. A 'tail-ender' picked up the direction signs and informed the marshals that he was the last walker.

So, in 1975, Earthshine had its own bus. This made it possible for far more schools and groups to use it and it was our most successful year. But it was a time of rampant inflation and rocketing property prices and it was becoming obvious that we were not going to get our farm. Inevitably, this led to a number of the older supporters drifting away, including those who wanted a part in running the farm. The organisation had become more Harrow-based, with most supporters quite happy to help clean and service the bus, help raise money to buy stuff, and indeed help on the holidays.

'My' group held a stall at Harrow Show, where people could throw a bucket of water over me for 20p or a whole dustbin-full for £2 and we raised nearly £50 just doing that. A disco raised over £70. This was a good sum in 1975. People have been saying lately that 'things were different in the seventies'. I can confirm that they certainly were! No-one questioned that two of my youth-club members often helped out on the holidays and that I was a youth-leader without any paper qualifications whatever. Things were beginning to change though, and become a little more formalised. After a year of resistance from me, Harrow Borough eventually persuaded me to go on a 'Youth and Community' course and get a certificate, in 1976.

A journalist who worked for the 'Harrow Observer' newspaper said he'd give Earthshine £10 if I 'mooned' out of a van past the 'Gateway' pub in Harrow one Friday evening.
I did this rather obscene act and was rewarded not only with the £10, but also with another bucket of water thrown (accurately) over my bare backside.

Ah, 1976. The year of the long, hot summer. 1975 was the most successful for Earthshine but 1976 gave us the most glorious, perfect summer for our holidays and it was a momentous year for me.

Our first holiday that year was at Easter and we took pupils and staff from the school we first took two years before to Tywyn where, if I remember rightly, we camped on the beach. I had two youth-club stalwarts with me, Colin Hugill and Clive Eustice, and I seem to remember that we didn't start at the school but at a number of pick-up points in Birmingham itself. At one, one of the pupils, a boy, had a panic attack and we had to use all our powers of persuasion to get him to board the bus. His mother was quite determined she should have a week off from him, and blocked his every attempt to get off. It was a while before he stopped crying but as we cleared Birmingham and he realised there was no turning back, he calmed down and I was more than pleased to notice that Colin was making a special effort to talk to him. We had a grand holiday and our proudest achievement was getting this disturbed child up to the top of a mountain on his own steam when he had been convinced he couldn't do it. The look on his face as he stood on the top, and his wonder at the view, made it all worthwhile. He returned to his mum, I think, with a lot more confidence and lots to tell.

After the Easter holiday we had another highly-successful sponsored walk, the same route as the previous year but notable for my friend Douglas, who was driving my mother's car with four walkers aboard, crashing the car on a bend approaching Henley. One of the girls, Leslie Eteen, broke her arm in this incident and had to be taken to hospital. I was amazed when she appeared later on the walk, her arm in a sling, insisting she would do the entire distance. She kept her word - I was very moved by this as she was only thirteen, and I and others doubled her walk money in appreciation. The car was a write-off.

I spent the entire summer holidays in 1976 driving and camping in the bus. The sun just kept on shining and the mountains of Wales were turning brown rather than green. On one trip, we stayed in a youth hostel near Llynne Brianne and used the bus to go to the beach at Porthcawl and to show the kids some of the best of the local scenery. This was the time I drove the bus on that tiny road between Llanwrtyd Wells and Tregaron, and I felt quite proud that I could do it! One of the parents who came along wasn't so impressed and suffered a panic attack as she was convinced we were going to go over the edge. The children loved it, of course.

Throughout this time, the bus proved totally reliable and it put in an enormous mileage. All of the groups who used it fell in love with it and wanted to book it again next year. For me, who went on every trip, it was some compensation for not being able to afford a farm and I was a lucky b.

to have such holidays, with good appreciative company, that cost me nothing at all. Best years of my life!

Part of my connection with Birmingham was through my cousin Ann, who had been the only child of my father's brother, Cyril, and his wife Kathleen. They had lived in Kingswinford west of the City. Ann, who is a little older than me, had gone to Oxford to study and had become involved with the Cyrenians, a group that helped the homeless. After she'd moved back to Birmingham and got married, she produced an irregular magazine called 'Uncareers' which advertised jobs that helped poorer and disadvantaged people but paid little or nothing, appealing to those with a social conscience who might have time on their hands. Earthshine of course appeared in the magazine.

Ann started, and ran for some years, an 'Open Christmas' project in St. Martin's Youth-club Hall in central Birmingham, where homeless people could come for three days and nights to get warm and have good meals. I helped for four years, I think, up to Christmas 1976 and on the last one a youth club member, Tony Kirk, came up to help as well. It was very hard work but great fun and a worthwhile thing to do. That year, 1976, was notable for a homeless lady giving birth on the floor! I don't think Tony has ever been quite the same since.

After the holidays that summer, I needed to find better-paid work than at the nursery as I was completely broke. I started to work for a coach firm in Harrow called 'Parson's Coach Service', which was, frankly, a cowboy outfit but paid £50 a week - a lot for me at that time. I was used to driving very old buses, so was in my element here! One of them was older than the Earthshine bus. How Bill Parsons had landed a contract with the Inner London Education Authority (ILEA) to transport inner city children to a rural centre in Bucks every school day defied logic then, never mind now. He also had a contract with the electrical firm Thorn-Eriksson, taking employees from the Harrow area up to Millbank in Central London each day, and back again in the evening, which fitted in well with the ILEA contract.

I was given this job every day, which made it a long day - about twelve hours. I would first get the coach, which was simply parked-up on a road near me, at about a quarter to seven, pick up my passengers and take them into London. I then had time for a breakfast before picking up from schools - a different one each day - all over the western part of London, some in very narrow streets! I would then drive them to the Harrias Barn Rural Studies Centre in Beaconsfield, Buckinghamshire, where the children would learn about the countryside. An ideal job for me. After returning the children in the afternoon, I picked-up the Thorn-Ericsson employees and dropped them as near to their homes as I could. At weekends there was private hire work.

The first time I did the Rural Studies job I got lost trying to find the Centre. Not really surprising when what passed as my work-ticket (a page torn from an exercise book) simply said 'The Barn, Beaconsfield'. We arrived about half-an-hour later than scheduled and the leader of the centre, Mrs. Dora Hinton, dismissed my apologies from 'another bloody coach driver'. I was not required during that day, so skidaddled off to spend some time in the nearest large town, High Wycombe, lunching at the 'Café de Nosh'.

Mrs. Hinton, in her mid-forties, was an extraordinarily attractive and intelligent woman who did a fine job getting her charges interested in rural matters. Harrias Barn centre was part of the Hall Barn Estate, which covered many acres and often the children would see some of the work of the estate in practice as they visited different parts of it. Occasionally I was called to transport the children to and from a remote part of the Estate, and quickly was accepted as being OK and started being invited to stay for lunch and then take part in some of the walks.

After such a glorious summer, the autumn turned out to be one of the wettest on record, starting almost immediately after a Labour minister, Denis Howells, was appointed 'Minister for Drought'. This meant that many of the walks had to be cancelled, and the children confined to the centre for the day. Once Mrs. Hinton learned about my own activities with getting kids involved with country matters, I was welcomed as a friend and helped with dealing with the children on a regular basis. This was brilliant, I was now being paid to do the work I loved best. Mum said 'You always fall on your feet - you really must have a guardian angel looking after you!'. I do actually think she was right.

Mrs. Hinton was very interested in the idea of Earthshine. I was invited to her home in Slough for a Sunday lunch with her and her husband, and took the bus so she could see it. I was amazed when she said she'd like to help out on some of the holidays, and maybe even drive the bus.

On one of the days taking the children, I was asked to drive a Bedford VAL coach, the first chassis by Bedford made exclusively for coaches rather than commercial vehicles as well. These had smaller wheels than was usual and two sets of wheels at the front, known as 'twin-steer'. They even had power-steering as standard and they gave a superlative ride, but the brakes were less than adequate and on this particular day part of the floor was missing. On all coaches then, inspection hatches were provided down the centre aisle of the bus, and one large one was missing! The children had to worm their way round the gap, holding on to the seats, and on the move of course the draft and noise were terrific. The teacher in charge said he'd have to make a complaint, which I heartily agreed with; he duly did but, amazingly, no action was taken by ILEA.

It was in this coach, a year or so later, that I very nearly caused a serious accident. Coming back from Bournemouth after a day trip, on the old Winchester by-pass, I had almost completed overtaking a small car when I noticed a long queue of traffic stretching back from the traffic lights ahead, in my lane. With a full coach I knew there was no way I was going to stop in time. The nearside lane, however, had a much shorter queue, so I swung the coach over, missing the overtaken car by inches, and of course stood on the brakes. I noticed I would have hit the last car in the outside lane at around 30 mph., which almost certainly would have caused a fatal accident and I was approaching the nearside lane queue all too rapidly. Just in time, the lights changed and the cars moved forward and we avoided a collision, but it was a very close shave.

The remarkable thing was, all my passengers were playing Bingo and none - not one - noticed what had happened. I mentioned this to Bill Parsons afterwards and he said 'you're very lucky. The shoes are down to the rivets, I meant to warn you about it!'. No-one, I hope, would ever send a coach out like that now, and if they did get picked up by VOSA - then known as the 'Ministry' - there would be a STOP order put on the coach and probably the firm as well.

After the 'Open Christmas' at Birmingham in 1976 came the usual pantomime put on at the Church, only this time there were more youth club members involved in it than there were church members. The group persuaded the committee to donate the proceeds to Earthshine this year, which was fantastic news for me as by then we needed to replace some of the camping equipment and the bus needed new tyres on the front. And, by their own choice, the youth club wanted to call itself the Earthshine Youth Club. There had been some opposition from other quarters in the organisation to Earthshine becoming more Harrow-based but in reality it was these youngsters who were the power-house behind the whole thing and without their support, it would have folded.

I resumed the coach contracts after the Christmas holidays. I'd now got to know where all the schools were in West London and the best way to get to them, and despite some pretty foul weather early in 1977 was never late again. We even got a much newer coach with fairly effective heating, and good brakes, as Bill was coining it in on these contracts. Luxury of luxuries, this one even had a power-operated door. All the others had to be slid back manually.

On one bus, the one older than the Earthshine vehicle, the passenger door (which was set back towards the centre of the bus) was operated by a huge lever situated to the left of the driver; you had to heave upwards on this to open the door. You quickly learned to commence this movement at the exact moment the bus stopped, to add a little momentum - if the bus was facing downhill it was near impossible to do. On one occasion when I was driving this, I heaved on the lever only for it to snap off abruptly, so then that was the end of the 'driver operated door'. Bill continued to use the vehicle in service, however! For coach aficionados, this was a Bedford SB1 coach with a rare - even in those days - Burlingham body. It would be a treasured classic now if it had survived to this day.

No such problems with this much more modern Ford vehicle, but it was still odd that the door opened from the leading edge, so then it swung into the step-well rather than - common practice now - slide open flush with the windscreen. One day for some unknown reason a small child had ventured down the steps without me noticing before I'd opened the door, then of course when I opened it he was swept into and then squashed between door and front 'wall' of the coach. As the door wasn't fully open I could not get it to close, so had to empty out all the air-tanks to release the pressure and close the door manually. Then, once screaming child was freed, I had to start up again and build the air pressure up to get the door to open and stay open to let the passengers off. Just as the point was reached, an elderly gentleman descended the first step only to be whacked in the face by the opening door. It just couldn't happen today. I took to warning people about it but there was still the occasional incident.

On the 14th. February I received a Valentine Card. I had been so absorbed in work, with the kids at the Youth Club and with Earthshine that my love life didn't exist - 'romance' was going away in the Earthshine bus. I'd had a few girlfriends over the years, one or two of them fairly serious, but once Earthshine had gained momentum there was simply no time for anything like that. I hadn't received a valentines card for years, nor sent one either. Where had it come from, who had sent it? I was, truly, mystified by this - and intrigued. The message read 'I can do italic writing'. That really didn't help much. It got me thinking, though. I was twenty-eight, and still, ahem, a virgin. The 'sexual revolution' had passed me by. Perhaps it was time I indulged in a little romance. Mum said it was certainly time I left home! Dad was approaching retirement and they initially planned on moving to Reigate in Surrey.

On my next trip to the Rural Centre I was asked if I'd received a Valentine. Completely innocently I replied that unbelievably I had but I'd no idea who'd sent it. Mrs. Hinton smiled and handed me some notes - in her italic writing. I was, understandably, shocked. We were obviously on the same wavelength and got on extremely well together, but she had given no hint that she fancied me. Even if she had I probably would not have recognised it. Not only was she married, and had three children (all grown-up and moved away) but she was over eighteen years older than me. She said that she admired the fact that I didn't just talk about doing things but actually did them. She was sorry if she'd shocked me but her feelings were genuine.

To say I was gobsmacked would be an understatement. I was being pursued by an older woman! At the same time, it was enormously exciting and flattering. I had enough 'nous' to realise that an affair would cause hurt to others, but here was a most attractive, vivacious woman seeking me out; could I resist? Dora, as I can henceforth call her, wanted more than an affair, though - she wanted to live with me. She also wanted to play a bigger role in Earthshine. I confess that though this change seemed momentous, I didn't hesitate for very long. We took long walks together, had serious and intimate conversations, and consummated our relationship within weeks. I must have been too self-conscious to have been much good, but she was kind enough not to say.

This momentous change was comparatively easy for me. For Dora it was far more difficult, obviously, as she had to inform not only her husband but her three children as well as her parents who were still alive. I was very nervous telling my parents and they were understandably upset and worried. I ducked-out of telling the people at the church for a while, though I did tell many of my youth-club friends.

I was charged with finding some rented accommodation, and through 'Ray's Bureau' in Eastcote (near home in Harrow) secured the upstairs of a typical 'semi' at 62 Rugby Avenue, Sudbury, just a stone's throw from the swimming baths at Vale Farm where I (didn't) swim much in my schooldays. We moved in in June, 1977. The rent was £92 a month, plus gas and electric. Within the six months from the previous Christmas my life was totally transformed, and I took to it like a duck to water.

THAT'S THE SPIRIT!

It astonished me how quickly Dora and I were accepted as a couple. The youth-club members liked her, friends immediately took to her, and we were not banned from my parent's house. I don't think I was ever really accepted by her children, but that was not surprising given that I was only a few years older than the eldest one. Dora's husband was amazingly accommodating. Bill Parsons was amazed and amused in equal measure. He took to interrupting us on Sunday afternoons, on the pretext of giving me my work tickets for the week and then staying for tea.

We seemed to have a lot of time to spend together, although in the autumn of that first year, in addition to the normal contract work, Bill gave me many a Blackpool trip. This meant picking up on a Saturday morning and driving to Blackpool for people to see the lights; we would arrive there at around two in the afternoon. I then had a few hours off before picking up the people at a pre-arranged point (on the Front) at around 8 in the evening and driving, ever-so-slowly, along the front to the very end, where the lights finished. I seem to remember it took about two hours from start to finish. Then we'd drive home, dropping the passengers off at around two or three in the morning. It was exhausting. This was about the time that tachographs (discs that record a coach driver's speed and driving hours) came into force but I don't ever remember using them with Bill. My driving hours were 'flexible'. He gave me £50 a trip, so some weeks I was bringing in £100 a week - very good money. Plus, people tended to 'tip' the driver more in those days. The flip side was that almost everyone smoked and many ate on the coach, so it meant a thorough cleaning of the vehicle when we got back in the early hours. Prising out chicken bones with the dog-ends from ashtrays was pretty unpleasant. But we had Dora's salary, too, and we weren't short of the readies.

Dora often accompanied me on the private hire trips. One day I was asked to take a group from a Catholic church in Edgware to the shrine at Little Walsingham in Norfolk. We left quite early in the morning as the A11 was still single-carriageway, unchanged really from the 'fifties. Dora sat behind me and the Father - called Father Patrick - insisted on sitting next to her. I couldn't believe my ears when I heard him ask her, in a strong Irish brogue 'Are you highly-sexed, then?' I knew Dora could take care of herself, but he was pretty insistent in his questioning all the way to the breakfast stop at a place called Red Lodge on the A11.

We both fell about laughing at the situation, and continued to mention it for many years afterwards. Partly as a result of being so distracted by the ongoing conversation behind, I missed the turn to Walsingham and ended up in a place called Great Snoring. We found our way back and our passengers enjoyed the delights of 'England's Nazareth'.

Personally, I think the best thing about Little Walsingham is the narrow-gauge steam railway that takes you out of it, to the coast at Wells. But it wasn't built then.

Despite Father Patrick's questioning, we had a lovely day out and enjoyed travelling through the Norfolk countryside.

I still carried on with the Earthshine trips and we had a splendid sponsored walk in 1977, raising enough to keep the bus going for at least another year from that event alone. We also had T-shirts printed at a favourable rate from a supporter called Richard, who designed a lovely logo for us with children dancing round a sheaf of wheat. Badges and other paraphernalia were also produced. It was another successful year for Earthshine and for the youth club, but the farm idea had drifted further away. Both Dora and I wanted the farm to happen, but we thought more and more that we would have to do it ourselves rather than it happen as a group pulling together. The coach holidays were almost too successful in that they took up a lot of time and resources. They were, though, tremendous fun and I do hope that those who went on them remember them with affection and perhaps say, 'those were the days!'.

Christmas 1977 - our first of course - was somewhat unusual. We had planned to go to Birmingham to do 'Open Christmas', but ducked out on the way there and came home again. I can't remember quite why we did this, but we had virtually no food in the place. Christmas dinner was a (shared) boiled egg! But we were blissfully happy. On Boxing Day we did go up to Birmingham and visited the youth centre and stayed a few hours. We then travelled in our beaten-up red Mini to Leeds, where we stayed overnight, and then on into Northumberland. In the Cheviot Hills the fuel-pump gave out late in the evening and we were rescued by the local bobby who towed us to a guest house with our car attached to his by his wife's washing line. The kindness of strangers. . . I don't know why we went to Northumberland in the dead of winter in a dodgy Mini, perhaps I wanted to show Dora my grandparent's home and the area I had loved so much as a child.

Our landlady lived below us in her semi. She was quite an elderly lady called Mrs. Sidwell, and told us one day early in 1978 that she wanted to go and live with her daughter and her husband, and would we move out? This was at a time when it was almost totally impossible to move a 'sitting tenant' out of their residence; but of course a sitting tenant would lower the value of a house if it was sold with them in situ.

We had become quite fond of our little abode, but we saw her point and said we'd try to find somewhere else. She was grateful for this. Dora was still working at 'The Barn' (though Bill's contract had finished and I was doing more local work) and one of the teachers offered us the upstairs of her own semi, and at a favourable rate. Unfortunately this was in Stonebridge Park - anyone who knows Stonebridge Park will know why it was 'unfortunate'. However, we duly moved in only to find that virtually no preparation had been made for us - no cooker or anything, we had to create our own kitchen! We bought one of those old kitchen cabinets for a song, which were incredibly useful and had served generations very well, before the days of 'fitted kitchens'.

The area was incredibly noisy. The West Coast Main Line passed close on one side, together with a vast area of shunting yards and carriage sidings, the North Circular Road was on another side - busy at all hours of the day and night. And our road, though a cul-de-sac, had people working on their cars and driving in and out all the time, and shouting matches and occasional fisticuffs from the local 'yoof'. I found it astonishingly unpleasant. Dora had a very old cat called 'Guinness' at her home in Slough and as her ex was not looking after her as well as he might have done, she came to live with us.

I was amazed at how quickly the cat adapted to her new surroundings, and became very fond of her. In fact she adapted better than I did, especially when we discovered that the teacher was working as a prostitute in the evenings! Time after time I answered the phone and had to deal with her clients, who were often not pleased to be talking to a man and presumed I was her 'pimp'.

Dora also had a fox-terrier 'Foxy' who now had to share homes with us and with her husband who continued to live in their bungalow in Slough. I'm ashamed to say I didn't like Foxy much and understand how children who are the product of a previous relationship can suffer with a new partner. Much more on this subject, later. Dogs have always been drawn to me, right from my young days - and I do love them. But I really didn't understand them then. I found Foxy intrusive and demanding. I wasn't patient with him and he was an early cause of friction between Dora and me. And it was me who was in the wrong. The unsatisfactory nature of the place we were living in did not help.

I approached Dad. He'd lent my brother Antony a few thousand as a deposit on a property and I asked if he would do the same for me. Surprisingly, he agreed. Dora and I started looking for a flat and I must have taken along my 'guardian angel', as we found a lovely downstairs flat in a spacious Edwardian house in Cunningham Park, Harrow, with its own garden and near a beautiful recreation ground. I remember sitting at the outside door of the conservatory, looking at the bees hovering around the flowers, thinking how beautiful and peaceful it was. It didn't take long for the deal to be done, and for the princely sum of £15,250, we became property owners together, for the first time. The flat was a gem. Spacious, light, solid - we couldn't believe our luck. We moved in just before the end of the summer holidays in 1978.

Quickly we made it our own, discovering that under many of the 'improvements' were period features. Many will remember Barry Bucknell who hosted a DIY programme on the Telly in the sixties, making everything 'flush' and dust-free - and totally bland. Our doors were thus - until we pulled off the hardboard covering to reveal the original beautifully panelled originals lurking underneath. We took a lot of pleasure restoring proper round handles and fingerplates to these doors, and restoring the open fire in the living room.

Guinness the cat came with us of course, and settled in very happily. In the kitchen there was a chimney breast that had obviously once served a coal-fired range cooker. This had long gone of course and the bottom of the chimney breast had been sealed off from the room, but there was a vent near the ceiling.

One day we heard an odd fluttering noise and traced it to the chimney. A bird had obviously fallen down into it and was fluttering around unable to get out. I removed the vent but still the bird was too far down for me to reach and help it. I have no idea why I thought of this, but it occurred to me that I might be able to get the hose of the vacuum cleaner down from the hole; it was quite a small diameter hose and I thought the bird would be too big to get sucked into the machine, so we agreed to give it a go.

It worked, spectacularly - almost immediately the noise of the vacuum changed to indicate the hose was blocked and I quickly brought the hose up, complete with beautiful thrush (looking somewhat startled) attached to the end. On switching the machine off, birdie flew straight back to the hole where the vent was and flew down into the chimney! Unbelievable, I thought, how could it be so stupid? So I had to do it all again, but this time the bird's head had got stuck in the hose and Dora was able to grasp the bird before I turned the vacuum off. She then carried it outside and we watched it fly up into a tree. We came back inside, feeling really pleased with ourselves at such a novel and successful operation, pausing to look outside through the window only to see Guinness munching on a freshly-caught thrush.

Dora had had enough of the 'Barn' by this time and wanted a change. I, too, was tired of just driving coaches and got my job at the Nurseries back. Dora went to work at a 'special school' in Acton, West London, for children who were labelled 'Maladjusted'. This was quite a challenge.

With a mortgage to pay, and my father to be paid back (with interest), money was somewhat tight and I found I couldn't spend as much time with the holidays as before. Also, many youth club members were leaving school and getting jobs, and some were moving away. Earthshine reached a crucial point. Paul Crouch agreed to buy the bus back and to carry on doing as many holidays as he could, but the writing was on the wall. Earthshine was formally wound-up in the summer of 1979, and the few hundred pounds left in the Bank were given to a 'farm for children' in North Devon. (This is still operating, incidentally). I felt very sad, but I knew that my life now was with Dora and we still hoped that, together, we might achieve the original aim of a farm which would cater for children.

Dora's job was a tough one, but it had some hilarious moments. One day she was complaining to her class about their bad behaviour, and one piped up 'Well we are maladjusted, you know!' In one lesson, the subject was helping people in trouble. The story of the Good Samaritan was told. 'So what would you do now if you came across someone in trouble?' asked Dora. A hand shot up. 'Yes, Bobby?' 'Don't go near 'em Miss. You might catch summink'. I think the journey was the most tiring for her; a long trek up through busy suburban streets every day. The pay was good, though.

I enjoyed being back at the nursery, having a break from driving. Then I saw a part-time job advertised in the local press 'Lecturer wanted to teach gardening in evening classes one evening a week'. I'd never taught before, (except in Sunday school) but Dora encouraged me to apply and just before term-time in the early autumn of 1979 I had an interview with an affable man who was recruiting tutors. I outlined my experience but said I'd never taught before. 'You'll pick it up' he said, and I landed the job. Later, I learned I had been the only applicant!

I decided to break up the classes into 'Gardening in Autumn', then 'Spring' and 'Summer'. I loved it. I had a small class of about a dozen people, all interested in learning how to propagate plants, grow vegetables, herbs and flowers, prune fruit trees and all the rest of it. I looked forward to this every week, and I think they did too. Once a year, in the summer, I organised a visit to the Council nurseries - the amount they did there was a revelation to us all. We also had 'open evenings' at my allotment, with people then coming back for coffee and a chat afterwards. Most of my 'pupils' were young married couples, or one half of a young married couple. One year, three ladies became pregnant more-or-less at the same time - nothing to do with me, honestly. However, word got round that if you were trying for a baby, it might be a good idea to pop round to the gardening group. . . .

One of the pregnant ladies was Michele, who has kept in touch with me ever since and been a very supportive friend in times of difficulty. Her daughter, Natalie, is now twenty eight as I write.

Dora and I visited Paris for a long weekend in 1979, which was lovely. We visited all the sights of course, but also explored some of the lesser-known parts. Looking back at this time, it seems we were so blessed. We were in love, we had the means to take time off like this, and we had the energy to do these things. It was a magical time, never to be forgotten.

Dora and I on holiday in Paris, outside Notre Dame Cathedral in 1979.

Dora was divorced by now and wanted to marry me. I felt happy as we were, I didn't feel the need for us to change anything. I really wasn't keen

71

but one morning Dora just took me by the hand and led me down to Harrow Civic Centre. I think she thought that we could find a witness and get married on the spot. When we got there, we found the office was closed due to a public sector worker's strike! I had to laugh, and so did she - and she didn't try again.

Throughout 1980 and most of 1981 I continued to run the youth club and did the gardening class. But during the summer of '81 I found what looked like a suitable cottage, with land, where we might start our rural activities. Whilst at Cunningham Park we'd managed to afford another convertible car, a Sunbeam Rapier, and I'd joined the Sunbeam Rapier Owner's Club. Through this I'd met a man who knew almost everything there is to know about these cars, Bernard Guest, who ran a small country garage at Yorkley in the Forest of Dean. He owned a convertible Rapier too. We became friends, and one day whilst visiting him Dora and I looked in Estate Agent's windows and found out that properties in this region were far cheaper than anywhere else we'd looked at. So we started looking at properties and one day I spied one at, I think, £23,000 on Blakeney Hill overlooking the Severn Estuary. The agent for the property was called Kevin Toombs, which we found wryly apposite after we'd moved in. It was down a narrow track (you had to leave your car in a space at the top) and it was semi-detached, but it had about one acre of steeply-graded land and a couple of outbuildings. I went to look.

It was a sunny afternoon, and the views across the Severn to the Cotswolds were stunning. The young couple who occupied the property had done some terracing of the land, which made it easier to work, but they were moving to a cottage further up the hill. I was shown around what was a poor little place, really, but nevertheless had two living rooms and a kitchen and bathroom on the ground floor and three good-sized bedrooms above. It had obviously been two cottages once, now made into one. Next door was even smaller, yet housed a young family. I was more interested in the land and the surroundings than the cottage, and missed quite a few disadvantages of the place. I drove home quite elated, so the next weekend Dora and I drove down to view the place properly.

By this time we had a dog, called Rags. He had been found wandering the streets by a neighbour and we'd taken him in. He was a sweet, silly, scared old thing and on his very first walk in the nearby recreation ground slipped his collar and disappeared. I dreaded going home to tell Dora, but when I reached the gate, there he was, sat on the doorstep. I'd put a notice up saying 'Found - brown-haired collie-type dog', etc. and ended with 'We cannot keep him long'. In the end we had him for nearly ten years. We'd also acquired a cat, Squatter, who'd simply turned up and moved in. He'd been a visitor from the start, but when we found him curled-up in the conservatory on our return from the French trip, we knew he was really ours now.

Rags accompanied us down to the Forest. In those days, sheep roamed freely in the Forest and it was obvious Rags was more than interested in chasing them. People who lived in the Forest had ancient commoner's rights to keep sheep and although the sheep were often a bloody nuisance, and created a lot of mess even in the towns such as Cinderford, the rights were jealously guarded. On my last visit to the Forest, there didn't seem to be so many of them, so maybe the tradition is on the wane.

However, it was obvious that Rags loved the Forest but not the little place I had found. He wouldn't enter the cottage. He was quite happy lying on the 'yard' at the front of the place but didn't like the cottage itself. Looking back, I'm surprised that neither Dora nor myself read very much into this. The people selling it seemed reluctant to let us stay in the cottage for any length of time, and ushered us out for tea - quite normal, as it was a lovely day.

We left, quite elated. We thought that, although the access was poor and the cottage rather uninspiring, we could make a go of it. We made an offer which was accepted immediately and looked forward to a change of lifestyle. Dora loved the Forest, I must say I never really took to it. It took me a long time to work out why. Partly the reason for the comparatively low property prices was the fact that the area was rather isolated, which for us was part of its charm. But it was also that the towns were, frankly, unattractive and with many unattractive houses in them. The sheep were everywhere, making a mess and getting into people's gardens and to me it seemed rather insular.

However, one of my favourite places of all time remains May Hill, just to the north of the Forest, a National Trust property which offers wonderful views over the Severn Valley and over the rich, varied Herefordshire countryside to the west, stretching to the Welsh mountains. And Ross-on-Wye I think is a lovely town, and that's just to the west of the Forest. So it's all a bit of an enigma, and I still don't fully understand it.

At the end of the summer holidays, Dora started work at another special school, much nearer our home in Harrow, but we still put our flat on the market, for a little more than the asking price of the cottage. It was quickly sold 'subject to contract'. How we were going to make a living in

Gloucestershire, wasn't properly considered. Dora could get a teaching post almost anywhere, but I wasn't so sure about coach-driving there or nursery work. We had become friends with a lovely couple over the road from us and in the end it was agreed that Dora could stay with them during the week, retaining her London job, and I would move with the animals into the cottage and start decorating it and looking for work in the Forest. Dora would drive down every weekend.

I made arrangements to hand over the running of the youth club to others, and gave notice to Harrow Council that I could no longer do the gardening classes after the end of term in December. This latter caused panic; there was no-one else available to do it. Off the top of my head, and without consulting her, I said that Dora could probably do it - she was a qualified teacher and I would give her my notes. Without any hesitation or checking, this was gratefully accepted - they did talk with Dora a week or so later, and confirmed that she would do the job. It would have been justifiable if she thought she had been dragooned into it, but she accepted it with aplomb. My last night at the youth club was an emotional affair for me, they had a disco in my honour and I was given cards and gifts which I still proudly possess. A lot of tears were shed.

As the time approached for the move, scheduled for just before Christmas 1981, the weather deteriorated. The winter of 1981/2 was the harshest since the famous one of 1962/3 and we had heavy snowfall early in December. It did not bode well for an easy move.

The day of the move dawned bitterly cold. I had managed to borrow an old Commer truck but on collection it wouldn't start. A spray from a tin of 'Startyerbastard' and a lot of swearing got it going eventually, but it delayed getting our stuff out of the flat.

My brother came to help us and we took turns in sliding down the front path with various items of furniture. It always takes longer than you think to empty a home and position it safely in a van but when everywhere is sheet ice it's a nightmare. We got away in time - just - and started the slow journey down towards Gloucester and the Forest of Dean. There was a lump in my throat when we finally moved away from our flat for the very last time. It had been a very happy home.

I don't think that either of us had fully appreciated how on earth we were going to get our furniture down from the top of the hill at Blakeney to the cottage, never mind in snow and ice and in the dark. Very fortunately we had Dora's youngest daughter and her husband to help, plus a friend and his partner who'd volunteered to help also. Dora and these helpers all travelled separately from me, and arrived after I'd got there, expecting blazing fires and food in the oven. But nothing had been left in the cottage. Not even a sack full of coal! Or any wood. It was absolutely freezing. Dora somehow remembered that there was an elderly man who lived in a house at the top of the hill who sold coal and logs, so pleaded some from him; but in general it was a rough baptism to our new 'enlightened' lifestyle. Then we had to get the beds and some chairs out of the van and down the snowy track; we'd not even considered how difficult this would be. We had been very naïve. The following day, we got the rest of the furniture down the track and slowly started to sort ourselves out. I returned the truck to London, taking our helpers with us, and got back just in time for Christmas, which I don't remember at all.

The haunted house in the Forest of Dean.

It was much more difficult to make the cottage feel 'home' than we had expected. This was partly due to the fact that we'd had large, airy rooms in Harrow and now we were confined to cottage rooms. Our furniture didn't really fit in too well. Also, it was unnerving that although it was so cold, Rags - and Squatter the cat - didn't want to be in the house. They had both been so happy to enjoy the warmth of the rooms in Harrow. When I took Rags for a walk through the Forest, Squatter would come too. We became a familiar trilogy sauntering through the woods.

Dora went back to Harrow, of course, in early January. There were mini-icebergs floating up the Severn. It was desperately cold, so much so that a news bulletin on the radio informed us that workers in a freezer plant in Ross had actually gone into a freezer for lunch as it was warmer than the temperature outside. On the A40 Northleach by-pass, trucks had come to a standstill as the diesel 'waxed' in the bitter cold, and had been broken into and contents stolen. Worse than that, for us, the cottage did not feel 'right' somehow. At first I put it down to my familiar feelings of loneliness when in a new environment, but it was more than that. I couldn't put my finger on it, but there was something sad and disturbing about the place, obviously being picked-up by the animals.

Was it haunted? Had something really horrible happened here? I tentatively mentioned it to the previous occupiers, and their laughs of disdain only increased my suspicions. And their reasons for moving only a short distance up the hill didn't really ring true. I didn't mention it to next-door, but it transpired that they were waiting for a day when they could move out. Then, one night, Rags shot out of the kitchen door, nearly taking it off its hinges. I caught up with him, barking and howling in the field, and refusing to come back in. Eventually I persuaded him, and although he stayed, he was uneasy and did not sleep. Neither did I, and we lay cuddled together for warmth and comfort for the rest of the night. I couldn't feel a 'presence' at this time, and I'm not really much of a believer in ghosts - well, I wasn't at that time.

It was just an overwhelming sense of sadness and of loss, a dispiriting feeling which got into your head and your bones and made everything an effort. I phoned Dora and she said we'd discuss it next time she was down.

We decided that there WAS something amiss here. On the evening after I'd gone with the truck back to Harrow, she had felt very uneasy in the place. One evening the place was overwhelmed with the smell of dank, musty dampness, like a vault, and when I rose from my chair I entered a distinct band of chill in the air. But cold air drops, doesn't it? Warm air rises. I felt a cold draught but couldn't make out where it was coming from. I lit a candle, but the flame burnt totally upright. The occurrences of the dank smell became more frequent, and always preceded the chill 'draft' and sense of utter dejection. I began to want out of this place. The feelings were becoming stronger, and more sinister - almost menacing. The animals were most unhappy. One morning I awoke to all the windows being open. I hadn't done it, and I don't think Rags or Squatter were capable of it. We struggled through January and February but by March I'd had enough. Very kindly, my mum and dad agreed to put me up for a while, and occasionally I could stay with Dora. The relief I and the animals felt, was palpable.

The winter hadn't helped, of course. One evening I had to take a taxi from Gloucester because of severe weather disrupting the bus service, and had to walk from Newnham home - about four miles. When I got home, I had mild frostbite on my big toe. Instead of being curled up by the fire, Squatter was waiting for me in a tree at the corner of our land, Rags was with me - the taxi-driver had relented his 'no dogs' rule this evening.

We felt we had no choice but to put the cottage back up for sale. Our dreams had been ruined, but it was partly our own fault for not making sure the place was suitable for what we wanted to do and was viable or practical. I don't think we could have prepared ourselves for the spirit-world though! We often went back over weekends but were never happy there, though the feelings were less if we were both there together. The place sold, through an ad in 'Exchange & Mart' in the late summer 1982, much to our relief. It wasn't very long before the new owner was telephoning us asking if we had known the place was haunted. In some respects, this was some comfort - it wasn't just us. It seemed to affect him more than us, and drove him and his family out very quickly.

The family who followed him suffered even worse. The wife set herself alight, twice, in the kitchen, by sheer fluke each time. We didn't dare go near the place once we'd vacated it and heard about this from our former neighbours, who had been found a pleasant detached house in Blakeney village. Once settled there, they seemed a lot happier and more settled, though we didn't discuss our experiences in the cottage. I just didn't want to raise it with them, and I think the feeling was mutual. During the transaction to the new owners, we had the Deeds - Dora brought them down to the cottage to see whether there was any clue in them for this odd haunting. I met her at the coach station in Gloucester with Rags, and as soon as Dora got in he howled all the way back to the cottage.

Dora also felt extremely uneasy with the Deeds in her possession. Afterwards, when the crimes of Fred West came to light, we wondered whether he had any connection with the cottage. It would have been a safe place to hide bodies and he certainly worked in the area, but we never found out anything.

I cannot explain any of this in logical terms, but every word is the truth. Also true is that my hair turned from almost black to white over this time!

BACK ON OUR FEET AGAIN

With the money received from the sale of the cottage, we purchased another downstairs flat round the corner from our previous one, in Beresford Road. We both craved some peace and stability and indeed familiarity; I went back to driving coaches and doing the evening classes. I landed a job at what was known as the 'Marks & Spencers' of mini-cab firms, Checker Cars in Pinner. The owner, Alan Fair, had just expanded into getting a couple of mini-buses and I was awarded a regular job driving schoolchildren every morning and evening in one of them. I even had a courier every day in the form of Pat Dalton, who, I am pleased to say, keeps in touch, thirty-five years on. The pay and conditions were top-notch.

The other mini-bus, though, took me back to the times of Bill Parsons. This was a Ford 'A-Series' bus known as the 'Jolly Blue Giant' able to carry twenty-five passengers. It had an old-fashioned 6-cylinder diesel engine which was the absolute devil to start in cold weather - Ford hadn't thought to equip it with glow-plugs. Instead it had a 'Start Pilote' system where as you cranked over the engine, you pumped a lever under the dash which then emitted ether into the engine (as in the 'Startyerbastard' tins). It didn't work too well. Time after time we had recourse to bump-starting it down the hill from the office. It usually started then, but on a couple of occasions I ended up across the main road in Pinner unable to proceed further, at the start of the rush-hour. The A-Series Ford was described as a 'blown-up Transit', and that was what we thought should happen to it! As I was the only member of staff at the time to hold a full PSV licence, I was gifted this wonderful machine on regular school runs, again with courier. I was well-paid for this, however.

The flat was the downstairs of an Edwardian house, detached this time. And it actually sat right beside the park entrance, and its garden backed on to it. I wasn't quite so keen on it at first as the Cunningham Park flat, but quickly warmed to it and I think we improved it considerably over the four years we lived there. We again had friendly neighbours and, at last, I began to really appreciate the nice things about suburban life. Each street was really its own little 'village', a small community, and at that time, in that area, a very nice community too.

After the initial struggle to recover financially, this was a time of increasing material prosperity for Dora and me. The 'greedy eighties' were here, a time of high inflation and spiralling wages. We didn't like this new culture but to some extent were swept up with it, and we benefitted financially from it. There was a garage that went with the flat, and I was soon to fill it with a classic car. This was followed by another classic car and then another, and I now look back at this period as a time of self-indulgence; partly as a result of our bad experiences in Gloucestershire perhaps, but mostly because I could.

Dora was generous with her money and I think she perhaps should have reined me in a bit on my spending. This is not to take any blame away from me. I did make some money from hiring-out cars for weddings and, best of all, to a firm called 'Action Cars' in Harrow, who supplied period vehicles for the BBC and ITV networks. My cars appeared on 'Tenko', 'Miss Marple', and apparently on one episode of the Muppets, though I haven't seen this. I was an avid attendee of classic car shows and every year we went on the RAC/Norwich Union Classic Car Run.

One year we took a huge Humber Super Snipe drophead to France with the Sunbeam Rapier Owner's Club, where it let us down first with a puncture and then with the exhaust falling off. This was subsequently mended by our friend Bernard who did wonders with what looked like a baked-bean can! It was almost a hedonistic approach to living and though I now feel we strayed somewhat off our path and missed other opportunities, I must say we had a lot of fun and enjoyed ourselves immensely.

In 1984 the Live Aid Concert was held at Wembley Stadium. We could hear it from Harrow. This brought us back a little to our senses and re-installed our ethic of helping others. My beloved Uncle John died that year and left me some money in his will. Then Dora's mother died (her father had passed away a few years before) and she came into a share of her mother's estate. We began again to think of a move to the country, but prices had increased dramatically in the three years or so we'd been at Beresford Road.

The thing to have now, according to the Estate Agents, was a cottage with a Pony Paddock. That meant that any cottage with more than a large garden had become prohibitively expensive. Despite our increased wealth, we simply did not have the wherewithal to purchase anything like what we wanted. If we were ever to try again, I had to think laterally; or consider going abroad. I did not want to do that, we valued our life and our friends here, and my own mother and father were getting older and I sensed we should not move too far away from them.

I came up with the idea of purchasing a nursery with or without a house on it.

Horticulture rather than Horseyculture. Nurseries were not 'fashionable' and it was difficult making a living on a traditional one, everywhere was becoming a 'garden centre' selling all sorts of stuff as well as plants. But there still remained, obstinately, traditional small nurseries and when they did come up for sale, the prices were far less than cottages with pony-paddocks. My idea was that we might purchase one of these at horticultural rates and, if there was no dwelling on it, somehow wangle permission to build one.

I put an ad. in a Nursery Trade magazine. At the same time, we went to look at a working nursery in Newent, Gloucestershire, that was being sold off as a result of the winding-up of the Land Settlement Association (L.S.A.). This organisation had, I believe, been formed between the wars to encourage and enable young people to get a foot on the farming ladder. It had thrived through the fifties and sixties but by the early eighties had been troubled by strife and corruption and was finally wound-up in the mid-eighties. Most of the holdings had a small but decent house on them. They were being sold mostly to the sitting tenants but a few came up on the open market. We seriously considered this one but in the end decided to reject it.

My advert in the trade magazine elicited several leads; we followed-up on three of them. The first was a three-acre holding at Bledlow Ridge in Buckinghamshire, in my beloved Chilterns. It had a small bungalow but the owners were retiring and were going to keep it. They had, however, applied for permission for a new bungalow to be built on the land. Very tempting, this. There were several polytunnels and it was a viable business, and the views from the site of the bungalow were glorious, facing south down the Saunderton valley. We seriously considered it, but declined it in the end as it was on the expensive side for us and we couldn't really see how we could adapt it for children's holidays should we do this.

Another was simply a semi-detached Victorian villa with the most huge garden in the Hughenden Valley near High Wycombe. The garden stretched right up the valley side to meet a beech wood towards the top. It was the cheapest of the three by a considerable margin and I now think we should have considered it more seriously - we could have at least lived a 'good life' at this place. It was called 'Nomads', and I often wonder if that land is still with it, or has it succumbed to 'development'?

Then there was a large nursery in Bedfordshire, at a price mid-way between 'Nomads' and Bledlow Ridge. This was a working nursery, mostly under glass, some of that glass dating from the 1930's. They were large greenhouses, up to 150' long and with very wide spans. There was also a stretch of open ground to the rear of the greenhouses, an office, a loo, and some sheds including a large packing shed. But no house, and no space for one either. It lay entirely off the road up its own driveway, and there was a wood on the western side and fields to the north, with extensive views. A pig farm lay beyond the southern boundary, and to the east between the nursery and the road there was a hayfield.

A serious contender, this. I didn't like the surrounding countryside much - this part of Bedfordshire had been treated unkindly by both the planning authority entrusted to stop ugly development and by many farmers who had grubbed-up hedgerows and this, combined with the rather boring flatness of it all, just didn't appeal. Most of the villages were straggly affairs with indeterminate endings and beginnings and the land was heavy clay. But, as Dora pointed out to me, we had to be pragmatic and realistic.

We paid a second visit. It was now March 1986. This time the owner, a Mr. Sanders, showed us round the whole place. Mostly, he grew tomatoes in the summer and lettuce in the winter months. An extensive irrigation system was set up and two of the greenhouses were heated by oil. Most of the greenhouses were occupied by lettuce, rows and rows of them that he took to the new Covent Garden Market, but in the heated houses were the young tomato plants that would grow into the huge crop he would plant out following the harvesting of the lettuce. The rear portion of land was planted-up with potatoes and the other small piece of open ground was destined for pumpkins.

It was a dull day with few signs of Spring, but the wood on one side was alive with the cawing of rooks as they constructed their nests. There was a pleasant, peaceful feeling about the place. And it was obvious that this stood head and shoulders above everywhere else we'd seen for value. The entire site occupied about two acres. We didn't make an offer then, but drove away through the adjacent village, and across towards the Barton Hills and Luton. I still didn't like the villages or the countryside, but 'beggars can't be choosers' was the expression that came to mind.

Mr. Sanders wanted to complete the tomato season, so the nursery would not be available until about September-time. This would give us time to enjoy one last summer in Harrow, which appealed, and with goodwill on all sides we agreed on a price and the die was cast. We'd take possession sometime in September. We asked if we could visit in the Spring and were told we could come up any time we liked. We made the journey in May, and even I was astounded at the transformation in the look of the countryside around - wild flowers were flowering profusely by the roadsides, the hedges green and cream with hawthorn flowers, the fields at least green, the gardens in the villages awash with colour. It wasn't going to be so bad after all.

We took advantage of the time we had left to enjoy a holiday in Madeira. This was the first and only time I have taken a flight. I loved the flight out, over France and the Pyrenees, and was scared witless by the landing on Madeira, where it seemed we would never stop in time before plunging into the sea. Dora had been to Madeira years before and wanted to show me what she regarded as a most beautiful island. It most certainly is beautiful, and full of contrasts, from the lush southern areas to the high (and cold!) mountains on the north side. We hired a car one day and took a trip past the highest cliffs in Europe, round to the northern coast and up to the highest mountain. Unfortunately it was smothered in cloud, but it was still a memorable trip. We walked through the woodlands and down along the 'levadas' (irrigation streams) along which grew magnificent agapanthus plants. I still have two of these, brought back from the Island, that grace our veranda. The flight home was unpleasant, with a lot of turbulence, but it was a holiday I will never forget.

We decided on our return to start looking for a house near the nursery. Bedfordshire was then the 'Cinderella' of the Home Counties, and prices were lower than in the surrounding counties. Hertfordshire and Buckinghamshire were a great deal more expensive; Bedfordshire was perceived as flat and boring with fields full of sprouts and cabbages. So we seemed to be in a reasonable position to look for a property. We looked at a flat in Bedford and various cottages, but none really appealed. Then Mr. Sanders, who was selling the place to us, suggested we put in a planning application for a bungalow on the land. In the meantime, we could 'commute' from our flat in Harrow.

The idea appealed to both of us. It would be an hour's journey each way, but that was OK., we thought. We loved our flat and our neighbourhood, so we decided to take up Mr. Sanders' suggestion and we took possession of the nursery that September.

The amount of land seemed huge, and most of it was under glass. Growing just lettuces and tomatoes didn't really appeal, we wanted to start growing our own vegetables and growing them organically. During this year there had been the Chernobyl disaster in Russia, and the risk of nuclear fallout poisoning crops, so growing under glass appeared attractive. But again, we hadn't really considered properly the amount of time and effort needed to cultivate such an area of land. Mr. Sanders had employed help and had machinery - we had neither. And we didn't have a really clear idea of where to start. We weren't downhearted, just a bit overwhelmed at first. It seemed a huge undertaking. No problems with 'atmosphere' or with the animals, though - this place felt lovely and peaceful. And in the greenhouses, all the local clay had been dug out in the fifties and replaced by Grade 1 Fenland soil, beautiful stuff that would grow anything. However, Mr. Sanders was not a fan of 'organic' growing and relied heavily on chemicals to keep pests and diseases at bay. He also used bromide to sterilise the soil every other year. This would cause problems for us the next year. . . .

We decided at first to grow bedding plants and pot-plants such as geraniums and fuchsias in the heated houses, and vegetable crops in the others. We rented out a couple of houses to a local grower who wanted to grow carrots, then when he decided not to proceed after sowing them we did well selling most of them to our vet at Harrow who was a great fan of carrot-juice. The rest we ate ourselves - they were delicious.

Over that winter, 1986/7, we considered seriously how we were going to work this. The journey to and from Harrow was onerous and costly, and we kept mentioning Mr. Sanders' idea of gaining planning permission.

But there wasn't really anywhere suitable on the plot for a house or bungalow. Also, how were we going to sell our stuff? This was relatively easy to solve; we took a stall at Hitchin market, first on Tuesdays and later, on Saturdays as well. In the Spring of 1987 we visited wholesale growers and bought in 'stock plants' - plants from which we could obtain cuttings to grow on and sell. We also commissioned a local grower up the road to sow and grow on a range of bedding plants for us. We employed a local lady, Maureen, to help us and we paid her well over the standard rate - she was worth every penny.

I bought a Ford Transit Luton-bodied van with a tail-lift and obtained some plant trolleys - we had lift-off. We had a fairly successful season for a first attempt, but it was a huge amount of work and it was this season that convinced us that we should seriously consider applying for planning permission. There was no time at all for keeping any stock or growing our own vegetables. The business took over all our time. We were growing without the use of chemicals - and for weeds and pests it was like taking the lid off a pressure-cooker. Weeds and pests had been suppressed by all those chemicals for all those years, and suddenly - wow, let's grow! We were inundated. There was no time for natural predators to make any impact, and I confess in the end we had to use some chemicals if we were going to have any crops at all. Weeds I suppressed by using a borrowed flame-thrower.

It was in the summer of 1987 that my father became ill. He had first started to feel non-too well whilst on holiday with Mum and things did not improve. It took a while before it was discovered that he had pancreatic cancer, and it was incurable by that stage. He had not that long retired, and had been busy learning how to pot - he'd just bought a kiln - plus he was involved in adult literacy and being a prison visitor. He had filled up his time of 'retirement' with doing really worthwhile things - I think he'd been busier in his retirement than he'd ever been in work - and had enjoyed himself immensely. After years of 'enjoying' the sun, sitting almost naked in an armchair in the garden whilst he turned beetroot-red, we thought he would get skin cancer if anything. But this pancreatic cancer got him, and he died in January 1988. His epitaph was 'a man with many interests and with many friends' - absolutely spot-on.

Although I say it myself, our market stall was a great success with the public. We decided we could expand our range and, through a friend, found a wholesale grower of all sorts of shrubs and perennials in Surrey. I motored down in the van to look, and came back with a full load, which kept our sales going right through the autumn. Then we had the hurricane of October 1987. The noise of it woke me in the night and I honestly thought we'd had a nuclear attack. There was miraculously little damage to our flat, but I dreaded seeing the nursery the following day. All that glass....

As we approached Bedfordshire, we heard over the radio that trees hundreds of years old had been uprooted, power lines were down, mobile homes overturned, houses and businesses damaged, the reports seemed endless. We turned into the drive leading to the nursery with great trepidation...but it looked totally unscathed. I couldn't believe my eyes, I really had expected a scene of devastation. We parked up and went into each of the glasshouses. One pane of glass was missing from one greenhouse and had smashed through a couple of others. And that was it. Nothing else.

I think it was Dora who said 'the wood has saved us!' She was right - the winds had come from the south-west and west and the wood to the west of us had absorbed the wind's force enough to save the nursery from destruction. I've had occasion to curse the wood sometimes in the autumn when the leaves blow and block up all the gutters, but I will never forget that without it the nursery would not have survived as it did. And I'd miss the rooks if it wasn't there. And the bluebells in the Spring and the colours in the autumn, oh and lots of other things too.

That hurricane spelt the end of our village being principally a horticultural settlement. All the other nurseries in the village suffered extensive damage and many gave up. Nearly all the greenhouses on these holdings were by then old and out-dated anyway; the hurricane only brought the end a little quicker. Since then, I have seen the village turn from an unattractive straggle of mostly horticulturally-based properties into an unattractive straggle of commuter-based properties.

We had bought a small caravan, a 'Sprite', early in 1987 and placed it on a small area of land not occupied by greenhouses, so we could have tea, lunch etc. in it and Rags could retire to it for a sleep in the afternoons. This too, was undamaged by the hurricane. I wondered if we might be able to fit a small house or bungalow on this bit of land, so we applied for permission. The Council were sympathetic to our having an 'agriculturally-tied' home but did not approve of the site I'd thought of. Again, I was forced into thinking laterally. In the meantime we had visited the 'Ideal Home' Exhibition at Earl's Court and seen a number of 'self-build' homes and mobile homes on display there. So much cheaper than buying a house in the village. . . .

THE ROAD TO HELL....

Dora had been brought up near the village of Fulmer in Buckinghamshire, and her parents and aunt had run a nursing home there until their retirement. Dora's son still lived there and on a visit, Dora had picked up a local paper. In it was advertised a mobile home to be sold 'off-site' at what seemed to be a ridiculously low price. We went to see it. It was occupied by an elderly travelling couple who wanted to have a newer one. We were attracted to it - it was immaculate - but it did not have a bathroom. We queried this with them and they immediately suggested we look at their daughter's 'van', which did have this facility. Fortunately this was on the same site, and equally immaculate - quite amazing as the land it was on was muddy and not paved. The daughter had just got married, and they wanted a 'twin' unit - i.e. twice as wide as this one. We were taken with this home - it even had a spare bedroom. It was a little more expensive than the parent's van but still amazingly cheap. Without thinking about obtaining planning permission, we said we'd take it, but could they arrange transport? No sooner said than done. We agreed a date for the journey and I was to drive ahead to lead the way, at no more than 45 mph.

Arriving at the site quite early in the morning, the van was already loaded onto a trailer and ready to go. I have almost always found that if you treat people, whatever their lifestyle choice or 'status', with respect and honesty, it is returned in full measure. I have fond memories of the warmth and sincerity of these people, and I hope they all ended up with the homes of their choice.

The journey to Bedfordshire was trouble-free until we reached Flitwick, not many miles from our destination. With absolutely no advanced warning, the main road through this elongated village was shut - and a weight restriction imposed on the alternative route! We came to a standstill, along with everyone behind, but fortunately I saw a police officer on the pavement ahead and got her attention. Quickly understanding our predicament, she just said - ignore the weight restriction, just go. As we were blocking the main road, this was a welcome solution and, of course, nothing untoward happened. We'd already got paving slabs down ready for the caravan, and the driver had no trouble at all in placing it on our site. We were thrilled - we could now sell our flat and use the money to build something, living 'on-site' in the meanwhile.

The flat quickly sold (for about double we paid for it, after four years) and we moved our stuff down to the nursery, most of the furniture being dry-stored. In contrast to the cottage in Gloucestershire, though, we found the mobile home very homely and convenient and we grew to love it. In retrospect, we should have either kept it or bought a larger one - not try and build a bungalow and run a business all at the same time. But I run ahead of myself. . .

Although we hadn't got permission to have the mobile home, no-one objected and no-one from the Council checked-up on us. It was pretty much hidden after all. I continued to think about where to have our 'permanent' home. Then it occurred - there were really too many greenhouses for us to manage, more certainly than we needed - why not demolish some and use that land for the house?

We put in a revised application. It was, somewhat reluctantly I felt, accepted. We had looked at a local firm that produced timber 'kits' of self-build homes and were attracted by their design and offers of help with various aspects of construction.

And I had, thank God, thought a bungalow would be easier and cheaper to build than a house.

In the eighties, we became relatively well-off and I was able to afford this rather magnificent Triumph Roadster, dating from 1948. It went very well with the Jaguar 2.4 engine fitted under the bonnet! Dora and I pose proudly beside it in 1989.

A local man offered to demolish the greenhouses and pay us for the aluminium ones. He did a good job of demolishing them quickly, but then disappeared without giving us any payment at all. But at least we'd got them demolished for nothing. We ordered the timber-frame 'kit' and got the foundations dug. I've forgotten the exact timing of all this, but I do know we were flat-out with the 1988 season whilst much of this was going on. I was chief builder - some of the brickwork was done by Mr. Sanders' son, a builder, the electrics were largely done by Dora's daughter Meg's partner Stuart, the plumbing done by a local firm and the roof done by a roofing contractor. But the erection of the main walls, the screeding, the insulation, the plasterboarding, was all done by yours truly - and I hadn't a clue. Builder without a clue. However, the bungalow still stands to this day and was recently sold for half-a-million quid - so I must have got something right. I completed it in just over a year, which I now know, was pretty good going.

Full production in one of the greenhouses in 1989.

But doing all this, working at building the business as well as building a home - was just too much. Dora and I were snapping at each other and blaming each other for various failings - we were tired, exhausted really, and of course Dora was approaching sixty years of age. We still had good times, but they were diminishing in number and in quality, and we were both fed-up with almost everything. Into 1989 and our relationship continued to deteriorate. We moved into the bungalow early in 1989 and I think we both felt we preferred the 'mobile'. Once our furniture was installed into the bungalow and we had decorated it to our taste it was better, but was it worth all that work, that expense, that hassle? Frankly, no it wasn't.

At one stage Dora suggested we separate, at another, I thought it. What I really wanted was a break - it would have done us both a power of good, I think. What made it worse, for me, was that Dora had heard of a goat that had been saved from some ritual slaughter and had agreed to re-home it. Goats will eat almost anything, and I didn't think it was a good idea to have it on a nursery. But 'Sheepie' came nevertheless and was not only often free to roam the nursery but was brought into the new home! He caused bedlam and it was extraordinarily unpleasant. There is a difference between 'domesticated' and 'domestic' animals. We had a coir mat on the floor, and as Sheepie defecated a lot, the little 'currants' fell through the gaps only to stay there. A couple of years later, when the house was sold, the new owners removed the coir matting and discovered them still there. . . . If I was eating, he'd nudge my arm quite violently, sending my plate crashing to the floor whereupon he'd eat the remaining breakfast/dinner.

Stalwart helper Maureen escorts Sheepie out of a greenhouse yet again.

As I'd invariably cooked it, it did not endear me to Sheepie. The worst, but now most amusing, episode was when we'd finally broken the one-thousand-pound barrier at our market stall. Jubilant, we came home and Dora counted out the twenties, tens and fivers and put them on a table. Sheepie came in and ate the lot - a bit like Paddy McGinty's goat. I tried pulling his tail, but alas no money came out - just the usual. This was a serious loss to us at the time.

Later, and Dora and I were sleeping in separate rooms, he once barged his way into my bedroom, jumped on the bed, and then pissed all over me. My God, goat's pee stinks. I've heard of 'golden showers' but this was ridiculous. Then, hens were invited in. I'd go to lie back in my chair and feel a wodge of hen poo squash into my back. It was becoming intolerable. The last straw was when I was rolling-out some pastry in the kitchen, and a load of poo was picked-up in the pastry. I threw the poo-pastry out of the back door, and followed it out myself. I slept, alone, in the mobile home that night.

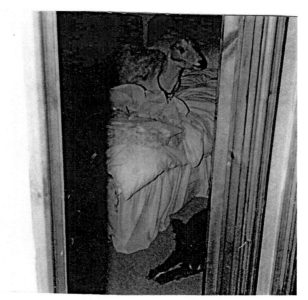

Sheepie on the bed with Rags the dog relegated to the floor, looking suitably sheepish.

Dora and I had been so happy for so many years, we must have both felt miserable, but I still can't fathom why she would want to spoil our life even further in our hard-won home by this behaviour. It seemed to be a desecration of our home. When Sheepie ate some of the agapanthus plants that had been lovingly brought back (by Dora) from Madeira, and she

90

didn't seem to give a toss, I considered, seriously, leaving. But when one has put so much into something, it is not easy. And how could I leave Dora on her own, with the business?

I decided, instead, to have an affair. I did not wish to hurt anyone, but I did crave a bit of excitement and pleasure. For some while, we had been taking the satirical magazine 'Private Eye', and those who are familiar with the magazine will know that in the small ads. at the back is a column 'Eye Love' which often contains - or contained - amusing pleas for people seeking love or romance - or affairs. I had always been physically attracted to the larger lady, so thought I would advertise in that vein. At the time, Les Dawson had a very amusing show which occasionally featured a mature group of ladies called the 'Roly-Poly's'. So I wrote the following advert, and sent it off:

'WANTED - ROLY-POLY LADY FOR ROLY-POLY FUN, OCCASIONAL AFTERNOONS, WATFORD – LUTON AREA', plus box number. It duly appeared in an August 1989 issue, featuring English cricketers on the front cover. They'd done extraordinarily badly that year, and the caption was 'can we bowl underarm?' or something similar.

At the time this appeared, Dora and I managed a holiday with my Mum in Minehead, Somerset. Things were better for us over this time, and I did have feelings of guilt over my behaviour, particularly when Dora read the bloody advert and found it highly amusing - not knowing I'd placed it of course. But when we got back, things deteriorated rapidly between us again.

I got one reply. It contained a few brief details and a phone number, with instructions when to ring.

I hesitated over ringing. It seemed such an enormous thing to do. Several times I put my finger in the dial (still dials then!) and then bottled out. But, after a particularly acrimonious exchange with Dora, I did it. And I got through and found myself talking to Shirley, a thirty-six-year-old lady with the most gorgeous, sexy voice. We exchanged pleasantries and agreed that we should meet initially on neutral ground 'sometime soon'. I had no idea into what deep, and rather murky, waters this seemingly simple conversation would lead me. You're right - I didn't have a clue. At the time I felt elated, confident, and optimistic that life was going to get better for me, and hopefully not hurt anyone else. I'm sure that this all sounds naïve and foolish, and I readily admit that that is exactly what I was. Selfish, too. Both Shirley and I were. We first met on a gorgeous early October day in

Aylesbury. She chose the venue, a little café over a newsagents in a large shopping centre. I was amazed at the change in Aylesbury since I had last been there. When I first visited the place in the early 'sixties it had been a thriving, busy market town full of interesting buildings.

A book of 'Chiltern Strolls and Rambles', produced by the Metropolitan Railway in the 'thirties, said that 'from the vale, Aylesbury promises a store of interest - it redeems the promise'. In the early sixties it was still true.

Now it had become just like anywhere else, with bland, soulless shopping centres and arcades. The rot had started in 1964 when a so-called 'architect', Fred Pooley, was commissioned to erect a huge Council Offices building near to the railway station. This appalling excrescence, in grey concrete, was the beginning of the end for Aylesbury as it had been. Dominating not only the town but the countryside for miles around, it is now regarded as one of the ugliest buildings in Britain. Pooley, I remember, was immensely proud of his work and went on to produce some further dreadful additions to the town including the most ugly style of lampposts - that became known as 'Pooley's coolies'. Aylesbury was special; it was individual. Now it's just another town. Thanks a bunch, Fred.

Anyway, I didn't come to mourn the loss of a Buckinghamshire town but to celebrate meeting a new lady. I found the venue with some difficulty, and found Shirley with some difficulty too as she was hidden behind the pages of the 'Guardian', still a broadsheet then. I introduced myself and got the coffees in. Shirley was not at all the person I had imagined her to be - though goodness knows why I had any preconceptions at all; I'd not received a photograph of her or really any information. I now can't even remember what my preconceptions were, but whatever they were, Shirley was not like them! Short, plump of course, with long dark wavy hair, and easy to talk with. We found we had a fair bit in common, including a love of the country and of animals, and I also learnt that she was married with two children, both boys. The eldest was interested in model railways, which I fully understood - I think he was twelve then. The younger boy was, I think, seven or eight. They lived near Thame. Neither of us mentioned sex. We kept to general topics and although I'm sure that I wasn't the handsome bloke she'd hoped to meet, we agreed to a further meeting. To be honest, I wasn't too sure, but Shirley had a certain 'je ne sais quos' I felt - and I wanted to learn more of her life. I'd told Dora that I was visiting a friend in Birmingham whose daughter had become gravely ill - and after the meeting with Shirley, I motored up and did just that. It remained a lovely day and I remember being pleased to see a genuine gypsy caravan and horse by the roadside on the way, near Banbury.

Dora and I took a short break to visit friends who had recently moved from Harrow to Barry in South Wales, later that month. It didn't help. What we needed was a break from each other. Our friends must have been puzzled at our awkwardness and it was not a happy time at all. On our return I contacted Shirley again to arrange a further meeting. This time we met in Ashridge Forest and we learned a bit more about each other. I still didn't feel really attracted to her and she was obviously not really at ease, either, but we agreed again to meet up one more time before Christmas. I liked her car, adorned as it was with stickers saying 'Nuclear Power - No thanks!' and various other 'Green' or left-wing things.

We met again as arranged shortly before Christmas, exchanged cards and had a pleasant few hours but I felt we weren't really getting anywhere. However, again we agreed to meet-up early in the New Year.

Shirley must have made a decision over the Christmas period to take our relationship a stage further, because when we next met she -er – 'came on strong' as the expression has it, and we had lift-off. But not take-anything-off yet. However, it was obvious that this would now happen. We had our first 'proper' kiss, and it magically changed everything for me and, I hope, for her too. I cannot explain why but I suddenly became extraordinarily physically attracted to her - it was almost a 'Damascene moment' if I can use that expression in this context. We debated where we should next meet, and I remember saying that it could be a hotel room but it seemed a bit tawdry. However, that's what we did. I felt awfully naughty hanging a 'Do not Disturb' notice on the door.

Almost straight away, Shirley started talking about leaving her husband. This wasn't in the plan at all! But the attraction between us seemed stronger than we could cope with and took over our lives. After our afternoon in the hotel, I told Dora that I'd met a lady friend. She initially took it very well saying 'why not?' but soon she realised that Shirley was becoming a threat to everything we'd fought for and achieved together. Dora was not really a jealous person, but she saw, far more clearly than I, that my actions could be disastrous for us both. It focussed her mind on how much she still felt for me as well, and indeed how much she had sacrificed in order to be with and stay with me, for so long. She started to become very angry indeed, and concerned for me I think, too.

Shirley did not tell her husband or, of course, her two boys. But one morning Adrian came down and looked in Shirley's bag for some keys and found a cache of letters from me, and predictably, hit the roof. I'm still not sure to this day whether he was 'meant' to find these, or not. Shirley said not. Adrian soon found out where I lived - I'd given pretty clear directions in one of my letters - and within a couple of days I received a visit.

It wasn't pleasant, but I was glad that the affair was now out in the open. He pleaded with me to desist visiting, telephoning or writing to Shirley for 'a couple of weeks' while he tried to reason with her and point out the probable repercussions of what we were intending to do. What were we intending to do? I still was at the stage where I really didn't know, but Shirley was adamant that she would leave Adrian once I'd found a house for us. If I expressed any doubt of the viability of my procuring a house, she would fly into a rage and say it was because I lacked commitment, didn't love her enough, or/and still loved Dora.

I have never met anyone, before or since, as acutely jealous - and indeed envious - as Shirley, and I was ill-equipped to deal with it. My mind was a complex whirl of emotions, but above all of them towered an overpowering need to be with this woman. I couldn't explain it logically then and I cannot explain it now. Of course I was concerned at the effect any change would have on her two boys. I assured Adrian that as far as I was concerned, he would have unlimited access to his boys and Shirley concurred with this. Knowing what I know now, I wonder indeed whether this would have been the case.

I told Adrian that I would comply with his wishes and, I think, managed all of a week before I broke the promise. I couldn't bear not to be in touch with Shirley, and she had been distraught at my compliance and sent me heart-rending letters and tried to phone. When we met, after this break, we were both overwhelmed and I promised I would not agree to a 'separation' again. Throughout 1990, which was blessed with a glorious summer, we met as often as we could. We made love in fields, woods, and commons all over Buckinghamshire and made plans for our futures, together.

It wasn't easy to fulfil any plans, as I had no money. I had agreed that I should move nearer to Shirley so that the boys wouldn't need to move schools or forego the excellent treatment they needed to have regularly at a hospital in Oxford. But houses in Buckinghamshire and Oxfordshire were vastly more expensive then than they were in Bedfordshire, so it wasn't going to be easy. Bedfordshire was still, then, considered to be the 'Cinderella' of the Home Counties, nowhere near as desirable as its sisters Buckinghamshire, Hertfordshire, etc. etc. And Dora was in no hurry to sell our place. She still hoped I might come to my senses.

The 'elephant in the room' with my relationship with Shirley was her over-riding jealousy, particularly over Dora or anything to do with my past life. Whilst she was still sleeping in the same bed as Adrian, and going on holiday with him and the children - who still knew nothing - I was 'not allowed' to enjoy anything I'd previously enjoyed or liked because it would 'remind me of my time with Dora'. Of course, she could continue as normal - 'because of the children' - but I now believe this was a blind as they say.

Adrian asked to see me several times during that summer, because he had no idea of what was happening and I agreed he had a right to know. Apparently Shirley wouldn't tell him anything at all. He knew all about Shirley's jealousy of course, it had been a constant problem throughout their marriage he said, and even after she had started a physical relationship with me and before he knew, she had accused him of fancying another woman. Adrian was a decent man. He detested lies and deceit and would have been the last person in the world to have been unfaithful. A better man than me, then.

He asked again whether I would give him time to try and reason with Shirley, and at least I had the honesty to say that if I made such a promise I knew now that I would break it. Adrian never threatened me and seemed defeated after the initial meeting, and I look back with remorse at the way he was treated, not so much by me as by Shirley, but with my compliance. He did warn me that Shirley was 'insanely jealous' and there would be frequent tantrums and shouting matches, but I was besotted and really didn't pick up on any warning signs, not for any length of time anyway. Shirley often accused me of being a liar. For many years, I had noticed that people who often accused others of various failings did it to conceal the very same failings in themselves. But I didn't apply it to her! What was the matter with me?

We continued our passionate relationship until autumn brought the rains, and the only practical place then became her home. She lived in a rather small cottage in a village near Thame, which Adrian had been trying to enlarge - the basic shell of the extension had been erected. I knew from my own experience how long it took to do anything like this, but Shirley had lost patience. The cottage was set back from the road, up a narrow drive, and was quite private, having in front of it a large garden in which Shirley kept chickens and ducks. I was somewhat amazed when I entered the cottage for the first time. It looked like it was just used for dumping stuff down, though the tiny sitting-room was reasonably clear. The 'dining room' which adjoined the kitchen was stacked with all sorts of stuff, and the table (covered with a classy Laura Ashley oilcloth) had but a tiny area available for putting a plate down.

The kitchen was stacked high with dirty plates, dishes, and other stuff - I admit that I was taken aback by the general air of neglect. I didn't dare say anything of course. Upstairs, the main bedroom had clothes strewn everywhere - on Shirley's side of the bed the clothes were piled so high on the floor that she appeared as tall as me as she undressed, when she was a good six inches shorter!

We had wonderful times though, I usually brought a sparkling wine which we quaffed (I remember particularly one called 'Omar Khayyam') and after our passionate times in bed we played the then-popular game of 'Trivial Pursuit' or read from the adult comic 'Viz'. We were often rendered helpless with laughter reading this and then we'd suddenly realise what the time was and I'd skid addle before the boys were brought home by the school bus. On one or two occasions I'd have to wait in the 'extension' whilst the boys walked up the drive and Shirley got them safely out of the way, before I deftly made my escape. One day, Adrian appeared unexpectedly, almost catching us in flagrante and I had to hide behind some curtains, realising too late that my feet were protruding from underneath them. We might as well have been in a French farce, but if Adrian had discovered us it would not have been so funny.

Naturally, the nursery business suffered, particularly after the Spring season. However, Dora had befriended a quite elderly lady who had recently been widowed and was preparing to move. Mrs. Cobbing was no ordinary lady and she lived in no ordinary house. She occupied a part of Bendish House, in the Hertfordshire hinterlands south of Hitchin. She owned all of it, (and acres of surrounding grounds), but she only occupied part of it because the rest was falling down. She also had a large vintage motorcycle collection. And loads of heavy furniture. All this had to be moved to her new home on the outskirts of the Forest of Dean. And she wanted me to help, at £5 an hour (quite reasonable then). She had a large Mercedes van which she insisted had to be renovated and put back on the road in order to transport all this stuff.

I've never seen so many motorcycles, in varying stages of decay, in my life. Some of them must have been very valuable even in their dilapidated state (I don't think any of them actually ran); there were makes such as Rudge and Brough, long since gone. Some of them had no wheels! I said that a motorcycle without wheels was like a pub with no beer, an expression totally lost on Mrs. Cobbing. She had many qualities, but humour wasn't really amongst them. We - I say we, for there was a couple from Luton who helped also - had to lift these into the Mercedes, which had no tail lift. Plus motorcycle engines of all sorts. I never found out how or why Mrs. Cobbing had all these machines, but the money I earned moving all these and driving them down to Gloucestershire more than made up for any income lost from neglecting the nursery business. There were at least two day's work every week, for many weeks. And they were long days.

The wonderful collection of dilapidated vintage motorcycles at Mrs. Cobbing's home in Bendish, Hertfordshire, before removal to a new home in Gloucestershire. What happened to them all?

Her new place was a farm, up an extraordinarily long lane and then a track. The farm buildings were going to be used to store the motorcycles. The farmhouse was in a good state of repair, as were the majority of the outbuildings, but she was elderly and obviously was never going to restore even one of the bikes and we all felt she should donate them to a museum. She was aghast at the idea - so possessive was she of them. And what about her? She wasn't in very good condition herself, she couldn't walk far, and she would be so isolated up there with no near neighbours - it all seemed totally daft, almost surreal. But who were we to tell her what she should or should not do? She obviously had plenty of money. I wonder if she, and the bikes, are still with us, twenty-five years on. . . .

Shortly after Mrs. Cobbing moved, I was trying to lift a heavy paving slab at the nursery when I slipped a disc. It wasn't too bad at first and I made an elementary error by keeping on working. The next day I could hardly move. It had seemingly locked into position and was agony. I couldn't straighten-up and moved around like the hunchback of Notre Dame. The Doctor gave me painkillers and Dora very kindly found me an Osteopath in Harpenden. I could just about drive, and about a week after suffering this I was due for an interview at a school in Aylesbury. I'd been looking for work in Shirley's area, and not had any luck, but this school needed a caretaker so I applied, and was granted an interview.

I drove over and met with Shirley before hobbling in. There were four other applicants waiting, all with caretaking experience, and fit! I was the third to go in, and shuffled along like a modern Quasimodo saying apologetically that I didn't usually walk like this. After the interviews we all had to wait for the verdict, and it was me who was called-in. They said that they liked me, and that the job wasn't so demanding, so I was offered the place. It came with a house, which I duly went to see - it was frankly awful. Doors were hanging off, the kitchen I remember didn't even have a cooker, it was dreadful. I was given a tour of the school, shown the enormous heating system which I would have to maintain, and told that I would be responsible for the cleaners doing their job properly.

Somewhat shaken, I then 'left the building' and Shirley and I went for a drink at a nearby pub. The little house was not suitable for a family. I couldn't ask Shirley to bring the boys to live there. I was overawed by the responsibilities I would have to take on. Shirley had a go. 'You're not enthusiastic, are you' she said 'you get an opportunity and you don't want it'. Both true, but I knew if she saw the house she'd say 'not suitable for my boys'. And I couldn't have done the job in my present physical state. I wrote a polite letter declining the offer and explaining why and apologising, and I heard no more. Perhaps they were relieved, too.

The Osteopath was brilliant. After three sessions he 'clicked' my spine back into position, and although I was not cured, he had put me on the road to recovery.

Christmas 1990 was the most miserable ever, for both Dora and for me. I didn't want to be where I was, and she was unhappy and anxious. We shouldn't have been there, working at Christmas for the homeless would have been much better. For months up to December, Dora had verbally laid into me almost every evening and I felt powerless to stop her; she had every reason and every right to chastise me, but it was becoming almost obsessive. After Christmas I said I would have to move out. 'Good!' she said; 'Good, good - do it NOW!' I couldn't do it just then, I had nowhere to go, but made arrangements with my friend Tony (who'd been a member of the youth club and helped with Open Christmas) to move temporarily in with him. He'd married another youth-club member, Rosanna, and originally they'd managed to get a flat in the suburb of Neasden, made famous by Private Eye magazine, in north-west London. Then they'd got a semi in South Ruislip, but unfortunately had split up a few months earlier and he was living there on his own. He agreed to let me live there for free, as long as I bought the food. So, in January 1991, I left Dora. I did not feel elated, in fact I felt very upset and guilty. I did not do it lightly.

...PAVED WITH GOOD INTENTIONS

I often visited Shirley on a Saturday afternoon, when Adrian took the boys out to see his elderly mother and treated them to a fish-and-chip supper (or maybe it was just chips for the vegetarian boys). The day after I moved in with Tony was a Saturday, so I rang her at an agreed time to confirm. Instead of being delighted that I'd finally moved, she started, with some hostility, asking questions about 'I bet you feel guilty!' and 'do you feel sad?' I felt both, and told her, which of course infuriated her. I was barracked unmercifully so instead of receiving some much-needed solace I found I was being shouted at by Shirley instead of Dora. Tony was present and murmured 'Don't go over! If she can't understand why you feel like you do, just don't go'. I took his advice, and of course was shouted at again when I phoned and told her, explaining why of course. She started crying, but it was too late now for me to go.

South Ruislip was - and probably still is - a depressing place. You get the feeling that you're living on the wrong side of the tracks. Most of the streets are dead straight, it seemed miles to the nearest station, the roads were clogged with parked cars and all the houses looked the same. Tony's first home in Neasden at least had a bit of character. Neither he nor I knew any of the neighbours: these streets didn't now have the saving grace of a friendly 'open-door' community (have we really progressed since the fifties?). But he'd offered me a roof over my head, and I was more than grateful for that. I discovered, by accident, that I was now living just around the corner from where my maternal grandmother had looked after me for a few weeks before my adoption.

Now I had to find a job. I still walked with a stoop and couldn't do much physical work, but I could drive, so went over to Pinner to see if there might be a job at my old firm, Checker Cars. They were very surprised to see me, but after a brief explanation of my situation, I got taken back.

Over the four years between leaving them and coming back, they had turned from being Checker Cars into 'Checker Travel', with a full-sized coach now on the fleet. The 'Jolly Blue Giant' had disappeared - I wonder why? The full-sized coach was a Ford, though - and incredibly old-fashioned for its years. Almost all coaches now had their engine under the floor or at the back, but Ford had persisted with mounting the engine at the front, which made it noisy to drive and put a great 'hump' at the front beside the driver. Shortly after I returned, another coach was purchased, a Leyland Leopard which was a more advanced design. At first, there wasn't enough work to warrant me being only a coach driver, so I borrowed some money off my mother and purchased a Rover Van den Plas car which was used as a mini-cab and I did some of this work as well.

Everyone was working on a self-employed basis, so I could legitimately say I was not available and had plenty of time to visit Shirley. On these occasions I worked evenings, and soon got a regular slot driving a Mercedes mini-coach on a series of runs from around 5-30 pm. 'til 10-30p.m., receiving £40 cash an evening - really good money indeed in 1991. These runs picked-up cleaning ladies from all over Borehamwood and took them to Haberdashers Girls School and an Edgware Care Home, followed by a late run from Aldenham School for the 'semi-boarders' who only went home to sleep. I felt sorry for these kids. They were at school from eight-thirty in the morning to nine-thirty at night. The mini-bus was old and shabby, so the cleaners and I were vastly amused when one evening an unfamiliar couple at one of the regular stops asked if this was the bus to Athens! With the money saved from Mrs. Cobbing's work and now this, I soon built up enough to put down a deposit on a modest home near to Shirley. Only renting, though - not enough to purchase at Oxfordshire's prices. I considered it important that we lived within the catchment area of the boy's schools, so that at least they would not have their education disrupted. Financially, it would have been far easier for Shirley and the boys to move to Bedfordshire but I am pleased that I put their educational needs before my financial ones, and also that I had told Adrian that he would be able to see his children as much as he - and they - wanted. Living in the area would make this far easier for him and for them.

Shirley seemed enthusiastic and she and I started to peruse the local papers for something suitable. We had considered a mobile home in Wheatley, but had not been particularly enamoured with it, but now an ex-council house came up in Chalgrove, south of Oxford City and known for its monument to John Hampden. (He had been mortally wounded at Chalgrove Field in the Civil War, and had been a vocal opponent of paying Ship-money to the King). The rent was £300 a month, but they wanted two month's rent in advance, repayable on ending the tenancy. It was a rather poor little house really, no central heating, downstairs loo, very basic indeed kitchen, no double-glazing; in fact it still had those iron-framed windows popular in the 'fifties. But there was nothing else, so after getting approval from Shirley, I went for it and secured it.

This was in May 1991. The house was let as unfurnished, so I had to buy everything in including a fridge, washing machine and cooker. It took a while to sort everything out, what with working as well, and having to travel each way, and to be honest I didn't really take to the house. I loved living in Chalgrove, though; it was a friendly village and I had very amenable neighbours. Ducks wandered around and sometimes came into the house - I didn't mind a bit. They were much less of a nuisance than a goat! And they just came in through the open front door, quacked a bit, and waddled out through the back. The house was on a corner plot so had quite a large garden, all down to grass. One of my neighbour's little boys came and cut it regularly for me, without being asked and not expecting payment. It was just that sort of place.

Shirley came over regularly, and having our own place was great, with not having to worry about being interrupted. She didn't really make any effort to move in, though, there were always reasons why not - usually my fault for not doing something or for allegedly wishing for my old life back. I did have to go over to the nursery sometimes, such as when pipes burst (as they did the following winter) and it was always viewed with suspicion and hostility. I took to not mentioning any trips but felt I should not have to be dishonest in order to try and keep the peace. Our physical relationship became even stronger, though, with the result that Shirley became pregnant in July. We'd never bothered with 'precautions' but nevertheless this came as something of a shock. A long time before, I had been diagnosed with having a low sperm count so hadn't expected this. Shirley said she'd double-check, and she did; the result was the same.

I am the first to admit that I was apprehensive at first. From merely wanting a 'harmless' affair eighteen months before, I had left my partner, my home, the security I had enjoyed, and my business, and was living in a rented ex-council house, having to travel nearly fifty miles to work, and now was going to be a father! Gulp. Now Shirley said the most extraordinary thing. She said that, as a vegetarian, she wouldn't hurt a fly, but if I wanted, she would have an abortion. If I wanted? I'd not even thought of the possibility and was genuinely horrified.

Taking into account what happened after this, I now believe this was a trap. I think Shirley wanted me to say 'yes, I think it's best you have an abortion', knowing it would be impossible for her to carry out, and then use my decision as an excuse to stay where she was, as I wouldn't be a suitable partner. I certainly believe that she would never have done it; so why say that? Unfortunately for her, I think, the idea horrified me. It did, though, focus my mind on my commitment to her, and now to my unborn child. That changed everything. I thought that at least, now, Shirley would tell the truth to her sons and move in.

But of course, she didn't. Excuse followed excuse, and I was always to blame. To be fair, she did make two half-hearted attempts; once, when the boys went on holiday with their grandparents and once when I wasn't there (though I'm not absolutely sure of this. There was no evidence of her having been there when I got back). At the time the boys were away, she seemed uneasy. Lovemaking became a desperate means of blocking out her feelings of guilt rather than acts of unbridled pleasure, I thought. It was different, somehow.

I was still totally in love with her but becoming more and more concerned that I'd been incredibly foolish and that we both should have stuck to our original idea of a passionate affair. Adrian had told me he'd tolerate this, Dora might have come round to the idea, but Shirley would have none of it. 'All or nothing' was her maxim, only the 'all' was on my part, not hers. Her jealousy didn't abate one jot.

I will never forget one incident. I was now driving the coaches more-or-less full-time, and (I think) become respected as a hard worker who got on well with passengers and the other members of staff. I always worked both days at the weekends as of course Adrian and the boys were at home so Shirley and I couldn't meet. I think the boy's trips to see their paternal Gran had finished by now. The firm was taking on a lot of 'booze cruises' - i.e. day-trips to Calais or Boulogne, with only the more experienced drivers allowed to do this. The hours were long, often requiring two drivers, and the money was really good, plus the fact we were able as coach drivers to purchase wine and beer at even cheaper rates (to take home of course, not to drink immediately!). There was a certain cachet to being chosen to do these jobs.

I was asked to do this trip two Saturdays running, and, feeling really pleased with myself, rang Shirley on the second Friday to tell her. 'You can't wait to get away, can you!' she said. I couldn't believe it. She was pregnant with my child, and unable to see me because of her own commitments at home, and yet resented the fact that I was earning extra money for us. It seemed so very silly, I simply put the phone down. It now seemed I couldn't be pleased about anything, even when it benefitted us. There were countless other incidents, often equally as silly, but I didn't just feel committed to her, I loved her deeply; and to put this in context, I phoned her every day without fail, and most times the conversations were loving. I now looked forward to her having our baby.

As the autumn turned into winter, (and 1991/92 was pretty harsh) I began to get seriously worried that not only was Shirley not going to move but that my daughter would be born without me being present. I had longed to be a part of the whole thing, a truly modern Dad! - a hands-on, involved father. I pleaded with Shirley to make the commitment, but by Christmas she had not even told Adrian that she was pregnant.

And he hadn't noticed. She hadn't told the boys, either. In January Adrian finally twigged, and said that Shirley would have to tell the boys as he was not going to. I think he meant 'tell them the whole situation', but of course she only told them she was expecting. They were delighted, I was informed.

I went with Shirley to the Radcliffe Hospital early in 1992 and saw our future child on the scanner. We were told we were expecting a daughter. We even went as far as discussing names, and at least Shirley agreed to a name I suggested: Heather. My exhortations to Shirley to move in still went unheeded, with the excuse now that it was all too much for the boys to experience with the baby coming as well. I was distraught, absolutely beside myself with grief, but I had no choice but to accept the situation and of course carry on working. Winter turned to Spring, and Heather was born, a large, healthy baby weighing-in at 10lbs. She was born a little late, but the birth had been an easy one. Adrian had been present, not me, along with Shirley's parents who also, of course, knew nothing of me. I did get to see and to hold our gorgeous little baby girl the very next day - she was perfect.

Shirley was home with Heather very quickly. I rang her as often as I could and within a fortnight I was able to go over to see them one day. For once, I had the courage to ask Shirley if Heather had been registered. She had, in Adrian's name. I leave it to the reader to imagine how this affected me. It was like a kick in the stomach. Shirley continued her promises that 'it didn't change anything' and would indeed move in with Heather 'once it was safe to do so'. I swallowed this bait hook, line and sinker because I wanted to. Anyone else would have seen through this as being the lie it was, and indeed they did when I told them, but I still had hope. . . .was Shirley lying to herself as well? I don't know. Perhaps she was.

I started to visit Shirley (and Heather of course) regularly as soon as it was possible, and we made love astonishingly soon after the birth, at Shirley's instigation. I learned how to change nappies, wind the baby, play little games with her. I found her enchanting. All this happened at Shirley's home for the first months, but then she started coming over to Chalgrove again, with Heather. I had got a room ready for her with 'mobiles' (not mobile phones! We didn't have them then), a cot, and other baby paraphernalia. As babies do, every time we went to make love, Heather would start screaming from the other room. Shirley was really annoyed with this but I found it amusing. A quick feed usually solved the problem.

Shirley and baby Heather in 1992.

One year after I'd started renting the place, the rent went up by 10% to £330 a month. I wondered whether I should try and buy it, and made a few enquiries. I would have had to borrow money for the deposit but the letting agents were also house sellers and offered a very good deal. I might have been able to manage it, just, but by this time - at last - I'd really started to understand that it was far less trouble for Shirley to stay where she was with the boys and for Heather to believe Adrian was her father than to move in with me. I now think she'd decided this long ago. As long as she could have the sex, (whilst accusing me often of 'only wanting her for sex') she would keep her home and everything, and be happy knowing that she'd entranced me enough to give up everything I had. I hadn't quite taken in that this would include our daughter in due course, but this would happen too . .

I made one last, desperate plea, that we should be a family. I never received an outright 'no' - Shirley wasn't brave enough to be truthful - but again got accusations and vague promises. I wanted so much to believe she was being honest with me, and still loved her so much, but it was killing me to carry on as we were and killing me to throw in the towel. For a further six months I vacillated, even moving enough stuff out to indicate I was serious about moving away, and I got tears, tantrums and shouting matches but no change, no indication of commitment.

As winter 1992 approached, I knew I had to leave. Tony had put his house in South Ruislip up for sale so I couldn't go back there; the only place was the nursery. We'd kept the mobile home on site, with no trouble from the planning authority after completing the bungalow, so I could move in there. I hired a van, got all the rest of my stuff into it including cooker, fridge and washing-machine, and finally left Chalgrove in November, eighteen months after moving in. Some of my friends thought it was eighteen months too late. I was truly sad to leave; I'd made many friends there and I would miss the friendly, unassuming and undemanding community. But I couldn't live there with the ghosts of ephemeral promises, and no baby enjoying her special little room.

I couldn't see properly when I got into the driver's seat of the van. My eyes were wet with tears.

TRAVELLING MAN

It was strange being back at the nursery after two years away. The mobile home had deteriorated in the time and was a really crap place to live, but at least I had a roof over my head even if it did leak. I made immediate moves to try and improve things and got a loan to buy another second-hand one, which I'd seen in the Auto-Trader magazine. Shortly before I left Chalgrove I had bought a home-converted camper-van very similar to the 'Jolly Blue Giant', even the colour was the same. I called it The Jolly Blue Giant Mark II. There must be a masochistic streak in me, but it was a bargain price (naturally!) and very spacious. I was still thinking in terms of Shirley, the boys and Heather, it was large enough to take us all on holidays and day-trips. The previous owners, a young couple who I liked immensely, had been to Istanbul in it. They must have been wearing ear-defenders and taken plenty of cans of 'Startyerbastard'! Shortly after moving in to the mobile home I moved out of it again and lived in the camper whilst the old mobile was burnt and then got the site ready for the 'new' one.

Dora was still living in the bungalow and had formed a relationship with Albert, a local man who had helped me with the building work. This took the pressure and awkwardness of being there, off a bit. Dora had put the bungalow on the market and I was to receive a third of the proceeds when it was sold. Why only a third and not half? Dora said she'd put more money into the relationship than me and I was really past caring to argue much. I felt lonely, our village in Bedfordshire was nowhere near as friendly a place as Chalgrove, and I was grieving over the loss of Shirley and Heather. Which is why I believe I capitulated when Shirley rang and asked to see me.

I needed to see her and I longed to see Heather. We resumed our relationship almost as if nothing had happened, with Shirley continuing to tell me she loved me and saying 'we' would try again to change our circumstances. She really meant 'me', not 'we'. I went along with it, wondering what would happen when Heather started to talk. I remember losing patience with Shirley only once. I was at her home and we'd argued over something, and I went outside shouting that Heather was 'my baby! My baby!' 'Oh the shame' said Shirley, meaning someone might have heard me, 'the shame!'. Why, oh why, couldn't I have seen the blindingly obvious even at that stage? Talk about not having a clue. . . .

The 'new' mobile home was a twin unit, twice as wide as the one we'd burnt. But it was still pretty much crap and was bloody cold in the winter. It didn't leak, though. I looked forward to the day the bungalow was sold and I could improve my accommodation. I decided I would re-start the nursery business in early Spring 1993 as a 'sole trader'; I still had many contacts who would appreciate my plants and I could continue earning extra money by driving in the evenings. This worked well; I could still take days off to see Shirley and Heather and often managed two days in the week, occasionally three. Checker Travel had begun a lucrative line teaming up with firms and individuals who dealt with groups of foreign students who came to stay for weeks at a time in England. We collected them from Heathrow, Gatwick or Stansted and took them to a number of collection points in the Harrow area where they were met and dispersed to various families. This often happened in the evenings, when many other drivers couldn't or wouldn't work. I could go straight from seeing Shirley or from home, wherever I happened to be.

It did mean I was doing an awful lot of travelling and really needed a better and more economical car. At this time, diesel cars were in the ascendant and, in particular, the Citroen BX diesel was being lauded for its refinement, frugality and reliability. They held their price well, though, and I didn't have enough to afford a reasonably-new one. At the time I was driving an ex-Checker Cars minicab, a Ford Granada, an excellent car but rather thirsty. Someone told me that a garage in Harefield, a village right on the outskirts of Middlesex and still fairly rural, had a nice Citroen diesel and might take the Granada in part-exchange. I went to look one lunchtime and met the 'salesman', a young bloke with long hair and a totally relaxed attitude, who said that as he was going for lunch in the pub and 'might be some time', I could take the Citroen for as long a drive as I wished as long as I left the Granada with him. If I liked it, we would do a deal and I didn't have to put fuel in it as it hardly used any.

I took the Citroen out, through the lanes to Chorleywood, then to Amersham, seeing how tractable it was and how she behaved over rough surfaces; then to Beaconsfield to see how she performed on the main road and finally back down the M40 to see how quiet she was at 70mph. The car excelled in every respect and I was amazed at how quiet and flexible it was; a world away from the 'Jolly Blue Giant'! After prising him out of the pub with some difficulty and perhaps somewhat taking advantage of his rather enhanced state of bonhomie, I agreed a favourable price with the salesman and a very good price for the Granada in part exchange. If you're still around, Dave, thank you.

The car only let me down once and I never grew tired of it. I eventually completed just 80,000 miles and sold it, still running, five years later. It's probably largely forgotten now but the BX Citroen changed people's minds about running a diesel car. Before that, they were recognised as being economical, yes, but slow, smelly, noisy and dirty. At many filling-stations you had to use the HGV pumps. Now of course, diesel is available on every forecourt and the cars are mainstream. But, to my mind, the modern diesels lack one quality the earlier Citroens (and Peugeots, Fords, Vauxhalls etc.) had, and that is simplicity. Today's cars are loaded with electronic gizmos which control this or improve that, which are fine as long as they work; but are incredibly expensive and complicated to fix if they go wrong. I still drive a twenty-year-old Vauxhall diesel which even I can fix, usually. It's fine for me.

I digress. But with my very economical and reliable diesel car, driving over to see Shirley and Heather didn't stretch my finances so much and this made it possible to do it more often. I didn't see Heather's first steps, but she proudly showed me how well she could walk very shortly after she'd started. It was a reminder that she was growing, fast. . . .

Throughout the rest of 1993 and much of 1994 I saw Shirley and Heather at least once a week and often two or even three times a week. We used to go out to lovely places and sometimes do the shopping; Heather loved to sit on one of those shopping trolleys in the supermarket and be pushed briskly along. One day we went to Banbury, and Heather became very excited at seeing one of those model horses outside one of the shops. We placed her on and inserted the money and she seemed to be in seventh heaven. Time and again we had to put more money in! This was a little foretaste of the future for Heather, as a few years later she started riding the real ones. Her little face was a picture.

I became very fond of our beautiful little daughter. She was enchanting. We went another day to a shop called 'Stacks' in Old Amersham which sold all sorts of reproduction furniture, bric-a-brac and unusual cards. I saw one with a picture of a little monkey on the front, waving, and I showed this to Heather who broke into a broad grin and waved back. Another time Shirley and I took Heather on a day-trip to France (via the Ferry) and we had a lovely time with her enjoying the beach at Wissant and playing hide-and-seek on the boat. That summer, 1994, Heather had started to learn words though she hadn't quite started to speak them yet. I would say 'knee' and she would point to her knee. 'Nose', and she would point to that. One day I ventured 'Daddy' and she smiled and pointed to me.

Very soon after that, she started to talk and I started to see her less. I last saw her in a shopping centre in Aylesbury, ironically, and I knew I was about to lose her - it was at the end of August. This time she waved goodbye and kept waving 'til she was out of sight. I made my way back to the car and broke down. I couldn't drive anywhere and was sat there for nearly four hours, unable to move. The parking charges were considerable and hurt my pocket, but it was less than the hurt in my heart. It felt as if a knife was being twisted in it.

> *The furthest star in the sky,*
> *Well that's the one that passed me by*
> *I tried to wish upon that star*
> *It didn't get me very far*
> *It fell on empty ears,*
> *It fell on empty hearts*
> *And my dreams. . . . they fell apart.*

Excerpt from 'The furthest star' by Amy McDonald from her album 'In a Beautiful Light' 2012

ROGER, ROGER!!

You may well ask why I didn't cause more of a fuss, or at least try to come to some arrangement with Adrian and Shirley over some provision on my part for Heather. I'm not quite sure how to answer this. Perhaps I was in a sort of shell-shock that this had happened; perhaps it was because at that time, the feminists had wielded such influence that we men felt superfluous - after all, Harriet Harman and Patricia Hewitt are on record as saying at the time that fathers were not necessary to a child's upbringing, and that attitude was pretty general. The Children's Act was passed in 1989 putting, for the first time, the rights of the child at the forefront and ending years of paternalism. Perhaps I still had hope. . . .I certainly still loved Shirley and she was still saying that she loved me.

The loss of any contact with my only child had a far greater effect on me, though, than I could ever have imagined. I must have had hope of seeing her again otherwise I could not have borne it at that time. I still motored over to see Shirley and she was quite insistent that she still loved me, but for the first time I started to have serious doubts about this. I had no doubts about my own feelings for her, however. I felt angry with her and betrayed, and also felt an increasing sense of desperation to get out of this destructive (for me) relationship; and I started to lose sight a little of how much I still loved her. Meanwhile, I had lots to do.

Dora had sold the bungalow and was swapping homes with the couple who bought it. They were upsizing as they had two young boys, and Dora was downsizing so it was a very handy arrangement. Also, the home she moved into was almost next-door to Albert. My new neighbours, the Coopers, knew all about my circumstances and Rick Cooper was a contractor with a JCB digger and offered to lay a concrete base for me for a new mobile home, for a bargain price 'as it's you'. For I had gone to look at brand new mobile homes. The firm 'Tingdene' of Wellingborough had just brought out a model called the 'Deene Cottage' which was aesthetically pleasing and done in a vernacular style. I was very taken with it; I had always wanted to live in a farmhouse and this was probably the nearest to one that I would ever be able to afford. It was quite unlike any other mobile home I had ever seen.

Mobile Homes (more commonly known as 'Park Homes' now because they are often parked out on designated sites, like rows of cabbages) in my view are brilliant. They could be the answer to our present housing crisis, if people had a less prejudicial view of them and the authorities were more flexible. And if they weren't always stuck on 'parks' where you can't have pets, or you can't have kids, or you can't do this or you can't do that, and presumably have to be dead from the neck up. Many people lived in 'prefabs' after the war and most of those who did, loved them. They lasted far longer than they were designed to, and some are still lived in today.

Mobile homes are essentially built on the same principle. They are constructed in a factory and then transported by low-loader to a site with a concrete base. They are then bolted together, the services connected, and you can move in within a couple of days. After spending a year building the bungalow this was a very attractive option.

The bungalow had sold for a little more than £90,000 of which my share came to just the £30,000. Believe it or not, this was enough (almost) to purchase the largest size of 'Deene Cottage', and have it delivered and assembled on site. The smallest cottage in our village was selling for about the same price, but had tiny rooms and an equally tiny garden. I would have the use of an acre of the nursery and a spacious bungalow, in effect. No competition, really. There was a fly in the ointment, though.

One day, after having ordered my home, I came back to my then-current abode to find a note from the local planning department pinned to the door. The pig farm next door had been sold and demolished, to make way for a new Nursing Home on the site - a planning official had been checking it out and espied my little home over the hedge and thought 'that's not on my map!'. So I was asked to contact the planning officer. I duly did and explained my position, but didn't mention I'd ordered a new one! He seemed pretty relaxed about it but said he'd contact me again, and an 'enforcement officer' would be making an appointment to see me. By the time he got round to this, the new home had arrived.

A firm in Oxford had removed my old one and I was again living in the 'Jolly Blue Giant'. I had stressed to Tingdene that could I have the home delivered as discreetly as possible, preferably around lunch-time which was a quiet time on the road. We had agreed a delivery date. The day before the agreed date I awoke at around half-past seven to a gentle rumbling sound outside the bus. Peering out I was astonished to find half my new home passing by on its way to the concrete base made ready for it. Not only had they come a day early (amazingly I wasn't at work) but they had come in the middle of the rush-hour and had to completely block the road in order to swing the two halves of the home in to the drive.

It couldn't have been more obvious or more inconvenient; two of the school buses that used the road had to turn round and divert, along with numerous cars. I quickly got dressed and introduced myself to the workers; they were good-humoured and it was too late to remonstrate. I was glad to see my home. The firm had actually let me visit the factory to see it under construction, which was interesting and informative, but to see it complete was brilliant. Perhaps I should have gone for a smaller version, but I still half-hoped that Shirley, Heather and the boys would come and share it with me. As I say, the home came in two halves and was joined together on site. I had the services connected the day after it was bolted together, and moved in the day after that.

Mobile homes usually come fully furnished but this is not compulsory, and I had mine delivered with carpets and curtains only. I had plenty of furniture to put in it. The model came with double-glazing, gas central heating, a pitched and tiled roof with dormers, and even a loft complete with light and ladder. You can more-or-less specify your own interior layout as the interior walls are not load-bearing; I enjoyed planning it and there are only a few things I would change, having learned many lessons from the bungalow. I ordered a 'proper' fireplace in the living room; and a large, farmhouse-style kitchen. A walk-in wardrobe and en-suite bathroom were part of the standard specification. It was absolute bliss after my previous one, with a good standard of insulation and quite tasteful decoration. I'd ordered a 'stable door' for the kitchen, which is the main entrance, and French doors for the living room. Rick from next door built some superb steps up to the main door. Once the furniture was in, I thought it looked really lovely and homely, but Shirley declined even to come and look at it. That was the final straw for me. I felt that I really had to sever my ties with her.

I had a twenty-year battle with the planning authorities to come, but of course did not know this at the time. For several months I was left alone, and I revelled in the space, convenience and the comfort of my new home. I mentioned that I didn't have quite enough money for it, and I should say here that Dora helped me out with a loan, for the shortfall. Whilst I was delighted with my new home, I couldn't help wondering whether I should have bought the house at Chalgrove. I could have bought it for around £45,000 at that time and perhaps Shirley would have moved in. I now know for sure she would not have moved in, ever, but I couldn't see it even at this stage. I still would have swopped my new home for that or anything else if it had included Shirley and Heather.

I continued working at Checker Travel, during the day as well as evenings quite often. The hours were long but I had lots of fun and several amusing episodes. One day I was designated to take a group from a school in Harrow to a theatre in Wimbledon. On the way back I mistook a turn for Wandsworth Bridge and ended up at the entrance to the Council dump. Emerging from his hut, the chap who regulated the traffic into the dump shouted 'Scrap vehicles over there, mate! Do you want to unload first?' I explained I'd taken a wrong turn and just wanted out, but he said it was a one-way system round the dump. 'It's a bit complicated - I'll get Fred down to act as courier'. Fred duly appeared, grinning like a Cheshire cat, and escorted us round, using the coach's microphone to give a running commentary on objects of interest en route. At one stage there was a mountain of toilet bowls, wash-hand basins and old sinks which he informed us was 'The Potteries'. They had been taken out of council properties during a modernisation programme. At another turn we were confronted with a giant willy someone had etched into a concrete wall before it had dried, which Fred described as 'modern art'. By the time we got back to the entrance hut we were almost helpless with laughter and we were quite sad to make our departure. I took the same group of children to London Zoo later in the year and of course got ribbed unmercifully; the kids had forgotten all about the show but remembered every detail of their diversion. . . . . particularly the giant willy.

On another occasion I took a group of Hindu people to a temple in Bradford and again got lost. Turning into a narrow road my vision was immediately blocked by a huge pair of pantaloons sliding down the windscreen from the washing-line strung across the road between the houses, with which I'd got entangled. An irate and very large woman ran out of the nearest house screaming obscenities at me as I backed the coach away, only to reverse into another line of washing in the road behind, completely demolishing it. All the clean clothes lay across the street and whilst my passengers thought it hilarious, this view was not shared by the residents. I was in a position now to make my escape, and I'm ashamed to say I did just that. I really didn't fancy facing the wrath of half-a-dozen very strong-looking Yorkshire ladies.

Once I took a group of policemen and women from their station in West London for a day-trip to Calais and the Hypermarkets. They were pretty inebriated before they even got on, and this was about 5-30 in the morning. On the way down the A2 past Canterbury a couple started 'mooning' - i.e. exposing their bottoms - out of the rear window. Unfortunately they were spotted by a patrol car from the Kent constabulary who pulled us over. On finding out who my passengers were, they issued me with a warning letter signed by 'P.C. Duncan D'Isorderly' and waved us on our way.

My favourite trip was with a group of hippies I picked up in Hampstead of all places. They were going to watch a Pink Floyd concert at Chantilly outside Paris. I picked them up at the appointed (late) hour and the organiser immediately gave me £100 cash. Astounded, I asked him what did he want me to do for this. 'Just be tolerant' he said. As soon as we were moving, the coach filled with the smoke and unmistakeable smell of about thirty joints being lit, and this continued all the way to Dover. The organiser had the presence of mind to stop all the smoking as we neared the port and opened-up all the top windows to at least reduce the smell. We got away with it and went through the French customs unhindered - we were just waved through. It was about 2 in the morning, and the officials looked like I felt - stoned! Then my passengers all lit-up again.

They wanted to see a bit of Paris before going to Chantilly, so I parked the bus within reach of the Eiffel Tower and they had a few hours to do whatever they wanted. I got some kip and then wandered around the shops near the Tower, and purchased the most beautiful material decorated with pictures of ships and lighthouses which I still keep in the bathroom at home. The time came to depart for Chantilly and we reached the concert venue with no trouble at all. I had taken a lounger and after my passengers had disappeared into the crowds I assembled it and relaxed on it, hoping to get a bit more sleep before the concert started. Almost immediately, huge drops of rain started to fall and the sky was rent with lightning. I hastily retreated back into the coach and watched amazed at the pyrotechnics of the storm which delayed the start of the concert by about half-an-hour. Then I enjoyed the concert - I like Pink Floyd - their well-known classic songs mixed with lesser-known ones. They played for around two and a half hours, even continuing through a further electrical storm which cut the power off at one point.

After the concert, we had to return to Paris as several had booked a hotel room there and were going to stay on for a few days. Somehow I had got on the old road rather than the autoroute, which turned out fortuitous as one poor bloke had contracted food-poisoning at the concert. Several times we had to stop, but it was fine as there was no traffic on this road at this hour. As we entered a small town just before the environs of Paris he again asked me to stop as he had the cramping pains of impending diarrhoea. The only place was the town square, so he leapt off and just squatted on the cobbled surface - there was nowhere else to 'go'. Just then a huge double-deck coach filled with passengers passed us, all seemingly awake, and they had a grandstand view whether they liked it or not! Fortunately it didn't stop.

Having dropped-off the people who were staying over, we headed back for

Calais. I could hardly keep my eyes open and it wasn't safe, so we made a stop at one of the excellent service stations on the way. It's amazing what a couple of coffees can do and we reached Calais without incident. However, the organiser was one of those staying over in Paris and of course almost everyone was smoking weed again. I pleaded with them not to smoke through customs but my pleas went unheard. We weren't waved through this time - we were stopped. As I opened the passenger door, smoke billowed out and immediately a dog was brought on board to sniff out the substance. There was so much, he didn't know which way to point and to me looked thoroughly confused. A great deal was confiscated and anyone found with stuff on them was fined, on the spot, the equivalent of £50. They didn't even look at me. As soon as they thought they had cleared the coach, they waved us through, probably glad to see the back of us. I do wonder, though, whether they enjoyed a bit of their haul. As it turned out, they hadn't found even half of it. Normal smoking was resumed almost immediately.

On our return, I was told I was the most tolerant driver ever and we parted on the most amicable terms. They gave me a further £50 plus, er, a considerable amount of weed. I did another jaunt with them, again to see a Pink Floyd concert, this time in Belgium, so they really were pleased with me. I didn't mind at all; there was never any hint of nastiness and it was easy to join in the spirit of the 'trip' (sorry).

I suppose here I should explain my stance on the smoking of cannabis. On the face of it, it seems that people become more aggressive after drinking alcohol than they ever do smoking dope. But most certainly if strong cannabis, known as 'skunk' is taken by youngsters there is a definite risk of psychosis. Moderate smoking of cannabis by adults doesn't worry me. I admit I've done it myself lots of times. It was actually Shirley who taught me how to smoke it properly - as I wasn't a regular smoker, I'd no idea about 'inhaling' (like, allegedly, Bill Clinton) and in earlier years had wondered what all the fuss was about.

Smoking cannabis enhances whatever mood you're in - if you're depressed or sad, don't do it. If you're happy, it won't harm you in moderate amounts. It will heighten the pleasure of sex. If you're prone to anxiety, it's probably best to avoid it - it can cause paranoia. I never found it addictive and now don't indulge, preferring a drink, and I don't miss it. But I did enjoy it for several years and honestly don't think it did me any harm. Some of my favourite memories with Shirley are those of sharing a spliff, watching the red kites wheeling in the sky over the Chiltern Hills and becoming high as kites ourselves....

One more excursion is worth a mention. For once we weren't booked on the Calais ferry but on one that then operated between Newhaven and Dieppe. It was a glorious day and the crossing was very calm and my passengers and I thoroughly enjoyed it; and the time we spent looking around the ancient port of Dieppe was a delight. Camping vehicles were parked all over the quay and I thought how lovely it would be to take the Jolly Blue Giant over one day and spend a night or two there. We then motored to Calais and predictably I got lost. My map didn't seem to tie-up with the actual road network at all. I took a left turn which seemed to go in the correct direction and the road just got narrower and narrower, 'til the coach was almost touching the banks each side. An opening appeared on the right, down which there was an ancient French farmhouse. I told my passengers I would ask directions at the farmhouse.

I walked down, to be met by a large French lady surrounded by hens in the yard, with her arms firmly folded and a quizzical expression on her face. My French is not good, but I managed a 'Pardonnez-moi, madam' and indicated I was lost and mentioned Calais. 'CALAIS?' she boomed, and shrugged her shoulders in a very Gallic manner. I tried to think of another town which might help - any town! - and came up with Amiens. 'Ah, oui!' she smiled and pointed, fortunately, in the direction we were facing. Then I saw the cars on a main road not half-a-mile distant as she said 'Anglais?' 'Oui Madam, merci'. 'Ha Ha! - mad cow, mad cow!' She wasn't referring to herself (or me) but associated England with the Mad Cow disease that was then rampant. As I thanked her again and started walking back to the bus, she expostulated 'Noir! - noir!'. Most of my passengers were black. 'Oui madam!' She burst into laughter 'Oh, ah, le jolie petite Anglais!' Did she mean them, or me? I shall never know.

Once we got to Amiens, Calais is easy to find. On going through Dover, a customs official shouted at me to stop. 'Excuse me, sir, but is your name Roger?' I said it was. 'You ran a youth club in Harrow in the seventies' he said. 'I did'. 'I was there! Martyn Thomas'. We shook hands warmly and after a chat where we delayed and annoyed a few people, I said we'd probably meet again as I often came through. 'Roger, Roger!' he grinned.

There is more to being a coach driver than coach-driving. You really have to be able to empathise with all sorts of different people, and be aware of their requirements. You meet all sorts. Children and teachers, foreign students, pensioners on day trips and longer excursions, church groups, football supporters, theatre-goers, clubbers; all relying on you to get them to their destination comfortably and safely. We used to take a lot of what we called 'twirlies', older people on day trips. I didn't know why they were called thus, until another (bus) driver told me that the free or reduced rates for pensioners on the buses started at nine in the morning but they often tried to board earlier and get away with it. 'Too early, too early!' was the driver's response - hence 'twirlies'.

A good driver will be able to converse easily with everyone. Occasionally you get drunk people and very rarely, aggressive people, and you need to be able to deal with these, too, and in a way that minimises the effect on others. Only once have I had to call the police and that was when I refused to drive a party who had been binge-drinking on a boat at Runnymede. Some of them were so drunk they could not walk, so would not be able to get out of the bus in the event of an accident. The last straw was when one of the party put his fist through a side window, shattering it and severing a vein. There was blood spurting everywhere.

But in forty years of driving, it's not a bad record. Most people are decent. I do wish, though, that teachers would not sit chatting with each other at the front of the coach, oblivious to what's going on behind them. They should always sit towards the back, where they can see what's going on. Many times I have had to ask them to stop the kids throwing things at each other, or standing on the seats or in the aisle. And they always appear vaguely annoyed that I've interrupted their conversation. Oi! Teacher! DON'T leave those kids alone!

OOOH, MATRON!

I met Rosa in November 1994. She was working as a matron at a Private Boarding School in Hampshire, but ironically enough, we met in Oxford. We got chatting and really hit it off, so agreed to meet up again, soon. She didn't tell me this until very recently, but when she returned to the school she told a friend there 'I've just met the man I'm going to marry!' Probably if she knew half what she knows now, she would have said 'that's the one man I'm NOT going to marry!'.

It was all rather whirlwind. I was honest enough to tell her about Shirley and Heather, of course, and I told her I still loved Shirley. I told her about my housing position, too. Nevertheless we spent Christmas together (at her home on the Isle of Wight with her mother, her sister and her daughter, and Rosa's son and later his fiancée) and, to cut the story a little short, we were married on the Isle of Wight on the 30th. December, the last to be married on the Island that year and under the 'old' rules - apparently they were changed for 1995. None of my family or friends were there; we'd only decided a day or two before and there was no time to tell them. We had our reception at French Frank's Café in Newport - I wonder if it's still there. They did us proud.

I hadn't gone over intending to get married, but I was determined now to make a clean break with Shirley and try to forget that I'd had a child and lost her. I thought that making the commitment of marriage would make it absolutely plain that I intended to put the whole 'affair' behind me - to everyone, including myself. We celebrated New Year as a married couple, and then Rosa had to return to the school and I to my driving job and the nursery.

I had dreaded telling Shirley, for all sorts of reasons, and had taken the coward's way out by writing her a letter just before Christmas and saying to her 'don't open it 'til the new year'. Of course I hadn't mentioned getting married as I didn't know, but I did explain that I'd met someone else and felt I'd been patient waiting for her for far longer than was reasonable, and that losing my only child was more than I could bear. I remember having a phone conversation with her that was fairly difficult, in the New Year, and getting an accusative letter which made no mention of Heather at all, as if she was irrelevant to all this. I'd done the right thing for me, but whether it was right to get married 'on the rebound' as it were, with me feeling still so bewildered and deeply disturbed, I cannot judge.

However, Rosa and I were very happy with each other and we enjoyed a belated 'honeymoon' in the early Spring in North Devon. We'd agreed that Rosa should carry on working at the school until the end of the summer term and put her house in the Isle of Wight on the market then, as well. This was not quite as simple as it sounds, as her mother lived there, and we discussed what arrangements should be made. I travelled down to the New Forest whenever I could and became friendly with many of the school teachers and other staff.

We walked on the Isle of Purbeck and in the New Forest with Rosa's dog, Belinda, and it was lovely to have a relationship without being constantly accused of wrong-doings and being suspected of all sorts of misdemeanours.

But, try as I might, I could not get Heather out of my head. I knew that she was happy, well-looked-after, secure. But she came to me in dreams, and suddenly when I was doing other things, unexpectedly, painfully. No-one with an ounce of humanity could 'forget' that they'd had a child - how could I have thought that I could just carry on as if nothing had happened? It was strange - I felt elated that I was married to a woman who truly loved me, yet at times I felt I was in mourning for my child and the lost opportunities of watching her grow and develop. I longed to give her what I had been given by my father, and rekindle my child-like wonder of the natural world and see it again through a child's eyes. I kept these feelings mostly to myself, but they weren't diminishing - they were growing stronger. How I missed her!

Checker Travel was going somewhat upmarket now, and we had two much newer coaches on the fleet - Volvo B10M's, one manual and one automatic. These were superb vehicles. Our own manufacturers had been slow to adopt some of the advances made by foreign competitors and when the Volvo was introduced to the British market it more-or-less did for Leyland, Ford and Bedford in the coach department. AEC had already gone. For a start, the Volvos had air suspension - ours still had cart springs. The engine in the Volvo was a masterpiece, rugged, reliable, long-lived and with a performance far superior to our home-grown products. When I first drove one, I thought it leaned rather too much on the corners until I realised I was taking the corners at about twice the speed as was normal! They were that refined. We now started to take on work that involved longer foreign trips and we not only took foreign students to various parts of the U.K., we took groups of them on to Amsterdam, Brussels and Paris.

I was really pleased to be one of the drivers selected to do these trips. A courier was required and I had the good fortune to be accompanied by Karen from the travel firm Nord Anglia on most occasions. She was not only brilliant at her job but very good company too. We often picked-up in Cambridge, then drove to Dover, caught the ferry to Calais and drove all the way through Belgium up to Amsterdam - a very long day! Two or three nights in Amsterdam, then down to Paris via a stop in Brussels or Bruges, and a few nights in Paris before waving the group goodbye as they caught a train for Germany and beyond. Then we drove back to Calais, though sometimes I was on my own if Karen stayed for a few more days in Paris.

I love Amsterdam - it's so relaxed for a city (can't think why!) and so full of beautiful buildings which include its magnificent railway station. There was plenty of time to stroll around and soak it all up, and in the evening there was, of course, the obligatory tour around the red light district looking agog in the 'shop' windows. One evening the coach was broken into and my passport stolen.

It seems that all Dutch people speak English as if it's their own language and the police were incredibly helpful, giving me a letter confirming I'd reported the loss in case I had trouble later in the journey.

I had no such trouble, fortunately. But later I got lost trying to find the coach park in Brussels. I kept following signs to the Centre, not realising that those signs were pointing to the centre of whatever suburb I was in! I asked a couple of policeman on their motorcycles where the coach park was, and they offered to give me an escort to it! Two further outriders were called-in and we were afforded the full 'escort' treatment, with blue lights flashing and cars giving way as we were guided through.

It seemed a hell of a long way to the coach park and as we finally pulled-in to it, one policeman said to me 'This is Belgium - assistance is very expensive! But no - we were bored, so this time, it's free!' Then with a wave they roared off, leaving my students, other passengers and their drivers (and Karen and me) gobsmacked. And extremely grateful.

I did many of these trips, and it was wonderful to come back from them and be welcomed rather than be accused of any shenanigans with Karen or any of the other couriers, which undoubtedly would have been the case if I had been still seeing Shirley.

At the end of the summer term I was with Rosa at the school to celebrate her time there and listen to the good wishes expressed for her future life with me. We've still got many of the gifts that were given to her on that day. And then Rosa moved in with me and put her home on the market. It was quite a momentous time, really.

Rosa loved the home. I'd told her that there were problems with the planning department, and sure enough, one of our first visitors was the planning enforcement officer for Mid-Beds Council, Mr. Ron Searle. He was courteous enough, but it was a gentle start to what, in the end, became almost a campaign of intimidation which deserves a chapter on its own. Rosa helped me expand the nursery business (I had been limited in what I could do because of lack of time) and we settled down to a happy newly-married life. We had a great holiday in the 'Jolly Blue Giant' which Rosa loved more than I did (she didn't drive it!). In fact she loved this 'hippy' type vehicle more than any other we've had, though the current one comes pretty close. The Jolly Blue Giant had a tail-lift, which we occasionally used as a raised 'patio area' which amused fellow-campers when we took evening drinkies perched on chairs on it. After one-too-many, I fell off once.

Any fellow-campers were even more amused at the antics we had to indulge in to start the bloody thing in the morning. If the 'start pilote' wasn't enough, and it usually wasn't, we had to resort to a can of 'Startyerbastard' squirted down the air-intake hose which looked like an elephant's trunk, having initially been disconnected at one end to facilitate the operation.... happy days.

With Rosa came her lovely old dog, Belinda, a chocolate Labrador, and two cats, Pansy and Arfur (because he only had 'arf a' tail). We soon added two more cats from the Blue Cross rescue centre, Bruiser (so named because he beat up several other cats at the centre!) and Willow, a tabby. We've only recently lost Willow. Soon we were being visited by a collie from the Coopers, next door.

This dog had been one of Dora's daughters' dogs, but Meg had recently separated from her husband Stuart and could no longer keep Tramp, so Dora had asked the Coopers if they would have him. He'd originally been a Battersea Dog's Home dog, and he'd been there twice because his first owner had found him too boisterous. But Tramp was obviously not happy at the Coopers. We're not sure why, but he didn't seem to get on with their terrier, and he kept sneaking up to us. In the end, we all let the dog decide and he came to live with us, living to the ripe old age of 21. I'll talk a little more about him later on.

SLIP-SLIDING AWAY...

The nearer your destination, the more you're slip-sliding away

(Paul Simon)

My longing to have news of Heather grew stronger as Christmas approached. It had been over a year since I had last seen her, and I had always contributed to her Christmas presents and if I thought about her too much it felt as if my heart would break. I longed to ring Shirley and ask about her, but at the same time, I feared to. Instead, I wrote to Shirley's cousin Julia, the only other member of her family to know about me, and I asked her if she could tell me how Heather was. She, very generously I thought, replied saying that she was fine. She knew all about my actions but she wasn't hostile and I was grateful to her. She added that she thought Shirley would appreciate a call from me. I doubted it very much, and didn't ring at Christmas-time. I did ask Julia to give her my best wishes, though.

I couldn't get Heather out of my mind and one morning telephoned Shirley. There was a shocked silence at the other end of the line, and a coldness that she had previously shown Adrian; but at least we got talking and she seemed happy to tell me what Heather was doing. Shirley then indicated that perhaps we should meet and have a proper talk and she would give me an up-to-date photograph of our daughter. I agreed straight away; it seemed the mature and sensible thing to do.

The appointed day arrived and I drove over to Oxford. We met at Shotover Hill on a cold, grey day that February. After an initial awkwardness, we got talking and I learned that Heather was a happy, healthy little girl and Shirley actually said that it wasn't right that I had no contact with her. I obtained my photograph and an assurance that we could meet on a fairly regular basis and I would receive updates on Heather's progress. I then went on to work, feeling much better about it all and hoping that, if I played my cards right, I would at least have regular and up-to-date information of her progress. It wasn't much, but it was much better than nothing at all.

It was during 1996 that the Council began to get really heavy over the siting of the mobile home on the nursery. Notwithstanding that the home had replaced another which they had previously not known or worried about, they deemed our home as 'unacceptable development in a rural area'. This made me laugh. They had given permission for a gigantic Nursing Home right next to us, on land which had previously been agricultural and outside the 'village boundaries', which looked like a giant out-of-town superstore and was visible for miles - yet we were 'unacceptable' when you couldn't even see us from the adjoining road!

The mobile home arrives on site in two halves. Within two days I had moved in.

Well established a couple of years later.

They slapped an eviction notice on us, but we had the right of appeal and took it, to the Planning Inspectorate. A typically grey-suited civil servant represented them at our appeal, held in the small Council Offices at Ampthill. All the arguments were delivered and then we had a 'site visit' by the Inspector and representatives from Mid-Beds. Council. One of their objections was that our drive - really, a track - didn't have a sufficient 'visibility splay' where it joined the village road, so a representative from the Highways Department had to come along too. Unfortunately she herself didn't have sufficient 'visibility splay' because she couldn't find us! She had to telephone us for directions. When it was pointed out that the Nursing Home driveway had even less 'visibility splay' and would be carrying vastly more traffic than we ever would, we won that argument. But it was

124

the only argument we did win. We lost the appeal. Then the Council lost interest for a while. We were expecting another eviction date to be sent, but it never did that year. We decided to keep very quiet. Rosa's mum was becoming increasingly less mobile as she had severe arthritis and found the stairs to her flat almost impossible. Fortunately a 'sheltered' bungalow became available in 1998 just down the road and she was eligible for it. She made it her own and lived there until her death early in 2014, aged 96, and very happy she was there, too.

Rosa had worked for a short time at the Nursing Home next door and did some nursing at various hospitals (she's a qualified nurse) but wasn't very happy doing this. I suggested she did a teacher-training course as she is good with kids and was used to a school environment. Somewhat to my surprise, she took me up on it. In September 1998 she started a one-year course at one of the Bedford colleges which led on to a degree course at the DeMontfort University, Bedford.

Back briefly to '96, we were kept very busy running the nursery and I was more-or-less driving coaches full-time. But Alan Fair at Checker Travel had been warned by HMRC that the coach drivers (who now numbered about six) would have to 'go on the books' or he would face prosecution. We could not remain 'self-employed' because we only worked, or primarily worked, for him. The financial implications for Alan were considerable and he decided to sell the entire business. He'd probably had enough of it anyway. Trying to run an expanding coach business AND a thriving minicab firm was onerous. Finding a place to park the coaches had been a problem, and eventually he'd come to an agreement with 'The Shires' bus company to stable and service the coaches at their depot at Garston, near Watford. This was brilliant for me, as it lopped about six miles off my journey to work each way and saved up to twenty minutes driving-time compared with his previous spot at Northwood in an unsecured commercial vehicle park. For all of us drivers, it meant we no longer had to fuel the vehicles ourselves or wash them by hand, as there was a huge bus-wash at the depot and the staff there fuelled the vehicles every day.

Driving hours rules were almost routinely ignored. One evening, quite late, I drove one of the Volvos into the yard at Garston after the drive from Paris. Alan was there and on seeing me, looked incredibly relieved and asked me his stock question when he wanted you to do something 'How's your sense of adventure?'. 'Pretty non-existent, Alan; I've just driven from Paris!' 'I'll give you double money if you can go to Cambridge and pick up a load of students and take them to Heathrow'. 'Alan, it's not about money,

I'm knackered, and out of hours'.

'Triple money' he said. 'Oh alright!' I took the tachograph out and handed it to him, he gave me a fresh one, and I was away. 'That tacho made a good frisbee' he told me days later. Oh, if I still had the energy and 'sense of adventure' of those days.

The new owner of the firm very quickly decided that he didn't want the coach side of the business, and sold it to Arriva, the big bus company that had recently bought-out 'The Shires'. The whole operation then transferred from Pinner to Garston, with the Private Hire and Contract Unit (as it became known) occupying a part of the office complex there. This worked quite well for a while, but Arriva are a bus and rail company, not a coach company, and after a couple of years they began to lose interest.....but again, I run ahead of myself.

After our first 'reunion' meeting, I started to see Shirley at first intermittently, and then it became a fairly regular occasion. It was great to be on good terms with her again and to receive news of our daughter on a regular basis. I was encouraged to take an interest, rather than be cold-shouldered, and received photographs of Heather fairly often at first. Then the inevitable happened, of course. My attraction to Shirley was a strong as ever, and I am quite sure that she knew it and nurtured it and wanted it - but no more than 'it'. The photos and information about Heather rather waned once 'it' had occurred. But again, I didn't see it that way.

I couldn't see that this might be a way of keeping me away from any closer ties with Heather, by 'stalling' my natural desire to see our child. Do I regret this? More than anything else in my life. How could I be so stupid, so ignorant, so blind to the bleedin' obvious? I can never again castigate anyone who pleads that 'they couldn't help it'. It's such a powerful force that it can take over your life, make you oblivious to the possible consequences or the harm it can do to others. Rosa was everything Shirley was not - selflessly loving, honest, sincere. . . .and not married (except to me). How could I be so unfeeling and so stupid? I have no answers. I can only plead that I was not truly myself, and was so very glad that at least I still had some connection with our daughter, however tenuous.

In August 1996, Adrian died, suddenly, unexpectedly, of a heart attack. The family were on holiday in Skye at the time, and his body had to be flown back to Oxfordshire for burial. I knew nothing of this. It was the school holidays and Shirley and I did not see or contact each other for the whole six weeks or more. Somehow, though, I had become increasingly wary during that holiday of reinstating contact with her. I left it a whole week after the start of term before ringing her, and I didn't want to, even then. I have no rational explanation for this. When she told me of Adrian's death, I was knocked sideways and didn't know what to say. He was only 54. Heather was only four years old, how on earth did she take it? I recalled Adrian telling me once that I had ruined his life, and waves of guilt and sadness engulfed me. I mumbled something about ringing her again when it had all sunk in, and said how sorry I was, and rang off. I don't think he had had any idea that Shirley and I were seeing each other again, so I am at least grateful for that.

Adrian rests in a little village churchyard just outside Oxford. From it, you can look past the old stone walls surrounding the churchyard, and the honey-coloured stone houses outside it, across the fields to the long blue line of the Chiltern Hills etched against the sky. He rests next to his mother, who died only about eighteen months before, and an aunt. At this spot there is a deep peace which I feel every time I visit, which I do all too seldom. It is, fittingly, a beautiful place. RIP, Adrian.

WAITING FOR A MIRACLE

I believe all children should know of their origins. I have known that I was adopted for as long as I can remember. It has never bothered me, as my adoptive parents were intelligent and sensitive enough to realise that the truth, for children and indeed for everyone, is of the utmost importance when it comes to lineage. We all need to know of our roots. At the time of writing there is a programme on the T.V. called 'Long Lost Family', co-hosted by Nicky Campbell and Davina McColl. It's very popular, and features people who have been adopted, or have had their child or children adopted, or have never known one parent, and have never been at peace until the missing part of the jigsaw has been found and placed. This programme helps the lucky few who have been accepted by the producers of the programme and it's very emotional, sometimes gut-wrenching, viewing. It's raw, because it is so basic. The basic need of a parent to know the child and for the child to know the parent. Of all human 'rights', this must be one of the most important.

I thought that Shirley agreed with this view. So perhaps I may be forgiven for assuming that now, with Adrian no longer with us, Heather would be told of her true parentage in due time and be introduced to her biological father. I had thought that she should have been told the truth by now anyway, as I had been by her age, but now there was no reason at all for her not to know. I had obviously overlooked the concern with which Shirley would have over her 'reputation'.

I didn't press Shirley too much for far too long. She described herself to me as truly 'The Merry Widow' and Adrian's death did not affect our relationship at all. I assumed far too much and was placated by her assurances that she would tell Heather 'when the time was right'. She meant 'when the time was right' for her; not Heather, and that would never be, of course. After all her previous procrastinations and broken promises, I still believed her! I really didn't have a clue. I was a total fool, putting my marriage at risk for a mess of pottage. The small comfort I have is that I continued to receive news of Heather's progress, and realised at last that I should be contributing financially to her upbringing. But I run ahead of myself, again.

Rosa and I were making a success of the nursery and were incredibly busy looking after the plants. We had expanded the season and had begun to grow shrubs and herbaceous plants as well as the more popular bedding plants and now we had a genuine need to live on the place for the sake of the business. It was great to be in the swing of these things again and there is a pride in running such a venture.

The season started in early March when I bought-in tiny 'plug' plants from a big concern in Wisbech, Cambridgeshire, which we then grew on and potted-up, often taking cuttings to start off a second crop as well. It reached a peak in May, when everyone scrambles to buy good-sized plants, and continued through June, slackening off through July and August then increasing again through September and into October. I was still driving coaches so I was very grateful to both Rosa and her mother, who also came up to help, as they kept everything well-watered and did a great deal of other necessary work.

The Council didn't share our opinion though, and after a break we started receiving rather unpleasant letters again. However, there was a new man at the helm of the planning department, Mr. Hill, who seemed fairly sympathetic to our position and who was as helpful to us as his position would allow. He used to send us a letter, he'd visit us or I'd visit him, then we'd hear nothing for some months. Then the process would be repeated, but we were aware that the problem was still not resolved and there was still a threat that we would have to remove our home from the site. In the end, we stalled the process long enough to become eligible for a further Hearing.

I'd become more savvy by now about the planning process, and we could produce figures for the nursery business that at least showed we had a viable business. I also joined a group called 'Chapter 7', after I'd written an article about the Planning system, as it affected us, in the 'Smallholder' magazine. Chapter Seven helped people who wanted to live on the land and were having problems with their local planning department. The group were - and still are - gifted with a most knowledgeable and articulate leader, Simon Fairlie. I, and many others, owe a great deal of gratitude to Simon for his vast knowledge of the planning system and his practical support. I went to several meetings in those early days, the first at Oxford - where else!

Despite all the above, we lost at the next Hearing as well. The Council suddenly started asking not only for a financial viability test (which we passed) but for something called a 'functional needs' test; in other words, we had to demonstrate that we needed to live on the place in order to run the business. We weren't prepared for this and didn't put up an adequate case. We felt that they had moved the goalposts and after a great deal of argument and correspondence, I went to the relevant Ombudsman, so stalling the process once again. The Ombudsman did not rule in our favour, but suggested that the Council looked at our case again. I knew that this would take some time. . . .

In fact, the Council took so long faffing about that we became entitled to yet another Hearing! But this wasn't until years later, so I'll spare you my views on the planning system for a while yet.

DOG DAYS

'Dogs are not our whole life, but they make our lives whole'
- Roger Caras

In 1998, Rosa's son, Simon, and his fiancée Dawn, got married, her mother moved into her little 'sheltered' bungalow, Rosa started her teacher-training, I met my birth family for the first time, and Snoopy came into our lives. Ah, Snoopy...

Throughout this period, despite running the nursery, I was still driving coaches more-or-less full-time. One late September Saturday in 1998 another driver, Les, and I took two coaches full of Hindu families to Cardiff for a huge wedding. Using a coach for weddings was not an unusual occurrence but having two coaches on one wedding was unusual. I'd once taken another extended family to South Shields and back in one day for a Hindu wedding there, and managed to include a coastal tour within the time - what's that about Driving Hours?

Anyway on this occasion Les and I drove in convoy down the M.4 and our passengers were blessed with the most beautiful day of warm sunshine and gentle breezes. I have always found Hindu people most welcoming and generous with their hospitality and we were encouraged to go in and partake of a form of 'wedding breakfast' before the actual ceremony. We came out after this for a chat and a rest in my coach, enjoying the sunshine and the calm of this glorious early-autumn day, with the passenger door open.

I was sat at the very front of the coach and was just about to doze off when a little Jack Russell terrier trotted by on the pavement. 'Hello' I said, and little terrier turned, looked at me, jumped up the steps of the coach and onto a passenger seat, curled up and went to sleep - all in the space of a few seconds! I looked out of the door to see if his owner was coming along, but no-one was visible. So I went to pat the dog who was already enjoying being stroked by Les but kept drifting off to sleep. 'He's exhausted' I said, and as I gently patted him, 'He stinks, too!'. God knows what he'd rolled in but he certainly was pungent. Then we noticed he had no collar. 'He's a stray, or lost' said Les. 'What can we do?' I offered to pick him up and take him round some of the houses to see if anyone recognised him, which Les agreed was a good idea, and he offered me his working jacket to protect my clothes. No-one said they recognised him, but one helpful lady with her hand full of clothes pegs offered one to me, 'for your nose' she said.

'We can't leave him' I said to Les, so I gently placed him back on the seat (this time covered with Les' jacket) and let him sleep. After about an hour, the wedding service finished and there was a commotion as the happy couple and crowds of relatives emerged into the sunlight. It was a truly beautiful occasion but the noise woke the dog and he skipped out and mingled with the guests, Les and I frantically trying to catch him. Les finally did it and apparently some of the wedding photographs show him and dog behind the newly-married couple, Les looking sheepish and dog looking jubilant.

Everyone was so kind and good-humoured when they heard about the dog, and miraculously agreed that he should travel back with them when the time came, as long as he was on the floor beside me and not on the seats! People were so kind - they brought out water for the dog, and food, though the little dog didn't seem keen on their vegetarian diet. I bought him a ham sandwich when we stopped at Leigh Delamere services on the way back, which he ate with gusto.

So began a five year relationship with a dog with the strongest character that both Rosa and I have ever known. After he died I wrote a children's book about his adventures, none of which I had to make up or elaborate, they were all true. I never published the book because I could not find an illustrator, and I think children's books really need good drawings to bring the characters to life. If any illustrator is reading this, I still have the script...

I telephoned Rosa from Leigh Delamere services and told her about the dog. She asked what sort he was. When I said 'a Jack Russell' she said 'Oh no! Four legs and attitude!' We still had Belinda and Tramp of course, so we didn't really want another, but of course Rosa would not hear of me abandoning him; not that I could have done that. I hoped Les might take him, but he definitely was not keen. So he came home with me. It was a late night, around two by the time I got in. Tramp came out to greet me as he always did, and immediately took the little dog to his heart; he accepted and loved him straight away, wagging his tail furiously and licking him like a long-lost friend.

The feeling seemed mutual - it was extraordinary the bond they had. Belinda was less keen but she was an old dog now and she certainly was not hostile. Despite the late hour, Rosa bathed him, which was just as well as once he was dried he jumped into the bed. 'Bloody cheek' I said, but Tramp already slept at the bottom of the bed. As I got in, the little dog growled gently but then snuggled up as if we'd had him for years.

Snoopy the dog posing at our front door.

The following Monday I rang the Police in Cardiff and the RSPCA to see whether anyone had reported a lost Jack Russell. No-one had, so it seemed fate had decreed that we were now to have three dogs living with us. But what to call him? We tried to see if he responded to any familiar dog-names. He didn't. I said 'He's just a twatty little thing' and at the word 'twatty' his ears pricked up and he jumped up at me. We couldn't call him 'Twatty' so we settled on Snoopy instead. He didn't seem to mind.

I'll leave the rest of the story about him for another book, another time, except to mention one incident that always causes amusement to those who hear it. One night, fairly early on in our 'ownership' of Snoopy, he decided he wanted to go out to explore the neighbourhood on his own. Slipping out of the cat-flap sometime after midnight and whilst Tramp was asleep and I was still working, he wandered through our neighbouring wood and out into the field, where an unofficial path led towards the middle of our village.

Trotting up the High Street, he disturbed a cat which he duly chased. Cat sought sanctuary through its own cat-flap but didn't expect Snoopy to come crashing through it as well! Snoopy lost interest in the cat when he saw a bowl of cat food on the floor, scoffing the lot before trotting upstairs and jumping into bed with the startled young couple occupying it. At around one o'clock in the morning, Rosa was awakened by a phone call and the caller saying 'Do you own a dog called Snoopy?' Rosa, still half-asleep, said yes. 'Do you know where he is?' 'In the bed'. 'You're right, but not in yours! He's with us!' Rosa had to drive up to collect him, and fortunately the couple saw the funny side of the situation and there were no hard feelings. I don't think the cat was ever the same again, though.

There were many, many other incidents, once when we had to call out the fire brigade to rescue him. We were devastated when he died of Weil's disease in 2005, preceding Tramp who lived for two more years until he died of (very) old age, at 21.
He never really got over losing Snoopy. When I buried Snoopy in our garden, he howled and tried to dig him up.

Dogs and people have had a special relationship for thousands of years, but occasionally you get an extra-special one. Dogs give their love unconditionally, which is more than can be said for many of us. I was not allowed to have one as a child, but it has been a pleasure and a privilege to have owned several as an adult. Many people seem to expect them to behave like people. Why? They are DOGS! Let them be what they are. Love them as they are! If you love them, they will want to please you and they will learn quickly through kindness and understanding, what you want them to do and how you wish them to behave. Love them unconditionally, too.

Time after time, I see people keeping their dogs on a tight lead for fear that they may sniff another dog! These are the same people who are often so anally-retentive that they struggle to acknowledge a 'good morning' when you encounter them on a walk, never mind actually offer one. They only seem to be at ease when bellowing down a mobile phone or texting someone, they are so far removed from the natural world you wonder why they have a dog at all. Let your dog be a dog, and be rewarded with the loyalty and affection that would put many of us to shame.

IN MEMORIAM, SNOOPY

Up from the street and into the bus
Leapt a little Jack Russell, and with such a fuss
Jumped onto the seats and pattered around
To find where he thought he could sleep, safe and sound.

He'd been walking all day, and travelled for miles
Lonely and lost, so he welcomed our smiles
And the warmth of the bus soon lulled him to sleep
And as we drove home I thought 'this one's to keep'.

So into our lives and into our home
Came this little Jack Russell, no more to roam
The mean streets of Cardiff, unyielding and bare,
But green fields and woodlands, and our loving care.

Five years we had him, years happy and sad,
He made us laugh and he drove us mad,
Wedged in rabbit-holes and stuck up drains,
Rescued by the fire-brigade, driving us insane!

Chasing the birds, the hens and the cats
We shouted in vain 'Snoopy, don't do that!'
Playing with Tramp, an old dog now,
Leaping and barking 'I'll show you how!'.

Wagging his tail, and tilting his head
When we spoke to him; all that growling in bed
Defending some pasta, a bone or some bread. . . .
Then, all of a sudden, curling up in my arms
Knowing that there he was safe from all harm.

And now he's gone. We all mourn our loss;
His best friend Tramp, his mistress, his 'boss'.
No more will the woodlands resound to his bark,
No more will he chase things just for a lark.

He sleeps in the garden, under a rose
Aptly called 'Mischief', the one that we chose
In thanks for his life. With flowers freely borne
In summer it will bloom for him
And in the winter, mourn.

R.C

135

BIRTHRIGHT

In 1998 I turned fifty, and after years of 'thinking about it' - but not very much - I decided that if I was ever going to find my birth family I really should do it. I'd made a half-hearted attempt a few years earlier, whilst living at Chalgrove. A neighbour of Shirley's worked at a charity called 'NORCAP' which helped adopted people find their birth parents and Shirley had encouraged me to contact this lady to find out what was involved in the process. That's as far as I got, though; Shirley became pregnant and other things just went out of my head. But now I determined to pursue it.

At this time, NORCAP was still being run by a lovely lady called Linda Savell who had, as I understand it, co-founded the charity. Its offices were in Wheatley, just outside Oxford. And Shirley was now working there taking the phone calls! Although she'd been well provided for in Adrian's will, she'd spent quite a lot on finishing the house extension and needed a job. Her neighbour had introduced her to Mrs. Savell and she'd landed the job through her. Mrs. Savell remembered my name and I now became a member of NORCAP, paid the fee for a search, and a lady in Exeter was assigned to searching the records for me.

It didn't take very long. She found my mother and father's address in Peterborough. This was actually out-of-date as it later transpired that my birth father had died the year before and my mother had moved to be close to her youngest daughter in Melton Mowbray. Yes, she'd had other children - five more in fact! And they were all my birth siblings, including an older brother. I had been the only one to have been adopted. This news was given to me very gently and diplomatically, but as I had enjoyed a great childhood and really have enjoyed a charmed life in many respects, I was not fazed by this news at all - just curious!

The lady in Exeter sent a carefully-worded letter to my birth mother and didn't immediately get a reply, as the letter had to be forwarded from Peterborough. I think we waited about three weeks before a reply was received. It said that she (my mother) would love to meet me but could we wait 'til after Christmas 1998 as she received the letter exactly a year to the day after my father had died, and she was still coming to terms with it.

Shortly after this, NORCAP changed from being a small charity living almost hand-to-mouth but with a warm, professional and humanitarian approach, to a larger business-like 'charity' under a new 'CEO' - Pam

Hodgkins. I heard that Linda Savell had been ousted and been treated rather shabbily. She was not the only one. I continued with my membership but I didn't like the new 'glossy' image being portrayed; however, I felt indebted to NORCAP and was too pre-occupied with meeting my birth family to worry too much about the direction of the charity now. Shirley kept her job there, and I kept up my membership.

I met my birth mum in January. I motored up on a crisp winter's day and our re-union was emotional. I realised I had been selfish in putting this off for so long, only thinking of what I wanted and not about what she may have always felt. In total contrast to my adoptive mum, Dorothy (as I will henceforth call her) was tiny, birdlike. She'd had a hard life and was keen to tell me how I had come to be adopted.

She'd met my birth father during the war. He was married to an Italian lady at the time and had, I believe, one child. The Italian lady was Catholic and although they were estranged, would never agree to a divorce. He was a partner (with his father and brother) in a factory in Islington, north London. A factory in Islington? It would be unthinkable now, but Islington then was not a rich place for yuppies and aspiring prime ministers, it was distinctly poor and run-down. It became gentrified during the late seventies and eighties. The factory enamelled metal items such as hospital beds. Most unusually Dorothy and he moved in together and had their first child in 1947, out of wedlock of course. They were desperately poor, so when I came along only a year later, my father persuaded Dorothy that I should be adopted. Dorothy had little option but to agree, but was so upset when I was taken she tried unsuccessfully to get me back, and swore that if she had any more children she would keep them, no matter how poor she was. So I was the only one to be adopted.

I think that this is quite an unusual story, but what is truly astounding is that whilst I was being brought up in Harrow, they were all living just two miles away. More unusual still, when I cycled to Wembley to school, I passed their house every day. And furthermore, when I got my first 'proper' car, that Hillman Minx convertible, my father was driving the very same model. They weren't that common and we used to wave to each other on the road when we passed, each not knowing who the other was. I find this quite extraordinary, but to top it all, one of my birth sisters, Lynne, lived for a while in a place called Mickle Trafford, just outside Chester. This was where my adoptive father, Charles, was brought up. It's a tiny village; a very strange coincidence, and the chances of it must be millions to one.

On the day I first met Dorothy I also met my birth sister, Brenda, the youngest in the family, who lived virtually opposite Dorothy. Dorothy had actually told Brenda's husband, Les, about me first, (he was the executor of her will) and he came across to meet me later. To my surprise he had a broad Geordie accent, much like my adoptive Mum. And I met their daughter, too. It was an emotional day, full of surprises, and was the start of a very warm relationship between Dorothy and me. I'm so glad I did eventually get round to finding her, and I hope - think - she felt the same. We met up a lot after that.

I didn't tell Mum that I'd done this - I had no reason to, and I didn't want to risk upsetting her although I really don't think it would have done. Over a relatively short period I met all my siblings, and there are still rather strange coincidences. My elder brother, Peter, lives in Stevenage, ten miles to the south of me and John, the younger brother, lives in Milton Keynes, around fifteen miles to the north. Lynne, the eldest sister, lives in Thame, very close to Shirley! My other sister, Pam, lives in Brighton.

It wasn't until much later that Dorothy told her sister, Olwen, that I had made contact. We have made up for lost time and have enjoyed a friendship for many years now.

Finding my family of birth was important. It made me realise with an increased clarity that Heather should know me and my side of her family. During 1999 I started to get a little more persistent with asking Shirley to tell Heather. I did not want to cause a rift between us but as Heather was now seven, and I hadn't seen her for over four years, I was becoming ever more concerned that she should know. As usual, though, I was fobbed-off with false promises and lame excuses, and, as usual, I swallowed them. But not for very much longer.

INDIAN SUMMER

At some stage I learned that my birth father had fathered another child, a girl, at more-or-less the same time that my younger brother was born. Again unusually, I believe that the mother was of Indian descent and despite his having an established family with Dorothy, his name appeared on the girl's birth certificate. Other than that, I have absolutely no information about her, but would be intrigued to know! This is not the reason for the title of this chapter, though, but the years 1999 - 2002 were the last flowering of any remaining confidence or hope I may have had that Shirley would do the right thing for Heather and for me, and tell her!

In 1999 we had the total eclipse of the sun in Cornwall and, along with thousands of others, Rosa and I decided to go down in the Jolly Blue Giant (Mark II) to witness this event. We booked a camping pitch near Marazion but by now the JBG. was not capable of passing an MOT. I was very naughty indeed, and would stress that no-one could do this today and get away with it. By this time, I had bought a Ford Transit-based motor home of similar age to the Jolly Blue from a specialist repairer of Transits, Gerrard Jonas, of Witney. This was a brilliant vehicle, even being equipped with an overdrive which enabled it to cruise easily at over 60mph. But it didn't quite have the same hippy-ish appeal or the interior space of the Jolly Blue Giant. So we - or rather, I - put the number-plates of the Transit on to the Blue bus and transferred the tax-disc to it. At least both vehicles were Fords!

With the JBG now ostensibly a Transit with an MOT we set off and after an overnight stop somewhere, reached Cornwall with a day to spare. Unfortunately I had noticed that the brakes were getting less and less effective as we approached Marazion but we arrived at the site safely. The day of the eclipse dawned disappointingly cloudy and we never saw the total eclipse although apparently people on the Lizard were more fortunate. We watched it on the telly! Outside, it just got dark for a short while. Later, the clouds dispersed and we enjoyed a further day or two exploring this part of Cornwall.

We decided to go to Land's End. The brakes were getting worse. I had looked underneath before we moved off the site and noticed that brake fluid was dribbling down one rear wheel - the wheel-cylinder had given up. I drove very cautiously after topping-up the fluid, and then we joined the queue for the car parks at Land's End. When we reached the pay-point we were told that there was really no room in the car parks but we could park for free in the coach park. They didn't tell us that the 'Ministry' were there....

Although this was not a public service vehicle, they didn't have anything to do so asked to check us. I told them that the brakes had become dodgy and as I was open about it, they were amenable. But they put an immediate prohibition order on the vehicle, which meant we couldn't drive it anywhere. 'You don't see many A-series Transits about nowadays' one of them said. A-series Transit? I didn't argue! In reality, the prohibition meant that when we got home, I wouldn't be able to drive the kosher Transit either! We asked them where a garage might be that would repair the brakes. They said some garage in Penzance, who quoted £250 simply for the tow to their place. The bus wasn't worth that. We got hold of a local garage who advised us to 'wait 'til they've gone, have a nice evening, and then drive to us. We'll fix it temporarily, then you get out of the county!'. So we did.

The people at the Land's End Hotel were incredibly kind and allowed us to have a shower for nothing, then we had a walk, a meal, and attended a magnificent fireworks display. Then back to the bus, and the bloody thing wouldn't start! I kept a rope permanently attached to the front bumper, and got Rosa to tie it around her waist and get the beast rolling - there was a gentle downhill slope. Amazingly she managed this, got the rope disentangled from her waist, I slammed it in gear and bingo! - she (the bus) roared into life. Then off we went through the narrow Cornish lanes and parked-up outside the little garage.

The following day we left them to it, and explored the neighbourhood on foot in a gentle, warm, Cornish drizzle. When we got back, the garage had blocked-off the rear brakes so there was no more fluid-loss (we still had a working handbrake) and told us to wait until dark and then get the hell out of it. All for £50. We got back without hurting ourselves or anyone else.

Then of course I had to get the rightful owner of the number plates (the Transit) MOT'd and passed as safe. This was easily done, and I was ruefully considering what I had risked at the age of fifty-two, still behaving like a hippy. Don't try this at home - the ANPR (automatic number plate recognition) cameras will get you these days! And in reality you won't be insured. If you had even a minor bump, you'd be in serious trouble, as indeed I would have been. It really isn't worth the risk.

Next time we went away we used the Transit, but I did get the JBG MOT'd once more and we had another couple of seasons before finally conceding defeat and obtaining a couple of hundred quid for her as scrap. Before this happened, I was stopped by the police because the bus, well, looked scruffy. 'Sorry, sir!' said the officer 'we thought you were a new-age traveller'. I replied that I was just an old age traveller and we all had a laugh and once again, my guardian angel saw me safely through. I hope this story does not lead to me being tried for 'historic excise duty abuse'.

After being taken over by The Shires, which then became Arriva, we continued to do the trips abroad for a while. I think my last one was around 2000 when I had a different courier with me, a young chap who was finishing his studies at Oxford (where else?). He didn't seem particularly at ease with either me or the group, but we had the usual itinerary through Holland and Belgium, only this time we stopped at Bruges rather than Brussels, and the trip was pleasant enough. We stayed in a different hotel in a suburb of Paris rather than one in the centre this time, and on the last night it was incredibly hot and stuffy. I had a room at the back, facing over a courtyard that was enclosed completely by tall buildings. The window was wide open but there wasn't a breath of air. Our entire group, including the courier and me, had a wonderful dinner at a little café opposite the hotel which looked so ordinary and unpretentious but served up superb, simple food and offered chilled red wine, which I had not sampled before. It was lovely.

I retired at around eleven o'clock but there was no sleeping, it was just too hot and the noise coming in through the open window was intrusive. Someone had a television on quite loudly, and it was a comedy programme. I seemed to half-recognise it and then realised it was 'Allo allo!' translated into French! Almost surreal. . . .and I'm not quite sure how they did that. After this had finished, someone was having a fierce argument that ended in doors slamming and something being thrown out of a window, smashing to pieces in the yard underneath me.

An interlude of reasonable quiet followed, then there came the unmistakeable sounds of a couple making passionate love, with the woman seemingly having multiple orgasms that carried on for ages. After this there was an intense thunderstorm, which at least cooled the air a little, but a gutter was obviously faulty and the sound of water dripping onto some corrugated plastic sheeting went on for at least an hour afterwards, during which the woman obviously enjoyed yet more orgasms. By now it was approaching two in the morning. After the final drips and sighs died away, there was a period of blissful quiet and I started to drift off. Then the peace was rudely shattered by the loudest, longest, most trouser-splitting fart I have ever heard - it actually echoed round the courtyard. The culprit must have had his backside hanging out of a window for it to sound like that. Ah, the romance of Paris!

The next day, we took the group to the railway station at Austerlitz and then had to hurry back to Calais to catch the ferry. I related my previous night's experiences to the courier and at last it broke the ice and I found him a relaxed and entertaining companion for the rest of our journey home. 'There's nothing like a good fart' he said. 'And that was nothing like a good fart' said I.

As I said, this was the last foreign trip. Arriva didn't really 'do' coaches and they neglected the private hire side of things. The coaches became rather run-down and we lost quite a bit of the more 'prestigious' work, concentrating more on school-runs and other mundane work. However, we did have a regular theatre group who used us, led by the redoubtable Heather Sorrell of Watford. She had founded and run, most successfully, a group that was large enough to warrant hiring a full-sized coach for every theatre trip; often there were two trips into London each month. It was often relatively easy for me to park the coach fairly near the theatre and when this was possible, I quite often went with Rosa. Going to the theatre was new for me. We saw Mamma Mia, We will Rock You, Les Miserables, Riverdance, The Producers and many others, often for free when Heather had spare tickets. And we still had lots of foreign-student work in the summer.

For a large company, Arriva seemed to take the regular maintenance of the private hire fleet as of little importance. Whilst we were given lessons in 'how to load luggage safely', 'how to drive economically' and suchlike, and threatened with 'disciplinary action' for the slightest transgression (all on memos pinned to noticeboards), the fleet became scruffy and run-down. One evening I pulled-up in Enfield to take a group of foreign students to Waterloo, which was then the terminal for the Eurostar trains. It's second-nature to check all the catches for security after loading the cases, so what happened next was due to the lack of maintenance of the vehicle rather than an oversight on my part.

We had to make a sharp right turn shortly after leaving the pick-up point and there was the most almighty crash from the nearside - one of the locker doors had swung open, horizontally as they do, unloading a pile of cases automatically all over the road, then crashing into a Transit van parked correctly by the kerb, completely demolishing it.

I used the same coach again a few days later after it had been repaired. This time I was picking-up at Waterloo and taking students to Watford, fortunately with another driver as it was a two-coach job. The coach park at

Waterloo was a very awkward and inadequate affair, involving some pretty nifty reversing to get into a space. We loaded-up and - especially - double-checked the lockers, each checking the other's coach as well as our own. I joked that it would be a 'double whammy' if it happened again.

I drew out first, turned right, and waited at the traffic-lights before turning right again, towards Waterloo Bridge. There was another almighty bang and showers of sparks as the very same lid opened again to a horizontal position and slammed into the electrical junction-box sited next to the lights. Luggage was again thrown out onto the pavement, one case narrowly missing someone as it skidded along. I couldn't believe it! Neither could Daniel, the driver following behind. What a great introduction to London for the students! There was nothing for it but to stop, phone the office and contact the police. They said they were somewhat busy as many of the traffic-lights had failed in the area I was in and it was causing chaos. I was careful to say that it was my vehicle (not me) that was responsible. 'Oh, you're the most popular man in South London then!' said the cheerful lady on the other end of the phone. They sent a most affable traffic officer to the scene who apologised for the fact he had to breathalyse me as a matter of routine. It was clear, of course, and all I had to do was fill in a form detailing what happened. Another coach had to be sent and the damaged one eventually towed away.

There was much amusement at all this (not from Arriva of course) but it could have been deadly serious, literally. Those side locker doors could easily slice a person in two even if they hit at a low speed. Sometime after this, I decided to leave and work for a small firm who only ran coaches, not buses. I continued to do part-time work with Arriva but I was relieved to be able to say 'no' to them if I felt like it.

By going part-time, I discovered I was exempt from many of their more petty regulations and requirements. They started banging-on about 'diversity' and 'equality' and how we were not to use racially-motivated insults. There were never any in the first place! True, we used the term 'black bastard!' occasionally and we were told we were 'white honkeys' (or was it donkeys?) but it was all in jest; jocular, not offensive to any one of us. But management frowned on it. The canteen lost a lot of its ribaldry and fun once these rules were imposed and we were all the poorer for it. No-one actually talked to the drivers except to give them orders or to tell them off. Posters just appeared on the noticeboards, telling us that there was yet another new diktat forbidding this or ordering that. I hated it. It was good to be less of a part of it.

We seem to be disappearing up our own backsides in our efforts to 'not offend' anyone. Just recently, as I write this, a young black guy, Mr. Chaka Artwell, was banned from speaking on the BBC about the protests over closing Temple Cowley swimming pool in Oxford; because he was wearing a golliwog. Mr. Artwell gives talks on black history. He's black. I hope he won't mind if I quote him. 'When I was growing up in this country, this guy [the golliwog] was a popular figure. Then, without anyone asking me if I was offended by it, people decided I was offended by it. White, middle-class liberal types decided I was offended by this guy and in the year 2015 I don't want people telling me what I should be offended by. People pick and choose what they want to highlight. This is ridiculous'. Amen to that, Mr. Artwell. The BBC's response? 'We asked him to remove the large doll [golliwog to Mr. Artwell, you and me] because it would distract viewers in a discussion about a local swimming pool and some viewers may have found it' - wait for it - 'offensive'. Fine, though, to 'offend' Christians, Jews, families, anyone with a sense of humour, even Mr. Artwell, on the BBC any day of the week. What has happened to us?

And quickly, on this, the latest example of state child abuse is the encouraging of teachers to label kids as young as four as 'racist' if they so much as ask a question of another kid like 'Do you come from Africa' if that child is black.

I'm told that this remains on their 'file' into secondary school. I have an idea. Why not have them wear a yellow star, say, so that everyone knows that child is a 'racist'? Perhaps you could have them dress up in stripy clothes too, so there's no doubt at all. In this manic pursuit of political correctness, we deprive children of their childhood and we lose our humanity little by little, piece by piece. May God forgive those that do this, for I never will. Now Labour say they want sex education taught to every child five and over. This would not merely be state-sanctioned child abuse; it would be state-ordered child abuse. Please God, let children enjoy their childhood. Bring this in and it will certainly be the end of the Innocence.

I was once asked to give a light-hearted talk to a group of drivers who were interested in older coaches, trains etc. I entitled it 'life in the steam age', and it was generally well-received I think but all the way through it a faulty lavatory cistern kept hissing away, constantly filling itself up, just off the room we were in. It sounded as if there was a steam engine in there and I kept dissolving into laughter. We all did. I cut the talk short and we went down the pub.

THE 'GATHERING STORM'

But I'll be free for what I believe:
And I won't sell my soul
Just to achieve my goal
And I've been holding back the tears
Dreaming all these years
And I'll sing from the heart if you listen to me
Everything I do is what I believe.

Excerpt from 'The furthest star' by Amy McDonald from her album 'Life in a Beautiful Light', 2012.

Over the years 1999 to 2002 not only were we growing the nursery business but I had started growing some of our own vegetables. I have never been able to understand why people pay to go to the gym when you can get just as healthy growing vegetables, in the open air, and for free; and have something useful to show for your efforts. But each to their own.... Every time I saw Shirley I would take her home-grown vegetables, which I hoped would be well received by her, the boys and Heather as they were vegetarian. It still gives me a small sense of satisfaction that Heather was eating the produce I had grown with her in mind, and it was grown without the aid of chemicals or artificial fertilizers, but with a lot of love. It was a small but positive contribution, I hope, to her upbringing. Sometimes I would pre-prepare a meal for them. I also started to contribute financially.

It had suddenly dawned on me that I should. After Adrian had died, Shirley had been quite flush for money for a while but much of it had gone by 1999. I couldn't contribute much. I had borrowed heavily for the home Rosa and I shared and for other things, and was feeling rather burdened by the repayments every month. So I started giving her £20 a week, or the equivalent - not much, but better than nothing. This was accepted quite graciously, somewhat to my surprise. After around a year or so I managed to increase the amount to £25 a week, and then to £30. I was working for the small coach firm but still had plenty of part-time work with Arriva, whose Private Hire and Contract Unit was headed by Kevan who had previously been the coach manager at Checker Travel and was generous giving me work he knew I'd like. So I was earning more.

Rosa was finding her studies at the De Montford University in Bedford quite taxing, but enjoyable. It did mean she couldn't help with the nursery as much, though. So I was working just about flat-out during the growing season, and having to drive coaches quite a lot of the time as well. We were still in locked horns with the planning department too, but Mr. Hill was continuing to be his tolerant self.

Heather was nine in 2001 and I was getting increasingly anxious that she should be told about me before she became a teenager. Shirley continued to stall, and became ever more non-committal as I became more persistent, and worried. This would be the second major issue over which she had promised so much but delivered nothing, and although I hope I did not show it, I was losing my patience. Once again, disillusionment was setting in. At the beginning of 2002 I managed to increase my financial contribution to £50 a week, which had been my goal since I started the payments. This was accepted without demur; I think Shirley knew I wasn't trying to 'bribe' her into telling Heather but simply wanted to help financially. Since Heather was born I had helped choose and pay for her birthday and Christmas presents, and also had put money into a trust fund for her, for when she became eighteen. So although I was quite impecunious and rather irresponsible with what money I had, I did at least help to provide for her in this way.

In the early Spring of 2002 I began to demand that Shirley tell our daughter the truth. She was approaching her tenth birthday and at last I had plucked up enough courage to become quite assertive. I knew, in my heart, that this would probably sever our relationship but it had become far too important, in my eyes, to ignore and I wasn't prepared to be messed-around any longer. I was right about the ending of our relationship; Shirley told me 'she'd gone off sex' one day in May, but she was clever enough to say she wanted to keep our friendship - no doubt thinking she could stall me further if she was nice enough.

She had, in the weeks previous to this, started to bring her lovely dog 'Harry' to our meetings. I'm sure she'd hoped that he would have disrupted our physical relationship, but he didn't! He simply went to sleep on the floor. Once Shirley had ended the sex, there was no need to bring him anymore; I never saw Harry again. I was quite happy to enjoy a friendship with Shirley but I was not prepared to be fobbed-off any longer over Heather. I warned Shirley that my feelings had been dammed-up for so long that if she persisted in stalling, the dam would break and my hurt and anger would just flood out. I didn't want that, I wanted this to be done as amicably and sensitively as possible and that when Heather was told, Shirley and I should be friends, not adversaries. 'Heather doesn't want a Dad' was her curt response.

How did she know this? Had she asked her? Of course not: it was Shirley who did not want Heather to have a Dad. After all those promises, and all my dogged patience, you may imagine that this was like a big kick in the stomach. And I felt a fool, duped over this for years and years. No fool like an old fool, dear reader, and I had been an old fool. At long, long last the scales began to fall from my eyes. Now I had to decide what, if any, options I had.

I took my time. I tried to weigh up the pros and cons and tried to think how Heather might feel if I started any legal proceedings. I certainly didn't want to go down that road. But all reasoning, pleading, arguing, had failed. Shirley and I were still talking and meeting-up, and although in some turmoil I am proud I never shouted at her or denigrated her. I still hoped she would show some humanity and some recognition that our daughter should know her father, who wanted to be a part of her life even if it had to be a minor part. Surely her work at Norcap would have shown her how important this was?

But she was being dishonest. She hadn't 'gone off sex' at all and really wanted me to gradually disappear without trace and without a whimper. I asked if she'd got a new man, she said no, there was no-one else. She was lying. I recognised that I was being treated in exactly the same way as Adrian had been, all those years ago. Any remaining faith or trust I had in her ended. I suggested we stopped meeting-up after that Christmas and she agreed 'if that's what you want'. She knew I didn't want this, but she was forcing my hand and trying to make me feel guilty for ending the relationship.

 I began to feel angry, and had to keep reminding myself that any way forward had to be measured and reasonable.

I went to the Citizen's Advice Bureau in Biggleswade and they suggested a firm of solicitors who were experienced in Family cases. I was pleased that a lady solicitor heard me and gave me the advice to try negotiation first. She wrote to Shirley that I would apply for the status, in law, of being Heather's father. Shirley herself obtained advice from a solicitor and she replied that having parental responsibility was not appropriate. I also received a letter from Shirley telling me that she thought that my seeking legal advice was 'vindictive'. Eloise, my solicitor, suggested professional mediation, and this seemed a good idea, so I started to look at this and what it would entail.

I contacted the Thames Valley Mediation Service at Amersham and a meeting was agreed, to be held in Aylesbury. Shirley put it off for as long as she reasonably could, but in the end a date was arranged and we duly were seen by a very professional-sounding young lady. A number of things were agreed (I cannot remember them all now) including, I think, a monthly phone call to keep up with Heather's progress. Shirley also agreed to put my name on Heather's birth certificate or at least make a formal statement that I was the father.

None - not one - of the agreements made were honoured, and I thought they were inadequate anyway. The one thing I did learn was that her boys - at last! - knew of me and that I was Heather's dad. No, Shirley hadn't told them. The youngest had found a letter from me and read it, and challenged his Mum. At last the can of worms had been opened! He'd found the letter in very much the same way as Adrian had found one of my letters all those years ago - a somewhat strange coincidence? I learned, naturally, that both boys were hostile to me, the younger more so than his elder brother. Shirley cited this as a reason for my not having any information at all of Heather. I said 'Surely this is not up to them' and the mediator seemed to agree.

I gave it several weeks, but it was obvious that Shirley was treating me with contempt. I left several messages on her phone but none were acknowledged. I contacted the mediation service again. They wrote to Shirley and tried to phone her three times, but didn't get any response. By the autumn of 2003 I knew I had no option but to go to Court if I was to pursue this. I knew nothing of the Family Courts in the UK, but I was very soon to find out. I cannot adequately express the heaviness I felt in my heart. Taking legal - court - action against Shirley was anathema to me. I felt a mixture of sadness, regret, hurt, bewilderment, betrayal and indeed anger but there would be no turning back now.

No more walks in the wood.
The trees have all been cut down
And where once they stood
Not even a wagon rut
Appears along the path.

Low brush is taking over.

No more walks in the wood.
This is the aftermath
Of afternoons in the clover fields,
Where we once made love
Then wandered home together,

148

Where the trees arched above

When branches were the sky.

Now they are gone for good,
And you, for ill, and I
Am only a passer-by;
We and the trees and the way
Back from the fields of play

Lasted as long as we could

No more walks in the wood.

(The Eagles, from their album 'Long Road out of Eden')

PREFACE TO 'COURTING EVIL'

If you tolerate this, then your children will be next (Manic Street Preachers)

This is by far the most important chapter in the book. Indeed, as I explained at the very beginning, this was to be the book! Those who only wish to read humour, or romance, or stories with happy endings will have to look elsewhere, I'm afraid. I am putting the events in Oxford Family Court and in the High Court into one chapter for continuity, so it will cover several years. There will be no point in my having written it if it does not help others to avoid the pitfalls I made, and I do not wish it to read like a 'pity me' saga. This chapter will be of no value unless it helps parents who risk losing their children through the ignominious 'Family' Court system to keep, or at least keep in touch with, their children. Those who are already embroiled in its clutches, or who have already lost their children through it, will find that this chapter strikes a chord.

I relate my story simply to illustrate that the Family Court is a must-to-avoid, almost at all costs. If you cannot avoid it, you will enter a different, dark, secretive world: one that purports to work in 'every child's best interests' but in fact works only in its own. A world where social workers practice a black alchemy and presume, lie and manipulate in order to get the results they want: where your voice is 'heard and valued' but then gagged and disregarded. You might as well be in North Korea. These are the Courts where no-one can hear you scream.

I don't have all the answers. In fact, to a number of the questions I have posed over the years I have never received any answers. Perhaps there aren't any. If you believe that British justice is the best in the world I will disillusion you. I fought the system and I lost, but if I can help clarify the way, warn you of the potential dangers so you may avoid them, or even inspire you to campaign for change, then the writing of this chapter will have been worthwhile.

I must also apologise in advance for some of the colourful - even intemperate - language in this chapter. I don't swear much as a rule, but on this subject I sometimes can't resist doing so. I hope you will understand, and forgive me. Looking back, the story seems to have had different phases, so I have used a couple of sub-headings to help separate them.

At the end of this book I have included, in an appendix, the stories and experiences of five different, but very articulate, ladies and I would urge the reader to consider these, as they give a female perspective to what is otherwise a very male account.

Dressed up as a vicar to protest at Christ Church in Oxford for my friend George Standen

COURTING EVIL

'Into my heart, a wind that kills
From yon far country blows.
What are those blue remember'd hills?
What spires, what farms are those?

That is the land of lost content
I see it shining plain
The happy highways where I went
And cannot come again'

(A. E. Housman)

Of course, before I made a Court application, I warned Shirley that I was going to apply to the Court for a Hearing. I gave her a date to comply with the very modest agreements we had reached at mediation, then another and then another - no response. With a very heavy heart, I found out how to lodge an application and finally did it. Two days later, I got a call from Shirley saying she was sorry she'd ignored my calls and letters, that it was her fault, and she gave me news of our daughter. I told her that I was sorry but I had already lodged a Court application, but that if she started to keep to the agreements made at mediation, I could withdraw the application. She went cold - I could almost feel the hostility down the phone! - and I don't think she thought for a moment, after all my previous tolerance, that I would actually do it. Instead of agreeing to comply, she more-or-less rang off. I did not withdraw the application.

I honestly don't believe I could have been more tolerant or tried any harder to stop this from going to Court. It tore me apart to do it. To be forced into this position by someone I had loved and known so long was immensely difficult. I was bewildered and shocked that Shirley could be so indifferent and not even carry out the agreements she herself had made over a little girl we had made together. At the same time I was bewildered and shocked by my own previous lack of action and my gullibility in the face of all the evidence. I was as angry with myself as with Shirley. Fortunately I had the unerring and strong support of Rosa who had wanted the father of her own child to be involved with him but who chose not to.

The initial hearing was listed for 15th. December. This was a 'directions hearing' that would hear a brief background to the case and decide what each party should do next. I am not a litigious person and had absolutely no idea what to expect. On entering the Court building, everyone is told to empty their pockets and any metal objects are put through separately after being checked. Then you go upstairs at Oxford for Family Court cases. Shirley was already there, and looked away as I entered the waiting area. She was as cold as stone and I got the clear message that she didn't want me to sit anywhere near her, so I didn't.

We were fortunate, I think, in having an intelligent, sympathetic lady judge for this initial Hearing, plus an officer from CAFCASS (The Children and Family Court Advisory Service) who seemed, at this stage, approachable.

I think the Judge was a Mrs. Pauphrey and I have often wondered since whether she is the same Judge Pauphrey who now sits in the High Court and has made several fine statements and good judgments in recent times. We were both properly listened to and Shirley was asked if she had ever doubted I was the father of Heather. She said she'd never denied it and I thought 'yes, you have! To the very person who should know!' but I didn't say anything. After this very brief appraisal we were asked to go into a separate room with the CAFCASS officer where we each put our point of view. I was surprised that Shirley intimated that I had never shown any interest in Heather and she was visibly discomfited when I said that she was receiving £50 a week from me. I stated that I had no wish to take anything away from Heather's life, just add a little to it. The CAFCASS officer, a Mrs. Kendall, told Shirley that 'Heather has a right to know' of her father. Shirley said 'I know'. For Heaven's sake, if she already knew then why the hell hadn't she told her before we had to go through all this? I was subsequently to find out. . . .

The Hearing was relaxed enough for Shirley and I to talk normally afterwards and I said 'why not come for a coffee?' She refused. 'Then, WHY all this?' I persisted. No answer. Not a murmur. It's a powerful thing, the Sound of Silence, and it usually means a cover-up. Again, I was later to find out. . . .

The outcome of this Hearing was that we were to attend another Hearing, where further progress could be made. This was listed for March 2004.

Shirley was left in no doubt that Heather should know who her father was. The CAFCASS officer had suggested, rather oddly I thought, that her G.P. might help with the approach to Heather as she was involved with child care. Christmas came and went of course, and I heard nothing further from CAFCASS at this stage.

In February my adoptive mother died after a series of falls and a short stay in a very small, very friendly and caring Nursing Home in Watford which my brother had found. As with charities, big does not automatically mean better. As my brother was an undischarged bankrupt at that time, and I was the elder brother, I was executor of her will alongside her solicitor. Because Tony still lived in Harrow, he had been her main carer over the last couple of years and I made sure he was included at every stage of the procedure following Mum's death. She had left £100 to Heather in her will, which was very nice of her considering that she had only met Heather once, as a baby.

Before we went into the courtroom, I sat with Shirley this time and told her about Mum and the bequest she'd made for Heather. She seemed unmoved, and said that I'd 'ruined her life' over the last year. I asked her how she thought she'd enhanced mine, but then we were called in and we didn't speak again that day.

Network Fail - Welcome to Dysfunction Junction.

The Court Hearing was on March 15th., under a new Judge - District Judge Michael Payne, and there was a different CAFCASS officer present, a Mrs. Feltham. I took an instant and instinctive dislike to her, but she assumed that Heather would want to meet her 'true' father and said so in Court, without hearing any of the circumstances leading up to this case.

Judge Payne came across to me as being bored by the whole process and of being uninterested in the case or, indeed, in the welfare of children. He made unnecessary and inane observations and I just didn't feel happy with this Hearing at all. Shirley's G.P. had expressed surprise that she had been asked to help and had politely declined. In effect, this Hearing was then adjourned until Wednesday 26th. May, and Mrs. Feltham was to be involved with 'direct counselling' with the parties involved. She had said that she was on leave for two weeks after the Hearing and then she forgot to notify her employers of the Court's order, so in fact nothing was done.

I left it a few weeks and then told my solicitor that I hadn't heard from CAFCASS and on the 16th. MAY - two months after the Hearing - we received a letter apologising for the fact that nothing had been done and asking for an adjournment so that Mrs. Feltham had more time to talk to the parties involved. I had no choice but to agree to an adjournment, the new date being set for 11th. June. To cut a very tedious (but utterly typical) story short, it was then set for 16th. July and then put back again until early September.

I was not at all happy about this, and rang Mrs. Feltham on my mobile seeking an interview. To my astonishment, this was refused. Hadn't the Court Order said that CAFCASS should engage with both parties? Mrs. Feltham then started to berate me, said that Shirley had agreed to tell Heather over the school holidays, that I was receiving a 'Rolls Royce Service' from CAFCASS, that she wouldn't be 'bullied', and that I was lucky that I was receiving any service at all! My concerns were irrelevant, she said, and if I continued to question her, she would walk away from the case. She reiterated this several times. Basically I should put up and shut up. She was not going to listen to anything I might say. If that is a Rolls Royce Service, I wondered, what was their Model T Service like? I remember I was at Whipsnade Zoo with a school party. I was by the Bison enclosure during this exchange and as I bade farewell to Mrs. Feltham, one of them defecated noisily and with great volume, which I thought was entirely appropriate to the occasion.

For some reason I had to ring Shirley shortly after this episode. During the conversation she mentioned that 'Hoonie said....' Hoonie? Who Hoonie? Hoonie who? It transpired that Hoonie was the first name of Mrs. Feltham. So Shirley was on first-name terms with Mrs. Feltham whilst I was not even permitted to speak to her. I was learning quickly why CAFCASS is held in such disregard by so many fathers, and we had only just begun. Dealing with CAFCASS was something akin to being in a Will Hay comedy - without the saving grace of steam trains. Or comedy. . . .

Rather than fight this dragon, I asked the solicitor to try and intervene. Kerry, the solicitor now advising me, got the most extraordinary, vitriolic telephone call back from Mrs. Feltham via Kerry's secretary Alison, again claiming that we were receiving a Rolls Royce Service, and claiming that she was undertaking this work out of the kindness of her heart! She actually said (and I have it on record should anyone doubt it) that she was being 'fantastically helpful' and had done more than had been asked by anyone. She asked why I had pursued this route and had to be told that it had never been my intention to do this but that I had been left with no choice. Then Mrs. Feltham telephoned my home and Rosa answered the call. Mrs. Feltham seemed astonished that I had a wife and astounded that Rosa knew all about the case. Ha! I thought. I'll write her one of my famous letters.

It started: 'Dear Mrs. Feltham, although you have refused an interview with me, I'm sure I am permitted to write a letter. You, of course, do not have to read it! I write it mainly because my wife, Rosa, tells me that you seemed very surprised that (a) I had a wife and (b) she knew all about the case.

This, if so, indicates that you may not have all the information I think you should. These personal details were all given to the Court at the first Hearing last December, and it is perhaps unfortunate that you were not present at that Hearing, and that I cannot remember the name of the CAFCASS officer who was. [I couldn't, then - it was Mrs. Kendall of course]. Despite your reservations, I cannot help feeling that some benefit may be obtained by your having the background knowledge to this case that was made available at that Hearing. In lieu of talking to you personally, I am therefore taking the liberty of informing you by this letter'.

I then went on at length about the history of the case and noted the fact that Mrs. Feltham had inferred that I was trying to 'bully' her. I resented this - if anyone was being bullied it was me. She was trying to bully me into submission! At the end of the letter, I wrote 'Whilst writing this, I may as well add my other main concern now, which is that as Shirley and her sons are so hostile to the idea of Heather learning of me, that they may attempt to dissuade her from contact with me. I am sure you will be aware of this possibility, as it would be far from unique'. I hadn't actually heard about Parental Alienation then, but it was a perspicacious observation. I've got to know all about it over the years since.

I never received a reply to this letter. People like Mrs. Feltham are attracted to the Social Services and to organisations like CAFCASS because they acquire unprecedented power over parents and they use it to mask their own incompetence and prejudices, and their intolerance of any criticism, suggestions, or protest. Her attitude towards me, and indeed her job, baffled me at the time but I was quickly to learn that it is very common. It's known as 'professional arrogance'. The really frightening thing is that Family Court judges almost invariably go along with their verdicts because they are perceived to be 'experts'. They are not 'experts' at all. At the time this farce was going on, CAFCASS officers had less training than parking attendants. Five days, I understood it to be. Then they were put in charge of decisions over the futures of children. No records have ever been kept by CAFCASS of the outcomes for those children, yet they claimed - and still claim - to act in every child's best interests! How do they know whether they do or not?

'In a child's best interests' is a handy catchphrase that is totally meaningless, designed to reassure people that they usually make the right decisions. In fact, they often don't. And those decisions are often irreversible. Now they have a jolly letterhead showing caricatures of happy children (with the obligatory wheelchair-bound one and a black one) dancing or moving around looking so happy to be free of one parent or of both and going into 'care', and safe in the hands of people like Mrs. Feltham! What an absolute disgrace. A picture of a desperate parent holding a gun to the head would be more accurate. One black guy told me he felt far more prejudice in the Family Court AS A FATHER than he ever did as a black guy. I wasn't surprised to hear this. And when I was dealing with CAFCASS they didn't have any recognised complaints procedure. The whole charade echoes that of the Social Services in general, and at last in Rotherham and of course in Oxford, and no doubt more places by the time you read this, the birds are coming home to roost. I'll come back to this later.

Meanwhile, back in Never-never Land (you're never- never going to win) I was still relatively naïve and still wanted to reason with Mrs. Feltham and at Court. But I had to wait now until Shirley had informed Heather of my existence. Over that summer I took my camper for a short holiday on my own (well, I had dogs with me) and I remember visiting the Severn Valley Railway and whilst at Bridgnorth, going in to the Church designed by Thomas Telford, to pray. This was very unusual for me, but easy in that beautiful, light-filled church with its simplicity enhanced by scented flowers. I lit a candle for Heather and prayed for the best outcome and that she would not be harmed by her new knowledge.

Towards the end of August I heard from CAFCASS that Heather had been told and that (predictably) she didn't want to meet me. Why was I not surprised? I wrote to Mrs. Feltham again and expressed the hope that she, at least, would now meet with me. She wouldn't. She suggested that I obtain a welfare report on Heather and if I did, she would then undertake the work and, surprise surprise, she would see me. I thought 'oh no you won't!'. I'd had enough of her. A welfare report is, if I remember rightly, carried out by Social Services and would have been very intrusive for Heather, with all sorts of questions being asked not only of her but of her teachers and other people as well. I had no concerns about her welfare in general at all and did not want her to have to go through this. Even my solicitor suggested we go down this route, but I refused, and asked at the very brief Hearing in September what any other way might there be to proceed. It was suggested that I try mediation again, through something called the Oxfordshire Family Mediation Children and Young People Support Service. The title is long but the service was free. Judge Payne gave us two more months to try and work something out.

Naturally I was sceptical, but my aversion to having Heather subjected to a welfare report over-rode my scepticism and I agreed. I was interviewed on my own initially, by a Mrs. Filkin, in their offices in Headington. I had to tell her 'my side of the story' and she agreed to help with the case. She would write to Shirley and ask to see her to obtain her version of events and then see us both together. She wrote to Shirley three times and received no response at all from her. The Court Hearing, by this time, was looming large. Ms. Filkin was kind enough to see me one more time, and in the absence of any response from Shirley also gently suggested to me that I should apply for a welfare report. Two days after this Ms. Filkin received a letter from Shirley asking for more time to consider her position.

I attended the next Hearing, on November 10th. almost on my own. Neither Mrs. Feltham or Shirley were present, but Mrs. Kendall was. It was the only time I saw old Judge Payne show any animation at all. He didn't like people not attending his Hearings! He even noted the fact that I had travelled so far and actually seemed to listen to some of my concerns this time. I told him that a welfare report had been suggested and said that I wanted to avoid Heather having to go through this if possible, so in the (long) gap between Hearings I had taken it upon myself to try mediation again but that Shirley had asked for more time to 'consider her options'. I said I didn't feel this was necessary, that she'd stalled enough, and Payne agreed with me. He fixed a date for yet another bloody Hearing, commenting that 'If Mrs. ..... deigns to appear next time, I'll listen to her'. I said I 'had some difficulty' communicating with Mrs. Feltham and would it be possible for another officer to take over the case. He quite readily agreed, and suggested Mrs. Kendall, the officer present, who had attended the first Hearing.

I agreed - she'd seemed pleasant and communicative enough to me. He also ordered a welfare report, but not at my request. I still didn't want this, but for once it was quite a good day for me.

I telephoned Shirley after this and left a message on her voicemail saying her non-appearance had done her no favours. I shouldn't have bothered - why could I not stop caring? I should have just left it. I was subsequently to learn that she then wrote to the Court apologising for her non-appearance and saying she'd 'forgotten'. How do you forget a Court Hearing which involves the future of your child? I began to wonder whether that welfare report might be necessary after all.

I was obviously concerned that Heather had been influenced at home to say she didn't want to see me. Mrs. Feltham had put in a report that she was convinced that Heather had expressed her true feelings, without being influenced by anyone else, and that Shirley was 'open-minded' to her meeting with me. I knew that last bit was bollocks! I was as equally sceptical about the first.

So a week before the Hearing I had written to Payne expressing the thought that Mrs. Feltham's report raised as many questions as it answered. No mention had been made in it of how Heather had been told of me, or indeed whether she had been given any information about me at all. Was she told anything about me as a person, what I did, where I lived? That I had always contributed to her birthdays and Christmases as well as the usual monthly contributions? That until a couple of years before, she ate the vegetables that I had grown, and eaten meals I had prepared for Shirley and the family? In other words, was Heather given a positive, encouraging picture? I said that if Heather had a 'right to know' of me, then she had a right to know a bit about me, too. I told him that I had the impression that Heather had been somewhat baldly told that I had disappeared off the scene when she was two and a half and had suddenly reappeared demanding access. And if this was the case, then she had been misinformed.

I wondered, too, what perception she may have had of me as a Father. Was she worried that I might try to 'take over' her life or even move in? Did she think I would tell her how to behave or what she should do? I could never, now, be a Father to her in the conventional, traditional sense. The best I could hope for was to be able to support her, encourage her, add to her life; help her discover her 'other' family in due course, to grow to love her and hope that she may grow to love me.

I noted that no mention had been made in the Report of the possibility of indirect contact (i.e. by letter). This would have been my first choice of approach, being a gentler way of introduction than by asking a twelve-year-old girl, so soon after having the shock of learning of me, whether she wanted to meet me face-to-face.

I had indicated at the previous Hearing that I was surprised and disappointed that no mention was made of this option. I also mentioned my concern that Heather would not have said that she was 'too young' to start a relationship with her Dad, without being prompted. She had said this to Madam Feltham apparently. I had sought the advice of a Child Psychiatrist who wrote to me saying that Heather was undoubtedly being prompted, and saying that CAFCASS officers were all-too-ready to swallow anything a child said without thinking things through, especially if the child was saying what the officer wanted to hear! She added that she could not understand why Mrs. Feltham refused to interview me before she interviewed Heather, describing it as 'very odd'.

At that last Hearing in September, I had voiced my concern and distress that Heather had been told that I had taken her mother to Court and that in her own words she was 'a bit angry about it'. Shirley had responded by saying that she had to tell Heather because of the involvement of Mrs. Feltham, but I thought it could have been handled with greater sensitivity. I reiterated this in the letter, and added that I thought she had been told because it was thought that it would further prejudice her view of me. I asked whether she was told also that I had brought the matter to Court only as a last resort, after every other avenue had been tried and had failed?

I signed off by saying that I could only place before him (Payne) these concerns and questions, and needed directions from the Court as to how to proceed.

At least to some extent, progress was now taken out of my hands as Payne had ordered a welfare report. I was very uneasy about this as it meant a lot of intrusion into Heather's life and she would no doubt be told that I had insisted on it, thus alienating her further.

Shirley and I were asked to attend a meeting at the dismal CAFCASS offices in Cambridge Street, Oxford, shortly before Christmas in 2004. I'd been to this God-forsaken concrete-grey building at least once before and had noted it was surrounded by razor-wire, cameras and warnings, presumably I thought for keeping angry fathers at bay. The meeting was somewhat awkward and I can't remember much of it except this was where I finally learned the truth - towards the end of the session - when Mrs. Kendall told us that we would both be subject to a CRB (Criminal Records Bureau) check. She said that Rosa would also be subject to a check and then asked Shirley if there was a man in her life who had contact with Heather. Shirley went bright purple and had to admit it - there was, a Len Leech.

I just looked at her steadily as she said this. So whilst I, Heather's father, had to jump through all these hoops and go through all this palaver just to see my own daughter - a strange bloke was able to simply walk in. Just like that! He could be anyone. Tom, Dick or paedophile. I was angry enough (think I didn't show it) but when Shirley said that Heather wasn't at all happy about the situation, (but 'well there you are'), I almost couldn't contain myself and was glad that the meeting ended shortly afterwards. I wanted to talk to Shirley in the reception area but she dived into the toilet. All my remaining hopes and any vestiges of trust went in with her.

At least it brought the curtain down on the whole pantomime, this charade of pretence and faux protectiveness. I walked back to my van, sat in it for a short while and then almost robotically began the long drive home. I turned on the radio and immediately heard the DJ announce the next track, a Leonard Cohen song - 'Everybody Knows'. What could be more appropriate?

Everybody knows that the dice are loaded
Everybody rolls with their fingers crossed
Everybody knows that the war is over
Everybody knows that the good guys lost
Everybody knows the fight was fixed
The poor stay poor, the rich get rich
That's how it goes
Everybody knows.

Everybody knows that the boat is leaking
Everybody knows that the captain lied
Everybody got this broken feeling
Like their father or their dog just died
Everybody talking to their pockets
Everybody wants a box of chocolates
And a long stem rose;
Everybody knows.

Everybody knows that you love me baby
Everybody knows that you really do
Everybody knows that you've been faithful
Ah give or take a night or two
Everybody knows you've been discreet
But there were so many people you just had to meet
Without your clothes;
Everybody knows. . .. .

And everybody knows that it's now or never
Everybody knows that its me or you
And everybody knows that you live forever
Ah when you've done a line or two
Everybody knows the deal is rotten
Old black Joe's still pickin' cotton
For your ribbons and bows
And everybody knows... .

Everybody knows it's coming apart
Take one last look at this sacred heart
Before it blows
And everybody knows

Leonard Cohen, 1988.

I couldn't have foreseen at the time how apt that last verse was going to be, and I don't remember anything more of the journey home or much of the weeks immediately after, or of Christmas that year. I've said before what a fool I'd been, a consistent fool, but I hadn't realised quite how much of one. I was worried sick about Heather and I didn't know anything about this bloke. I felt an incredible anger at Shirley and decided to try and do something. I have a friend who was once a bit of a private detective and went to have a chat with him just before Christmas. He told me he'd 'do a bit of digging'; I was not on any account to try and do anything myself but to leave it with him.

Mrs. Kendall called me in for a further interview in January, presumably after the Welfare Report had been completed but I have no record or memory of that Report. I remember the meeting, though. She told me that Shirley's, Rosa's and my CRB checks were clear. I asked about Leech. 'Oh I forgot about him' she said. I managed to remain civil but why on earth had Rosa and I been subjected to a check when it became obvious that we were never going to have anything to do with Heather, whilst a strange man who could see her every day slipped through the net? I asked her, very politely but firmly, that she should carry one out as Heather was at a vulnerable age. 'Are you asking me to do this?' she said. I just looked at her. To be fair, she did, and he proved clear, but I was not at all impressed over this episode.

Then came the bombshell. 'When I was speaking to Heather, she told me that she was surprised that you were still seeing her mum in 2002 as Shirley had been seeing Mr. Leech for a long time and they all went on holiday with him when she was eight'. By now, I was not that surprised. I had received information from my Columbo-type friend that indeed Leech and Shirley had been an item for a long time. Except for one act, this was the last time I received any sympathy from Mrs. Kendall, whom I shall now refer to as Mrs. Cafcass as she henceforth behaved like CAFCASS personified.

I had made a mistake in getting Mrs. Feltham dismissed from the case; they all club together and my 'awkwardness' was going to be rewarded by an increasing hostility and implacable refusal to heed any of my concerns and arguments. They also knew I had become a member of Fathers 4 Justice. They don't like that. I had started asking awkward questions and stating 'inconvenient truths' and they most certainly don't like that, either. I've always been a fully-paid-up member of the Awkward Squad.

I never asked 'Columbo' how he got his information, but he called me over to his place shortly after this meeting to tell me where Leech lived, where he worked, and how old he was! I'd agreed to meet and talk with Adrian all those years ago when the position was reversed, so I thought it only fair - and right - that I should meet and try to engage with this man; as far as I knew he had unfettered access to my daughter and it was almost my duty to her to make sure he was OK. I hadn't by then heard that Leech had cleared the CRB check, in fact I don't think he had at that time. I don't set much store by them anyway; so many have been cleared simply because they haven't been caught.

To my utter astonishment I had learned that he worked as a Jeweller in Hatton Garden. Shirley had always professed her 'socialist' credentials and her contempt for capitalism, so I was gobsmacked at this news. Not only had she betrayed her promises to me, she had, seemingly, betrayed her own principles too. I really couldn't take this in for several days 'A Jeweller?' I kept repeating to myself, 'I can't believe this!'.

Shirley the socialist
Impressed upon me
The need for social justice,
Truth, equality.

Human rights, and no more fights
Love and harmony
A caring, sharing partnership
Between herself and me

I fell in love with Shirley,
I gave her all I had
And in return she made me
A proud and happy Dad

But when it came to parenting
It really was quite weird
The socialist in Shirley
Completely disappeared

R.C.

163

One gloriously sunny January day I was given a job where I knew I had a good chance of parking-up the coach in Holborn, fairly close to Hatton Garden. I'd never been there before, so when I was successful in parking the coach in my usual spot, I sauntered down and walked the full-length of the street. Security guards and police were everywhere and I couldn't locate the actual building Leech worked in without looking suspicious. So I telephoned him, and got through to his elderly father who at that time still ran the business. I simply asked when Leech would be in, was told, and then rang again.

This time I got him! I politely wished him a good afternoon and said who I was - 'you know, Heather's dad'. There was a stunned silence. He must have been as surprised at hearing me as I had been at hearing he was a Jeweller. He stuttered a reply and I quickly said I had no wish to cause trouble but, as Heather's dad, wished to meet him. I suggested South Mimms Services on the M.25 as he lived fairly close. 'When?' he asked. 'I can be there this evening', I said, 'might as well get it over with'. I couldn't help giggling to myself at his total shock and discomfiture. I'd really caught him on the back foot. He muttered something about not being able to make it that evening, so I said I'd ring again or he could ring me. I gave him my number. Then I went to a nearby pub and had a double brandy, and bought the barman a drink as well. Just for once, I'd hit back and I confess it was very sweet. I tried to imagine the telephone calls or conversation between him and Shirley that evening. It didn't do me any good in the long-term though, and he never had the guts or the decency to meet me, or even telephone me. A poor show.

At that last meeting I had informed Mrs. Cafcass that my mother had left Heather £100 in her will, but I had no way of making sure that Heather received it. Mrs. Cafcass agreed that she would give the money to Heather, and also agreed that Heather should send me an acknowledgment in her own writing. I think that she went the extra mile on this one, for she actually did it. For that, I'm grateful. From now on, it was all downhill. . . .

Another bloody Hearing was scheduled for the second week in February 2005. In fact, like the subsequent ones, it wasn't really a Hearing at all, as I wasn't heard. The Welfare Report had been issued but I was given no chance at all to comment on any of it. Judge Payne had reverted to type, and as Shirley was present and allowed to speak he swallowed everything she said without question and with no recourse to me. I was allowed no contact, but a report on Heather's progress and health every four months. This was presented as a Big Deal - they only wanted me to get a report every six months. I had protested so strongly (in writing) that Shirley was tardy in giving me any information at all that they agreed to four months.

Payne commented to me that I should 'let her [Heather] go'. Go? You let a son or daughter 'go' at eighteen, not twelve! Did he think that a father's role was to be that irresponsible? What an unmitigated idiot! I returned from this 'Hearing' aggrieved, and I wrote to Payne to tell him so.

I wrote: 'It now seems evident that I am joining the ranks of broken-hearted fathers unable to see their children, and I have been forced to think long and hard over my situation and the findings and conclusions of this report. The question that shouts at me is; why is it that Heather, or any other child in a comparable situation, is given the choice of whether or not she sees or has contact with her father, when on equally important issues she has no choice? Did Heather, my daughter, have the choice as to whether Mr. Leech entered into her life, or whether or not she had to share a holiday with him? Why should such overwhelming priority be given to a child's right of choice over whether that child sees the father when the issue of choice is not sought, never mind considered, when it comes to meeting the new lover? Yet, who is the more likely to have the child's best interests at heart? There seems to be an anomaly here, and injustice. Shirley did admit at the meeting with Mrs. Kendall on December 2nd., that Heather would prefer it if Mr. Leech was not around. But he is. This preoccupation with giving Heather's wishes total precedence rings rather hollow to me, when such scant regard is paid to them on such a matter as this.

'I would like to suggest that it would be fairer to all parties to arrange a few meetings, or even an exchange of letters, before asking a child of Heather's age or younger whether he or she wishes to continue. Heather obviously has an aversion to seeing me, and she must have preconceptions of me, her own or instilled, and I have had no chance to allay (or even confirm!) them. I now believe, subject to the Court being convinced that he has the child's best interests at heart and can contribute to his or her life, and is consistent and sincere, a father should have the chance to know his child, and vice-versa. I think that not only is the father missing out, so is the child.

'There is only this one chance - too late, really, when the child becomes an adult. Too late altogether if the father dies. If, after an initial period, the child remains hostile, then obviously the child's wishes should hold sway. The father would have to accept it: but at least he would have been given a chance. The child's wishes would remain paramount: but not exclusively to the loss of the father's. And a child's wishes would be formed on a degree of knowledge rather than on outside opinion or mere conjecture, and perhaps most important, the father would cease to be some kind of ogre, or mythical figure.

'I believe these questions are important ones, and my suggestions valid. I regret not being able to ask them today, but hope that they can contribute to the debate over the rights and responsibilities of fathers in the future.'

Payne's favourite, most-used word was 'inappropriate'. It would be 'inappropriate' for him to comment, so he didn't. He used the word again in a later Hearing, which I will take some grim pleasure in relating a little further on. I regarded it as a lazy way to reply - just too easy. I have described him as 'bone headed, bone-idle, a blinkered, blithering idiot', and nothing I have heard since has altered my view.

When Len Leech failed to deliver on his promise to ring me, I wrote to him. I knew Shirley would have told him not to talk to me, she'd asked - no, told - me not to talk to Adrian, but I felt it unfair not to. Leech lacked the backbone.

I know this sounds self-righteous, sorry! 'But there you are', to coin a phrase. I wrote a civilised letter and undertook not to write to him again. No response.

Well, no response from him. Instead I got a letter from someone at Lightfoots Solicitors in Thame (the signature was always illegible and they never bothered printing out the name) accusing me of harassment and threatening me with legal action should I ever write anything again. I took some pleasure in demolishing the letter piece by piece and asked for an apology from them. I also asked if they would make sure that Heather would receive the money I'd put in a trust fund for her and make certain she'd receive it on her eighteenth birthday. They refused to apologise and couldn't assist with the fund. I wrote again asking to whom could I address any concerns I may have over Heather's welfare? They said I could ask them.

There were quite a number of letters sent to-and-fro but one day they simply said 'we are no longer acting for Mrs. ....., and will not respond to any further correspondence' so their claim that I could ask them about the welfare of Heather was bogus. In the meantime, I had discovered that my letters were simply being passed on to Shirley. This amused me greatly, as Shirley was now paying to read them! I addressed my first reply to 'Dear Sir or Madam' but after this, to 'Dear (signature illegible)'. I think their last letter did provide a name, but it was several letters and months later. How unprofessional.

During this (to me rather amusing) correspondence, I had decided that as I had no idea what Shirley was spending the money I sent her, on, (probably meals out with Leech) I would stop payments after the next monthly instalment. I got a letter direct from Shirley. She told me it was unfortunate that I was going to stop the payments because she would 'have to tell Heather, as I will have to cancel her riding lessons'. I wrote to Lightfoots, saying that I had no wish to prevent Heather doing the thing she most loved in the world, and offered to send the money direct to the Riding School. Predictably, this was 'not acceptable'. Shirley had no reason to tell Heather, or cancel her lessons, it was just another way for her to alienate Heather even further.

I began to think that Shirley must now hate me more than she loved our daughter. I didn't know how I could counter her cold heart and her closed mind. I was lucky we hadn't involved the CSA. (Child Support Agency). I now implacably believe that there should be no financial support from an estranged parent unless that parent is allowed to give emotional support to the child as well.

Emotional support is just as important as financial, but it's always only about the money. Many fathers were being treated as though they were walking cashpoints. Many have been totally ruined by the CSA. Some have committed suicide. I regard the CSA as indicative of the attitude of officialdom in our times. It's all about the money. It's only about the money. It's certainly not about the kids.

Here's a good example. It's already been written about in Matt O'Connor's book 'Fathers 4 Justice - the Inside Story' so I'll keep it brief. Michael Cox was a rare find for Fathers 4 Justice - he was a barrister who'd all his life lived within the law but was now prepared to break the law to uphold a principle. The Child Support Agency had branded him as 'a parent without care' or 'non-resident parent' - only this was not true. Michael had a rare thing - 50% shared residency. He looked after the children for 50% of the time. His ex-wife received child benefit and family tax credits, he didn't, yet the CSA said that he owed £42,000 in unpaid child support. He was hauled before Southampton Magistrates and told he would have to cough up - or be banged up. Michael's ex had written to the Court pleading with them not to imprison him as it would force her to stop work and resort to benefits. Mike's boys, at that time 16 and 13, were also distraught at the prospect of their Dad being sent down. Michael saw it in black-and-white. He looked after the boys 50 per cent of the time. He clothed them, fed them, took them on holidays and provided a roof over their heads. He didn't receive child benefit for the time they lived with him, so why should he have to pay the CSA for the other 50 per cent of the time? Why did the CSA brand him an 'absent father' when he clearly wasn't?

The magistrates decided to hold Michael's committal to prison in closed court (they would, wouldn't they?). Somehow the youngest son got in to the Court and shouted at the Magistrates 'Don't jail my Dad! I love my Dad!' He was ushered out in tears. The clerk of the Court had told the magistrates that their decision was not to rule on the 'children's best interests' as the CSA had already considered those 'interests'. Very handy! Michael was sent down, obviously that being in the children's best interests as the CSA had considered them. Nobody had asked the children of course. It is hard to think of anything that could be more in their worst interests.

It was shortly before the time I had the correspondence with Lightfoots that Sir Bob Geldof appeared in a short series on the T.V. about the 'The Real Love that Dare not Speak its Name'. He'd recently gone to the High Court to gain custody of his daughters after Paula Yates, the mother, had died of a drug overdose. He'd been warned, by a Court official, not to say that he loved his children, otherwise he might be viewed as being a bit extreme. You couldn't, as a father, say that you loved your children! That, indeed, was the prevailing attitude in the early days of this century and that attitude was the cause of huge distress and indeed the formation of Fathers 4 Justice. Fathers - certainly this one - were regarded at best as an irrelevance, and at worst a threat.

Sir Bob went on to make some very strong, very accurate comments about the way parents were being treated in the Family Courts. 'I cannot believe what they do to parents in the name of the law', he said. The trouble was, no-one else believed it at the time, either. Fathers 4 Justice provided the wake-up call.

Note the word 'parents' in the last paragraph. At the time I believed, along with hundreds of other disenfranchised Dads, that it was indeed only fathers who were being wronged and marginalised. I came to realise later that this was not really true, that mothers could also be treated with barbarity in these Courts, and sometimes even children too. But this was after my case had finally ended and I was active in taking part in and then organising demonstrations. For the sake of continuity I'll stick to the Court process, although my involvement with F4J ran parallel at this stage. My membership undoubtedly disadvantaged me in the Court. Authority doesn't like dissent, particularly high-profile publicity-seeking dissent. I revelled in doing it - it was a way of fighting back, of not being merely a victim.

In March 2005 Heather's birthday was approaching. However angry she might feel towards me I wanted her to know I felt no ill-will towards her. Rosa suggested I put an advert into her local papers. Heather would become a teenager in 2005 and so we composed an advert congratulating her on this landmark. I expected a bucketload of vitriol from her Mum or Lightfoots but received nothing at all.

I accepted the fact that probably no-one had noticed it so forgot about it quickly as I realised I was overdue a report and photograph of Heather from Shirley, so wrote a faintly sarcastic, but nevertheless polite letter to Lightfoots. I commented that I would use the words they'd used to me, (that they wouldn't hesitate to take court action if I wrote again to Shirley, and seek costs), if she didn't comply with the court order. I said I trusted that we understood each other. I got the report and photo almost by return! - but the photo of Heather was of her covering up her face.

This was obviously designed to wind me up as it wasn't even a proper photograph by my book - a computer-printed one of poor quality. I again politely wrote asking for a 'proper' one next time, and amazingly received a reply that I would indeed receive one that showed Heather's face clearly. Was there a hint of contrition in this letter? I didn't dare hope too much. When the next report and photo again became substantially overdue, I knew any hope I had was misplaced. Once again, I had to write and ask for it. At least this time the report included a good photo of Heather and a full set of school reports, all showing what a model pupil Heather was. I can't claim that she inherited this from me!!

I had to write again for the third report, and this time it was sparse, to say the least. I was worried now about the trust fund I had in place for Heather. The solicitors had said that they were no longer acting for Shirley and I wasn't allowed to write to her or contact her in any way. I didn't want Shirley to be entrusted with giving the money to Heather, I needed someone I felt I could trust to pass the money on when the time came - after all, it would be only five years hence.

It was my Columbo friend who suggested Heather's maternal grandparents. Shirley had shown me their house years before and I remembered the road - it was really straight and boring rather like Worcester Gardens in Greenford, and I remembered the number of it, (the date and month of Heather's birthday!). I remembered their surname, too. 'Leave it to me' said Columbo.

Within a day he'd got the full address! I thought long and hard over asking them. Should I call or should I write? Or should I not do it at all? I knew they knew nothing of me before all this Court stuff started but surely, with the boys and Heather knowing now, they would have been aware? I wrote a very carefully-composed letter, assuming they knew about me but couching it in terms that would be gentle and sympathetic if they did not.

I took hours over choosing my words and even then very nearly did not send it. My instincts were saying 'no', but what else could I do, where else could I turn? I posted the letter.

A few days later I received through the post a summons from the High Court in London. In my naivety I assumed it was Shirley seeking retribution. I later learned that my letter had reached Shirley's parents on their 58th. wedding anniversary - and had caused them huge distress, and huge embarrassment to Shirley. They didn't know anything about me, of course, and the news that Heather was not Adrian's child came as a bombshell to them. I felt awful; I couldn't care less about Shirley's discomfiture but upsetting her parents like that was not my aim. I should have known that Shirley would have kept the truth from them. Columbo told me not to worry, it was Heather that I was trying to consider and any Judge would see that. I laughed in his face.

High Hopes?

I travelled up to London on the specified day, and such was my luck, my boss at the coach firm suggested I 'did a job' for him and so I took fifty-odd people up to London with me! They didn't attend Court, of course, they went off and did what they had to do, and I parked the coach in the one coach bay in High Holborn for free for the day. I must be one of very few people who actually got paid whilst defending himself in the High Court and wasn't subject to either the congestion charge or a parking fee! I was very early, so went for breakfast at the Wetherspoons pub nearby, treating a 'Big Issue' seller to one as well as he told me his experiences in the Family Courts. We parted with a warm handshake, he to go on the streets and I to the Royal Courts of Justice. 'Oh well' he said, looking at the lowering sky, 'Just another day in Paradise!'. This poor man had, like so many others, lost his wife, children, home, job and income but was the soul of cheerfulness and optimism and made me feel very humble. If he by any chance reads this, I salute you, mate. I hope your ship has come in now.

(Oh and of course I bought a copy of the Big Issue - and I took it into the Court with me).

I went as directed to a building in Holborn only to find it was the wrong one, and then had to dash in a ferocious downpour to the Royal Courts of Justice just off the Aldwych, arriving looking like a drowned rat. I was directed to some form of annexe, but lost my way en route, ending up in a large and rather empty hall, dripping from all extremities. A couple of ladies were entering the hall so I went to ask them if they knew where Room whatever-it-was was, only to realise that one of them was Shirley, and the other was a particularly sour-faced woman I recognised as the CEO of Norcap. Ah, Norcap. I must remember to include my little episode with them later.

Back to the High Court, then. Here was Pam Hodgkins, CEO of a 'charity' set-up to reunite people with their birth parents, supporting her employee who was preventing the birth father of our child from having anything to do with her. Wonderful. I found the room I was looking for on my own.

This room was absolutely crowded-out with dads trying (mostly unsuccessfully) to have contact orders with their children, enforced. You could hardly move. We were holed-up here for what seemed like hours (I think it was two), and unfortunately I was button-holed by a desperate father with the worst case of halitosis I had come across in a long time.

I kept trying to avoid the fumes but it was very difficult in that crowded room and I was almost passing out by the time a court official came in and said that as it was approaching lunch-time, we could go out for an hour.

We agreed we'd adjourn to 'The George' pub across the road for a pint and a sandwich. This soon filled-up with other 'deadbeat dads' who were fighting to see their children. I got our drinks in quickly, and by God the taste of that cold lager was welcome! I breathed-in the aroma of it and it was as sweet as nectar. Then the court official appeared amongst us, informing us that we could stay here until we were called as there was no room across the road. They actually came into the pub to call us! Needless to say, several became fairly inebriated during the afternoon. Before I was summoned, I received a call from Rosa, saying that she'd had a call from Aylesbury police who had received a complaint from a Mrs. Shirley . . . . of 'harassment' and I had to 'make an appointment' to be arrested! When I relayed this to the assembled multitude there was uproar and huge merriment; I don't think I paid for one more drink that day. I was duly called, and with many expressions of goodwill and good luck, crossed the road, a little unsteadily, to await my fate.

A very sympathetic court usher explained to me that it was not Shirley bringing the action but my daughter, Heather. I didn't believe this at first. I had felt rather benign after all the pub merriment and the drinks, but this certainly sobered me up, big-time. How could a girl of thirteen bring an action against her own father, a man she did not know? The usher, most kindly, allowed me a little time to adjust outside the courtroom. Sometimes, the kindness of strangers can overwhelm one, and I wept with a mixture of despair and gratitude. This very kind lady also ensured that I sat well away, and to the rear of, my adversaries.

The Judge was Judge Janet Case from Chester, a circuit judge. Immediately she saw that Heather had no legal representation, only a McKenzie friend - Pam Hodgkins. She asked why Heather had no legal representation. The answer was that it cost too much. She couldn't believe this, as legal representation is free, and a right, for anyone under 16. She said it was extraordinary that a girl of thirteen was expected to stand up in the High Court with no representation. She as good as accused Shirley of lying, but asked Heather why she had brought her father to court. 'I don't regard him as my father' she said, 'I don't know him'. She spoke clearly and well, and despite what she was saying, I felt very proud of her. 'Well', said Mrs. Case, 'I think it is a huge pity, as he obviously cares for you very much and he's concerned for your future'. She looked down over her spectacles at Heather and said 'You are not of an age to know what is best for you. This sounds autocratic - it is, but it's true - sorry'.

The Judge saw the notice I'd placed for Heather's birthday, and it was passed to me. I'd not actually seen the paper and the advert was much larger than I'd expected. I was pleased they'd seen it. Judge Case said 'Is this what all the fuss is about?'. Then she read the letter I had sent to Heather's grandparents and other correspondence and said that this was certainly not malicious, just desperate. 'I'm minded to give Mr. Crawford a full contact order'. She commented that I would have a very difficult job after all these years to win Heather over, and I concurred. She criticised my being a member of Fathers 4 Justice, saying that there were better ways of changing the system than by dramatic protests, but understood why I did this. I was gobsmacked. I had not expected this at all. It was like a blinding light had pierced the fog of obfuscation, delay and politically correct crappery that was Oxford Family Court and I was caught off-guard, and blinded by the light.

It was obvious to everyone that Ms. Case saw that Heather had been coerced into doing this by her mother and Mrs. Hodgkins, and they had been in such a rush to take me to Court, they had not considered Heather's position or rights at all. She was able to see in minutes what old Payne could not ever see. My daughter, pushed and encouraged to hate rather than to love, not knowing me at all . . .my daughter, my daughter! I believe that Shirley and Pam Hodgkins were guilty of child abuse, no less, for this.

Have you seen 'Judge Judy' on the television? Judge Case was the English version. How I wished we had a 'Judge Judy' at Oxford! Anyway, despite 'minding to give me a full contact order', Judge Case said she had to refer the case back to Oxford, with the same judge as before - so I knew I would never get that contact order. I'm sorry, but seeing the total disbelief and shock on the faces of Shirley and la Hodgkins after the hearing gave me a huge sense of vindication and some hope.

They had obviously thought they'd played a blinder by coercing Heather into doing this, and they had been rightly knocked down. Even if Heather had wanted to do this herself, she should have been discouraged rather than goaded on to do it.

She looked distraught, but I shall forever be grateful to Judge Janet Case for giving her an alternative view. I wrote to her after the final Hearing in Oxford telling her so, and received the most kind letter back. This episode convinced me now that Shirley hated me more than she loved our daughter, and would go to any lengths to alienate her and malign me.

It's a hard life, it's a hard life, it's a very hard life
It's a hard life wherever you go,
And if we poison our children with hatred
A hard life is all that they'll know

(Nanci Griffith, singer/songwriter).

Next stop, though, was Aylesbury Police Station. We agreed a date, and I duly motored over on one glorious Winter morning. 'I've come to be arrested' I informed the duty sergeant. 'Yeah, yeah' he laughed, then, 'Oh yes, you're Mr. Crawford aren't you?' He directed me to a back room (no windows) where I awaited the constable to whom the complaint of harassment had been made, who was based at Waddesdon, just outside the town. A polite and amenable man, he talked to me briefly outlining the nature of the complaint and asked me if I had a copy of the offending letter (to Shirley's parents). I most certainly did, he briefly read it and said 'hang on a minute' and disappeared. He was gone so long I thought he'd forgotten

173

me but he duly reappeared and told me he'd shown the letter to the duty sergeant, he'd read it, and said 'let him go - we're not going to arrest anyone for this'. So I walked out, 'without a stain on my character' as they say. I'd had my day in Court, and now my day at the Police Station. It was a brief, but very welcome and needed, respite from all the crap I was being buried under at Oxford.

The Hearing at Oxford was on the 8th. February 2006. I'd had to prepare another 'position statement' and I'd been meticulous in doing so. I felt that Shirley was trying to malign my character so had asked various friends and colleagues to write letters of endorsement. I'd also mentioned the comments made by Judge Janet Case, and the fact that the Police had not pressed any charges against me.

I had letters from my cousin Ann, from members of my birth family, from my friend Hilary whom I'd known for over forty years, from my 'manager' at work, from my wife Rosa, a neighbour and another friend, from Michele who'd been a member of my gardening class, from my step-son and his wife, and from my previous partner Dora. All of them stated that I was not a malicious person, and I was overwhelmed by their generosity. I have never been able to express adequately my indebtedness to them. I've put copies of all their letters in the appendix at the end of this book, just to show that even the most glowing testimonials can be ignored if a Judge sees fit. I don't think Payne read one of them. I am of the opinion that he is a lazy bastard and he only wanted the case to end now.

But we had yet another futile stage to go through, a final Hearing, before which Mrs. Cafcass had to produce yet another meaningless report. How much was all this costing the taxpayer?

At least Heather had a solicitor at this Hearing and at the final one, a Mrs. Edwards, from Hodders Solicitors in High Wycombe. She took the trouble to take me aside after the Hearing and talk with me. She asked me why on earth had I contacted the Grandparents? Before that, she said, Heather had been coming round to the idea of meeting me. I explained why I'd done it, said I thought the letter I'd sent was measured and courteous, and asked her, politely, if Heather had told her that she was 'coming round' to the idea of meeting me. She answered that no, it was her mother. I said this had only been said to make me feel even worse, that it wouldn't have been true - and she did not dispute it. I found Mrs. Edwards approachable and to her immense credit she did try to broker an agreement. Unlike the Court, she was not adversarial. But the forces against us were too great and after all she was representing Heather, not me.

The last Hearing was held on 24th. May. Heather had been asked if a particular date suited her, and she said 'just not on my birthday'. She was visibly distressed. Before the final one I was called over yet again for an interview with Mrs. Cafcass in the Gulag Rooms in Cambridge Street. I spent a total of six hours that day travelling to and fro and having this pointless meeting, and drove over 100 miles. Though I felt that I was 'under suspicion', I have no argument with the questions asked, but it could just as well have been done over the phone, and in a kinder way. Mrs. Cafcass took the opportunity of being accusative and hostile. When I mentioned that Judge Case had said that Heather was still too young to really know what was best for her, she snapped 'Heather found that patronising!'. No mention of the evil that saw Heather there in the first place. I said I was distressed that the first time I'd seen Heather in eleven years was in the High Court. Cafcass said 'Yes, but what about Heather?' But Heather had, ostensibly, brought the action against me!

Mrs. Cafcass over-ruled a High Court Judge and airily dismissed anything that she'd said. She was Judge now and I've no idea why I was called in for this 'interview' - really a dressing-down. She said that Judge Payne would take her word for anything, and whatever I might say would be rejected out-of-hand. I didn't doubt it! She said that Heather had mentioned that she didn't want to have to come over to see me every other weekend. What? Who'd told her that? It hadn't even occurred to me.

Much was made of my letter to Len Leech, and again the term 'harassment' was levelled at me. I told her that when Adrian found out about Shirley and me, he didn't write me a letter or telephone me, he came over and roughed me up a bit. He was over six feet tall, so it had been quite intimidating. I had taken it as par for the course and would not have dreamt of pressing 'harassment' charges.

He'd also - once - physically attacked Shirley, I saw the wheal marks on her neck. He'd done it out of sheer exasperation at her emotional cruelty to him and I didn't remember her contacting the Police over it. Mrs. Cafcass countered this by saying it had all happened long ago, mine was now. A polite letter requesting a meeting with Leech, harassment? Causing distress? Oh really! What a wimp!

I tried for one last time to plead for a supervised meeting with Heather, so at least she could form an opinion on some knowledge of me, but of course Mrs. Cafcass said no, and she said it with a quiet satisfaction. When I asked whether CAFCASS kept any records of the outcomes for children subject to their rulings, she had to admit that they didn't. 'So how do you know if you are acting in any child's best interests?' I said. 'I haven't time to talk politics' was her answer. I asked for the meeting to be terminated, as it was obviously a waste of time for both of us.

I was most definitely back in Never-never Land and the brief burst of truth and light in the High Court had been extinguished for good. 'You're never going to see your daughter - get over it'.

I very nearly gave up at this point. Perhaps it would have been better if I had. The day after the last Hearing I had written a statement, as had been requested, to Mrs. Kendall and to Mrs. Edwards. It was to be my last throw of the dice and I put my heart and soul into it. Mrs. Cafcass didn't even mention it at our meeting. I write it down here just to illustrate exactly how I felt then, and invite the reader to judge whether it is a valid statement which merited at least some consideration. It was in response to Mrs. Edwards' and Mrs. Kendall's request, on behalf of Heather, that I drop the case to avoid putting Heather through the stress a further last Hearing.

'This is the most difficult decision I have ever had to make. It is made after a sleepless night and through countless tears.

'Yesterday I witnessed Heather's acute distress, knowing that I am largely the cause of it. The last thing any caring father would want is to cause his child this anguish. It is difficult for me to come to terms with the fact she must hate me. And I now have to make a decision which will either alleviate her unhappiness or add to it.

'I have been urged by both of you to drop the case. Of course, Heather would wish me to do so too.

'I have to make this decision as a loving and caring father, in what I believe to be Heather's best interests, long and short-term. I have to put aside completely my wishes, which is hard enough, and also try to think beyond Heather's immediate wishes and her anguish, and concentrate on what I truly believe would be the best for her. I find it incredibly difficult to be dispassionate about this.

'Having seen Heather yesterday I have been minded to drop the case. This would, at a stroke, be a source of relief for her, for her carers and indeed for me. I have no stomach to fight my own, my only child, and am weary of beating myself up over this.

'I am opposed in this decision by the strong support of my family. They say that I am really fighting FOR her, not against, and that, no matter how painful, I should continue to fight for what is right. Abandoning it would be the easy option. I would not only be letting my family down, I would be letting myself down and also, they believe, Heather.

'I personally don't believe an easy option exists, (and they did not witness Heather's distress). Any decision I make here is going to cause acute hurt. The only criteria that matters is Heather's best interests. As a child's best interests remain undefined in law, I have to try and untangle all the various arguments, and my own convictions, and I feel I am not best placed to do this.

'This is a poisoned chalice. Do I salve my own conscience and drop this case, possibly increasing the chance that Heather may forgive me in time, and start to wish to see me and my side of her family? Or do I pursue it, believing honestly and without any doubt that what I personally believe is in Heather's best interests, over-rides any distress that Heather now feels? And risk alienating Heather for ever?

'It must help if I try to articulate my beliefs on what are Heather's best interests. What are my core principles?

'That two decent, loving parents are better than one, for all sorts of reasons.

'That a culture of secrecy within families and between parents and children is not healthy and is fraught with difficulties and dangers, in that the truth will often emerge at the most difficult of times. Often secrecy equates with a lack of honesty and when the truth comes to light, people affected feel deceived and bewildered, and often very hurt.

'That I have a great deal to offer any child or young person as I seem to have a natural empathy. Given the chance, I would be a warm and loving father to Heather and could only add to her enjoyment of life. I can be rather too honest at times and of course could be a better person in many ways, but I believe that many on my side of Heather's family would make up for many of my deficiencies. We are an open, welcoming and loving family and I know that any child would benefit from having regular contact with us, and be proud to be a part.

''To thine own self be true'. I must make this decision in the totally honest belief that it will be in Heather's best interests, for the rest of her life. I said that I am not best placed to do this, but the decision has to be mine: and if I pursue this, the decision on whether I am right is then taken by others.

177

Perhaps this is the only way to go.

'I said that I believe that two decent parents are better than one. I feel it is wrong that Heather has not been aware until recently that I am her Dad, and that she must still be unaware that she has a side of her family that are inherently decent, open and loving. There are no Einsteins amongst us, no Mother Theresas, but in my birth family I have experienced a love, a closeness, and a compassion that is the essence of humanity and happiness. All the family know of Heather and want her to be a part of their lives, even if it is a small part. We, as a family, know that Heather is a bright and intelligent girl and we feel that a relationship with her would enrich and enliven our lives as much as we hope we could contribute to hers. Our family - her family - is open: there are no secrets, we all know the circumstances surrounding her upbringing and all of us are welcoming and uncensorious.

'I have seen, and been profoundly affected by, Heather's obvious aversion to having anything to do with me. Nevertheless, I feel she is making this judgment in ignorance. I have to ask the question again that why is she given the choice over whether she sees her father and his side of the family, when she has had no choice over other important changes in her life? Why is it that I, as far as I know, am the only person in the world who is forbidden to see Heather, by simple virtue of the fact that I am her father? I keep asking these questions because I have never had an answer to them, I feel it is wrong that we are putting these important issues, that should be decided by adults, onto a child's shoulders.

'I reiterate that I feel very strongly indeed that I should have the opportunity to put right the wrongs I have done in her eyes and redress the situation. I feel that if Heather does hate me, she would not, could not, if she knew me. I feel that those involved in her welfare should be encouraging her to try and draw closer to her family members rather than further keep them apart. I believe also that she should be encouraged to face up to her demons (i.e. me!) and surely would feel happier not regarding her father as a hate figure, lurking menacingly in the background of her mind and her life.

'For these reasons I feel I have to continue. I am most concerned that no records are kept on the outcomes for children subject to CAFCASS' recommendations. With my suggestion, made in my position statement, of supervised contact, there would at least be some follow-up. I do ask that you don't dismiss this out-of-hand.

'I am attaching copies of the various letters I have received in support. I would be particularly grateful if you would read the letters from my birth sisters, Brenda and Pamela, and the one from Mrs. Lawson, who has known me for nearly forty years.'

I also attached an addendum which detailed my financial provisions for Heather. I hoped that this might at least illustrate that I had thought long and hard and did not take any decision lightly. Mrs. Cafcass I understand told Heather about the addendum, but in a way that looked as if I was trying to 'bribe' her to see me. I'd wanted it to be kept absolutely confidential, but she used it to further Heather's resolve to not want to see me. Never give confidential information to a CAFCASS officer.

In-between seeing Mrs. Cafcass and the final farce - sorry, 'Hearing' - I had to deliver the above report to the Court. I was wearing a badge which simply stated 'I support Fathers 4 Justice'. I'd actually worn it in the High Court without a problem. But the clod who monitored people entering the building said 'You can't wear that 'ere' and insisted I remove it. I said I'd worn it in the High Court with no problem. 'Not 'ere' he said. It was a true harbinger of what was to follow. I had dealings with this officious prat a few times after this, as you will be amused to read (well I hope so. The best way to deal with these people is to laugh at them).

The final Hearing was listed for 24th. May. For the only time throughout these Hearings I was late, due to problems on the road. For the only time throughout these Hearings, it started on time. It was listed for 'all day'. Payne accepted that I'd had a difficult journey, (but had previously denied my request to move the whole farce to Watford. I'd expressed dissatisfaction with the goings-on at Oxford at the previous Hearing. Another mistake!). All-day Hearing? Fat chance. It lasted twenty minutes. Maybe Payne had an urgent appointment at the golf course that afternoon. I'd only received a copy of Shirley's statement (which contained several 'inaccuracies') the day before, and wasn't even allowed to comment on it. Payne acknowledged that I'd made 'profound observations' but when I mentioned that we were here to discuss Heather's best interests, he dismissed that as 'inappropriate'. What was 'appropriate' then? I made to walk out but was threatened with the Tipstaff (alias Court bouncers).

You guessed - no contact, no communication allowed, no nothing. Heather was not present as she was 'too distressed' to be in the same Court as me. The alienation was complete.

THE OXFORD BLUES.

'I'll tell her when the time is right
Though when that'll be, I don't know quite'.
I'll always remember those words she said
As I tried to allay the fears in my head.

The fear that my daughter would never be told
That I was her father, and longed to hold
Her, and love her, and no more to dread
Her saying one day 'God, I thought you were dead'.

So I took my case to the Family Court
And explained to them there that really, I thought
My girl should be told the truth at last
And we should catch up and redeem the past.

The CAFCASS lady said to me
'I'll think we'll just have to wait and see
What the mother says about it all':
This was the start of my long downfall.

"I'll fill her mind with poison
I'll fill her heart with hate
So when that bastard gets to Court
It'll be far too late:

I'll keep her love all for myself,
I'll let it not be shared,
If that bastard speaks the truth
Let it not be aired.

Get a gagging order, quick!
Stop him speaking out!
I'll get the Judge to order it,
Let there be no doubt

That I am in control here
And I couldn't care much less
If I break his heart in two
And leave him in distress.

180

She's my daughter, mine all mine!
I'll have the final word,
Who does the father think he is?
It's patently absurd
For him to want to share her life
And know her as a child,
I'll make sure he rots in Hell
Abandoned and reviled.

Besides, I've someone new now,
I think she quite likes him,
For her to know her Daddy now
Well - it wouldn't quite fit in."

The CAFCASS lady said to me
'I'm afraid your child you cannot see
She doesn't want you, I can't say why';
And I was left, hung out to dry.

'But I was promised, for years and years'
I protested through my tears
'She is my only child' I said
The CAFCASS lady shook her head

As all my pleas were firmly quashed
Like rotten fruit, trod on and squashed
Into a pulp, rent with a knife,
A broken man, a broken life.

The case was heard by District Judge Payne,
Never was there a Judge with such an apt name:
Your hopes and dreams will come to nought
If you take your case to his 'Family Court'.

R.C.

I wrote to Judge Payne and Mrs. Cafcass after this 'Hearing'. I commented that they had set me free. Free from any need to care, to support, to help, encourage or to love my only child. Free to squander any provision I had made for her future: free to deny her very existence. Free, in fact, to disown her, to turn her away if she ever wanted to see me, to abdicate any responsibility for her welfare, her happiness, or her future. In other words, they could rejoice in my being a truly feckless father; in the secure knowledge that this had been sanctioned by the Oxford Family Court. And

181

when this magical transformation was complete, no doubt the mother would then press the Court to 'honour my responsibilities as a father', and receive a sympathetic Hearing. I ended 'God help our children, and us'.

My view on how things should change

The two worst aspects of the present Family Court system are its secrecy and the fact that it is adversarial. It sets parent against parent and child against parent. In fact, it is the Anti-Family Court. 'The Family Division' of the Court is a far more apt title: nothing more divisive than these Courts. The whole system makes an awful lot of money out of it being this way, but that is no excuse for it being a huge contributor to the misery in this world. I went to the Family Court in Oxford out of desperation, when all else had failed, hoping - expecting even - that it would help resolve the situation. I could not have been more wrong. I most certainly did not expect cod professionals exuding faux concern, taking over as 'guardian et litem' and deciding my daughter's future and mine with a stroke of a pen. Or a Judge who simply took the view of the 'professionals' whatever they happened to say, and ignored anything else however 'profound'.

So my first change, were I in any position to do it, would be to make Family Courts into just that - Family Courts, where THE FAMILY is heard, not just poorly-trained CAFCASS officers. Many opponents of the present system say that the child's wishes should be paramount. I'm afraid I cannot agree. Certainly the child should be heard, and that would be a mammoth step forward - but the whole family should be heard, including grandparents and aunts, uncles etc. To heap the entire future of a child on its own shoulders would not be fair on anyone, including the child. What a child says he or she wishes is not necessarily what is best for the child.

Every report, every study shows that children are, in the vast majority of cases, best brought up knowing both parents, whether or not those parents live together. So there must be a presumption, in law, for both parents to see their children after separation. I'm not talking about a fifty-fifty share of time, that is often impossible anyway, but a presumption of equality is a good starting point for negotiation. Did you know you have no right in law to see your child? I kid you not. Yet the State, proved the worst possible 'parent', has the right in law to take your children away. This has to change, particularly in the light of the events in Rotherham and in Oxford (and probably nearly everywhere else). If a child has not seen one parent for years but shows an antipathy towards seeing that parent, the child should be gently encouraged to do so on a trial basis, so at least if the child subsequently continues to object to contact, at least it would be on the basis of a little knowledge rather than on the prejudice of the other parent, or on the child's own imagination. That, truly, would be in the child's 'best interests'. If the child simply refuses to see the other parent, then surely 'indirect' contact should be instigated (i.e. by letter or E-mail). Always with the caveat 'unless there is a very good proven reason why not'. Which brings me to my next suggested change.

Many fathers and some mothers are forbidden to see their kids on 'evidence' being accepted on the 'balance of probabilities', and not on the 'burden of proof'. This is wholly inadequate on such an important and emotive issue, which will change a father's or mother's or child's life, for the rest of their lives.

If, say, a mother accuses a father of sexual abuse then the accused party will not be able to see that child until the charge is disproven, which may take many months. In effect, the accused is guilty until proved innocent. If one partner accuses the other of 'emotional abuse', that accusation is often accepted on the 'balance of probability' after that parent has shown emotion in court, with often that parent then being forbidden to see the children. It's simply not good enough.

When I related the agreements we had come to at mediation to the Court, I was told by Judge Payne that they were 'irrelevant'. So in other words going to mediation was a complete waste of time and money, and the time was used by Mum to delay the inevitable proceedings. I believe that agreements made at mediation should be mandated in Court, if the case subsequently goes there. Otherwise, what is the point? I am not convinced that 'compulsory mediation' would work, but if mediation is used, it certainly should not be used by one party as a cynical stalling tactic.

This 'always working in a child's best interests' nonsense has to stop until it ceases to be a lie. It must be recognised for what it is - a meaningless mantra that seeks to cover-up all manner of injustices done to parents and children alike. Every study shows that children are more at risk from new boy/girlfriends and live-in-lovers than they are from their natural parents, yet a parent can be stopped from seeing their child or children whilst new lovers can simply walk in to the home of the child, no questions asked. New lover is presumed to be fine with the child from day one. No police checks for them - no court appearances. They simply walk in, no questions asked. Yet the natural parent has to go through the hell of the family court system to maybe obtain an hour or two a week with the child, and that's if they're lucky. How could this ever be 'in the best interests of the child'?

I agree with Mark Harris, who wrote in his book 'Family Court Hell' 'Personally, I believe future historians, probably well after my own children's lifetimes, will look back on what currently masquerades as 'in the interests of the child' by the family courts and will place what's routinely happening today alongside other historic, authority-led world crimes against its people, such as slavery and the holocaust'. We certainly suffer a holocaust of the heart. How can it ever be right that I can see any child, any child in the world, except my own? And that anyone can see my child, except me?

I must quote from Mark's book again, for he pinpoints exactly the lunacy of all this, far better than I. 'To completely round off this insanity. . . . .it came down to the inescapable fact that absolutely anyone could speak to my children if they saw them in a public place at any time EXCEPT ME, their father, unless of course it was during my allocated contact time, even though the mother wilfully obstructed it. And this is not an isolated piece of family court lunacy. When I set up the DADS protest movement [more of this later - Roger] a science teacher at my daughter's school in Plymouth joined us. He was divorcing and having problems seeing his two children. He taught my daughters, he worked alone and unsupervised at their large comprehensive school. But he was on SUPERVISED CONTACT with his own children. He was not allowed to see his own children without someone present at a contact centre. He worked full-time as a school teacher without any concerns from the authorities in a school with 1,000+ children, so just why was he on supervised contact with his own two kids? It's insanity.

'Now, neither of us were banned from speaking to or associating with any other children, anywhere, other than our own. To take this absurdity a small theoretical step further, if the science teacher took up a relationship with my ex-wife, and I did with his ex-wife, the ludicrous situation could have easily developed where both of us fathers could be living with the other's children, while restricted from our own children, by orders of the court. I made this point to Judge Munby during the committal hearing, but he just got angry and told me I was 'missing the point'. He never explained the point, probably because there is none. I still cannot see the point to this day, I cannot see any point to this madness at all'. Nor can I, Mark, nor can I. Can you, dear reader?

I believe that, as in the Magistrates Court, there should be three judges on every case. This was suggested by a Magistrate at one of the Norgrove Report's 'consultations' with the public, of which more anon. It was an excellent suggestion, I thought. In such life-changing situations, it seems wrong to me that the decision on where a child should live or if one parent should be excluded from the child's life, should rest with one person. So many cases have gone wrong and of course I would have welcomed other judges at my Oxford hearings who hopefully would have been less blinkered than old Payne. No doubt this would be regarded as 'too expensive' but I would say it would actually save money. It would also make hearings fairer, very important indeed in family cases for all parties.

The veil of secrecy must be lifted. To say that it is there to protect children is widely regarded as a nonsense. It is only there to protect the Family Court system with its legions of social workers, CAFCASS officers, incompetent Judges and flawed operation and to stop wronged parents from speaking out. The Children's Act of 1989 clearly intended that both parents should have an active part in their children's lives. 'Shared residence orders are likely to become the norm' they said, twenty-five years ago. As my friend Hilary has written in her piece in the appendix, many Family Court judges simply ignore the will of Parliament and 'don't do' shared residence orders, neither do they think that the Courts should be made more open. Considering their incompetence, it's not surprising. Justice must be seen to be done, otherwise there really is no justice.

Going back once more to the Courts allowing any new man/woman into the home of a child whilst excluding a natural parent. I'll quote Mark Harris one more time: 'In all practical terms, there is probably little that can be done' [to prevent any new lover entering the home of your children]. 'There is no realistic way to police just who a mother, or any parent, brings into their children's home. It simply cannot be done. You would have to post social workers outside the home of every single parent to check who's entering or leaving. So, the authorities simply accept the hugely increased risk of death or harm to the children posed by the parent's new lover, just as they accept that, statistically, the motor car will kill ten more people tomorrow, and every single day thereafter'.

HOWEVER - if the natural parent currently excluded from the children's lives was not excluded - those children, if they were being abused and harmed, would then have that parent to turn to for support and help. Knowing how much I was blinded by my passion for Shirley, I can clearly see that anyone could be in a state of denial over the abuse of children by a new lover. Who killed Baby Peter? The new lover, not the father.

'Contact orders' are routinely flouted, with no effective deterrent being applied by the Court. I have lost count of the times a shut-out parent has told me that time after time they have had to go back to Court to get the order for contact enforced, often with little success. Time after time I have been told that a Judge has refused to take any action, especially over Mothers, as jailing the mother would 'harm the children'.
Yet they will jail a mother, or any parent, for keeping the child off school,

or for persistent shoplifting, or persistently driving a car whilst disqualified. They don't consider 'upsetting the children', then. Which is more important? They are equally important. They are COURT ORDERS. I never received the fourth report about Heather from Shirley. Shirley said Heather had 'begged her not to' send it. This was accepted without question by old Payne, but in law it was no excuse at all. So I would suggest that the Court upholds its own rules, the rules of the land.

P.A. can mean two things in the Family Court - Parental Alienation and Professional Arrogance. They are both rife, but neither are recognised in law in this country. I'll concentrate briefly, again, on Parental Alienation. Parental Alienation is when one parent (always the resident parent) alienates a child against the estranged parent, and encourages that child to say that he/she does not wish to see him or her anymore. Mothers and fathers can be equally vindictive, and I have seen two cases where the mother has been subject to this, with devastating effect. Some people call it a 'syndrome' but I think it's just plain evil. To manipulate a child against one parent and one set of grandparents for personal convenience should be recognised in these courts, and when proved should result in the perpetrator serving a prison sentence. The long-term harm to the child and to the affected parent can be permanent, and the damage caused, irreparable.

There is so much wrong with the operation of the Family Courts in this country that my suggested changes will be seen as simplistic, but others far more qualified than I have gone into the minutiae of changing family law, so I will leave it there. As it is, I believe the Family Courts are a disgrace to the country that permits them to operate as they currently do, and a reflection on the mentality of many of those who work within them. I would go further, and suggest that anyone who wilfully prevents a parent who has done no harm to their child or children, from seeing them - be they the other parent, or a Judge, or CAFCASS officer, or social worker - belongs to a new type of underclass. Not in terms of wealth or standing, of course, but in terms of the most basic tenets of humanity. J'accuse. J'ACCUSE!

'You're obliged to pretend respect for people and institutions you think absurd. You live attached in a cowardly fashion to moral and social conventions you despise, condemn, and know lack all foundation. It is that permanent contradiction between your ideas and desires and all the dead formalities and vain pretences of your civilization which makes you sad, troubled and unbalanced. In that intolerable conflict you lose all joy of life and all feeling of personality, because at every moment they suppress and restrain and check the free play of your powers. That's the poisoned and

mortal wound of the civilized world'.

Octave Mirbeau 'The Torture Garden' - as found on the sleeve of the
Manic Street Preachers album 'The Holy Bible'.

AFTERMATH

I've been walking through the fields and on the streets of town
Trying to make sense of what you left me
Everything that I believed in has been turned upside down
And now it seems the whole wide world's gone crazy. . . . . .
When I feel like giving up and there's nowhere left to go,
That's the time I dig down deep, it's the only thing I know. . . . .
Do something! Do something!
Don't leave it up to someone else
And don't feel sorry for yourself. . . . .
Run away? You can't run away.
On your honour, for your pride
You'll sleep better knowing you tried (to)
Do something! Do something!
It's too easy not to care
And you're not ready for the rocking chair. . . . .
Don't wait too long, even if it's wrong
You've got to do something! Do something!
It's not over.
No, it's never too late.

Extracts from 'Do Something' by The Eagles, from the album 'Long Road out of Eden'.

Well before the final Hearing, I realised I was on a hiding to nowhere. I felt helpless, a victim even, and I had never before felt a victim to anything except my own naivety and stupidity. I became determined to try and help change things. First, I joined Fathers 4 Justice. I was attracted to their blend of campaigning, humour, non-violent civil disobedience and the fact that nearly one-third of their membership were women. I also liked the fact that they were 'Fathers for Justice' rather than simply 'Justice for fathers'. I quickly learned that my case was pretty small beer compared to others.

I joined at the end of 2004, just under three years after it was founded by Matt O'Connor. Actually the movement itself was NOT founded by Matt but by Mark Harris, who founded DADS - Dads Against Discrimination - in 2000. I would like to make sure that Mark is properly recognised for this, as it is seldom mentioned these days. Matt, far more savvy as regards publicity, thought up the name Fathers 4 Justice and Mark was quite happy for his group to be merged with the new one. DADS was, I believe, the first true campaigning movement for fathers post-feminism. Under Matt's guidance, Fathers 4 Justice became one of the most effective campaigning groups of our age. Anyone who lived through the first ten years of this century cannot fail to have heard of it, and more importantly, be aware of why it was such a success and why some of its members went to such extreme lengths to gain publicity. For me, virtually gagged and blindfolded by Shirley for so many years, unable to express my love for my daughter, and now being gagged by an arsehole Judge - sorry - the sense of liberation was really something else. I wanted to shout from the rooftops, and here was the very vehicle to do just that!

In 2004, Fathers 4 Justice were very much in the limelight. Jolly Stanesby had done a number of high-profile demos including on Tower Bridge in London and on the Royal Courts of Justice and St. Paul's Cathedral, and Tony Blair had been flourbombed in the House of Commons by protestors 'Big Ron' Davis and Guy Harrison, which really brought the group to media attention. They made the 'bombs' from self-raising flour, purple icing colourant and purple glitter, wrapped-up in condoms. I understand that Mates condoms were trialled initially but wouldn't burst on impact, so they tried Boots, Durex, and others, none of which split on impact (unlike sometimes, allegedly, in other situations!). Someone then thought of cutting into the condoms a bit, which then yielded the desired result of a powder puff of purple haze.

Guy was a wealthy man - a millionaire - and had won an auction bid for lunch with Baroness Goulding, a Labour peer. This included a chance to watch Prime Minister's Question Time from the VIP's gallery which did not have the glass panelling protecting M.P.s from the Plebs. Guy was an excellent sportsman, having gone to Public School, and could throw accurately. Ron was delegated the job of hanging an F4J banner off the edge of the gallery, but unfortunately hung the banner upside down so no-one could read it! However, the demo was a great success and the Speaker, Michael Martin ('Gorbals Mick') had to suspend the House.

This was quickly followed by a protest at York Minster during a meeting of the General Synod (the Church's governing body). The Church had (and still has) a feeble voice on the matter of family breakdown, and the shutting out of fathers from their children's lives. The last time it was debated was in 1992....

I love York Minster. It's an inspiring building and its beauty is awesome. But it's spoilt, for me, by the sound of cash-machines reverberating down the cloisters. You have to pay to get in. If Jesus was here today, he'd overthrow the lot of them. Matt O'Connor felt the same. 'In the name of the

Father, my arse' he said. 'In the name of the checkout, more like it. It's a f*****g theme park for counterfeit Christianity. They should stick a cashpoint in the pulpit and a bank sign above the main doors'. Matt gives details of the protest, and many others, in his book 'Fathers 4 Justice', but after being thrown out of the Minster he was invited back in to put his - our - point of view, by the then Archbishop, David Hope. Other activists, including our friend Jolly, had got through and formed an ecumenical shield in front of the altar and had refused to leave until Matt was allowed to give a sermon from the pulpit. It must have been amusing to see these activists, usually clad in lycra, dressed as a monk, a cardinal, two priests and a pope. I have to repeat this bit of Matt's sermon. 'The Archbishop of Canterbury is the Arthur Daley of the Christian World' he said. 'He flogs you this thing called marriage, but a few years later, if it breaks down, there is no roadside recovery and no after-sales service.' After finishing he asked to be forgiven for disrupting the service but why, he asked, should it be necessary for us to go to such extremes to raise the issue of family breakdown and of fatherlessness? A question that remains unanswered to this day. I think it's telling that the congregation broke into a round of applause after this.

In September a man called David Chick climbed a crane by Tower Bridge. He was a humble working man who had been treated abominably by his ex-partner and then by CAFCASS and the Family Courts, spending thousands of pounds in a futile effort to see his only daughter. Unlike me, he had been at her birth, and like me he loved and deeply cared for his 'little angel' as he described her. He was not a member of Fathers 4 Justice and had a deep dislike and was suspicious of Matt O'Connor, whom he regarded as solely a publicity-seeker. David was up there out of desperation.

Totally unnecessarily, the Metropolitan Police closed Tower Bridge to traffic, causing huge congestion and tailbacks of up to ten miles. The Police wanted to blame Dave Chick for all this, but it didn't work. When they took him to Court (open Court!) he was found not guilty. The police kept the road closed simply as a tactic to discredit Chick, and bring disrepute on the cause he was championing, and the police logs proved it. Later, Chick was awarded second place in the Evening Standard's 'Personality of the Year' poll in 2003, well ahead of Ken Livingstone who made some pretty dumb personal comments about David Chick. Just occasionally, there are some sweet moments amongst the dross.

Immediately after this came the *piece de resistance* of all protests. Jason Hatch managed to scale Buckingham Palace. It was an act of extreme bravery and audaciousness, or foolhardiness and stupidity, depending on your point of view. But by God it got the publicity. Everyone, but everyone, now learned of the desperation of parents who were forbidden to see their own flesh-and-blood. People now know about the secrecy and injustice of the Family Courts and many more have been emboldened to speak out about it.

It was against this background of audacious but peaceful and humorous protest that I joined F4J. I attended two protest marches, both held in London. They were both simply marches; the first from Green Park to the Royal Courts of Justice, via Piccadilly, Trafalgar Square, and The Strand. As I had been treated fairly at the High Court, I couldn't join in the chorus of 'Shame on You!' directed by the marchers at the Court. The last one, just before Christmas, started at Westminster and ended at St. Paul's Cathedral. This one coincided with the last day of operation of the famous Routemaster buses. I was heartened by the support of tourists and shoppers all along the route. They were sunny days and I suddenly realised it was forty-five years since I had last joined a protest gathering, against the threat of an airport at Wing.

In January 2006 I read, in a small article in the Daily Mail, that Matt O'Connor had disbanded Fathers 4 Justice. This was corroborated by a BBC News item later that evening. Apparently some of our members, after that last march, had been overheard by an undercover officer who'd mingled with the group in a pub. He then, allegedly, tipped off the Sun newspaper, telling a reporter that we were plotting to kidnap Tony and Cherie Blair's youngest son, Leo. We were in the business of uniting kids with their dads, not kidnapping them, and immediately smelt a rat. As an organisation we were deeply disliked by many in the Establishment and this was just the sort of dirty trick some would pull to smear us. The Blairs would not have allowed any information like this to have been made public, neither would the police have released such information if they were investigating such a serious matter. In fact, it was Tony Booth, Cherie's dad, who wrote a letter to the Guardian newspaper, berating the Sun - not F4J - for running this ridiculous story. He wrote:

'As Leo Blair's grandfather, I find it utterly unbelievable, actually unforgivable, that the *Sun* newspaper would endanger the personal safety of my five-year-old grandson by not only publishing details of the alleged kidnap plot, but also splashing this little boy's photograph across its front pages. There can be no excuse for this action.

I recall, at the end of last year, the discretion exercised by that same newspaper over the contretemps between its editor, Rebekah Wade, and her partner, Ross Kemp. Then, the only issue was of the personal dignity of a pair of adults, not the personal security of an innocent child. Shame on you Wade and your unthinking cohorts'.

I wonder whether Mr. Booth suspected, along with some of us, that the Blairs were complicit in this matter? Surely they would not expose their youngest son simply to pay us back for the flourbombing incident? We'll never know, but I'm somewhat bemused that a D-notice hadn't been slapped on it (a D-notice forbids the press to report or comment on something sensitive. B.liar had used such a D-notice before with regard to his private family matters). Matt had had enough. I had little idea of the nastiness he had already endured and felt no sympathy. I had shelled-out £30 for my membership and had received one newsletter and had no consultation over F4J's demise. It seemed an autocratic way of going about things. Shortly before this I had made an appointment to see Matt at his Suffolk home to talk to him about doing protests, an hour-and-a-half's drive away from me, only to discover he wasn't there. His secretary, Jenny, was most apologetic but didn't know where he was. I couldn't contact him by phone, and I wasn't impressed.

Not being a part of Matt's circle, I didn't know anything about the internal politics and discord that had begun to manifest itself within the organisation. I hadn't been a member long enough to get to know the activists and become one myself. I felt betrayed personally, but this was the year I finally lost my case at Oxford and I don't remember much more about this time.

Postscript. Since writing this I have heard 'from a reliable source' that it might have been Matt himself who orchestrated this. I was told that he'd received an ultimatum from his new and pregnant wife along the lines of 'it's F4J or me'. I don't know whether it's true or not, but nothing, now, would surprise me.

My step-grandson Ben, dog Pipsqueak, and me.
This photo appeared on the back of the campaign bus during my election
campaign.

NORCAP - MORE CRAP.

I mentioned earlier that Shirley had encouraged me to join Norcap, which helped people who had been adopted find their birth parents. I also mentioned that when I did, a lovely lady called Linda Savell still ran the charity. I mentioned, too, that Shirley worked there, manning the telephone line. Shirley kept her job when Linda Savell was ousted and a new 'CEO' was appointed, Pam Hodgkins MBE. The charity rapidly changed its status as a small, personal outfit to a more amorphous, businesslike operation. It started to produce a glossy, 'professional' magazine rather than a printed sheet or two, and seemed much more concerned about its 'image' than having a rapport with its members. Politically-correct measures were introduced, wasting money on first a 'smoking room' then a ban on smoking altogether in the offices shortly after the 'smoking room' was introduced. This did not go down well with Shirley's neighbour who worked there and smoked like a chimney, and neither did it with me: I thought our subscription monies were being wasted on this needless frippery. Smokers now were allowed time off to smoke outside the building; non-smokers of course, weren't.

Showy things were introduced, such as services for 'Truth, Reconciliation and Hope' which are fine if done sincerely but I began to feel that it was more to burnish the credentials of Norcap and of Pam Hodgkins MBE than to offer any real comfort to those affected by adoption. However, they did still adhere to the original concept of uniting birth parents with their offspring and vice-versa.

Sometime before the last 'Hearing' in Oxford, I attended one of these services of 'Truth, Reconciliation and Hope', feeling somewhat in need of all three. It was held in Aylesbury Parish Church one Saturday afternoon. NORCAP knew I was coming, as I'd applied for a ticket and been granted one. Shirley was there with her new - or not-so-new - beau. I didn't know how he'd got to be there, he wasn't a member. . . .they sat at the front, I sat towards the back amongst people some of whom were obviously very emotionally troubled.

Throughout the service, Len and Shirley were giggling, not joining in the service at all, pawing and fawning over each other, presumably for my benefit. I found it distasteful and was immensely heartened when the lady sat next to me commented on them saying she was offended and remarking that they should be 'removed'. 'Who are they?' she asked me. 'Norcap staff' I said; 'Quite nauseating isn't it?' 'If that's true, I'm leaving Norcap'

195

she said. 'It is true' I said, 'You've heard of New Labour - this is New Norcap!'. That raised a watery smile and she and I had a very pleasant chat outside the church afterwards. There were 'guest speakers', one of whom was Lord Filkin, Children's Minister, who arrived late. As I'd listened to Bob Geldof telling this man to 'eff off' on T.V. not long before, due to some inane remark he'd made about fathers, I was not impressed with the choice of this 'guest speaker'.

The service, whilst sympathetic and emotive enough, was ruined for me (as I think it was meant to be) by Len and Shirley and obviously spoilt for others as well. It was incredibly crass and insensitive of them to behave in that way. I felt like going up to them afterwards and saying in a very loud voice 'How's Heather? You know, my daughter?' There's still a bit of me that regrets not having the balls to do it. But two wrongs do not make a right.

For a while before this, I had stopped receiving Newsletters from NORCAP (though I was still a fully paid-up member). I wrote to Madam Hodgkins but received no reply. I wrote to a Mandy d'Souza (on the office payroll) and got no reply. I wrote to a trustee and got no reply. So I turned to my local representative and she kindly agreed to have lunch with me whilst I told her the whole saga. She was kindness itself and promised she'd get me all the Newsletters I'd missed. I understand she made herself pretty unpopular at 'The Coven' as I called it, but she succeeded in getting me the Newsletters. She'd been a staunch member of Norcap since the very start and I know it was difficult for her to cross the new regime (which she also had reservations about) so I remain very grateful indeed to her for her sterling efforts. She was also an immense help to me over my High Court case.

After the service for 'truth, reconciliation and hope', I went through a very dark period. I'd never had clinical depression before and I never want to have it again. I could keep working but I was not myself at all. I couldn't shake it off and it got worse.

For some reason Rosa was away for a while during this, and I tried to end it all. I've no wish to dwell on it, but I was rescued by a friend (by sheer chance) who I'd introduced to NORCAP a year or so before. He'd been adopted too, (and went to private school and drove coaches!) and had wanted to find his birth family, so I had suggested he joined the organisation. He was successfully re-united with them and he and I were good mates. He saved my life and at the time I was not at all grateful! He was so shocked that he wrote to Mrs. Hodgkins telling her what had happened and why. He got a very sniffy reply from her saying that if he wanted to help, he should renew his membership! Needless to say, he did not.

I'm so lucky I'm not a depressive person and I quickly recovered after this. Just as well, as I lost all hope of contact at the final 'Hearing' shortly afterwards. I also received strong support from my birth family and from Rosa at this time. But not from NORCAP. They'd hoped I'd just go away, I was an embarrassment and of course Shirley was a personal friend of Mrs. Hodgkins. As often happens, Hodgkins covered up her embarrassment with aggression towards me. I received several dismissive and frankly nasty letters, and of course no newsletters. I retained my cool and always wrote plainly but with courtesy. Eventually, my local representative gained me the Newsletters I was due but then I was refused a renewal of my membership because I had spoken to her about my case which of course involved a child.

'Norcap specifically does not involve children'. The hypocrisy of it, when Hodgkins had taken time off to accompany Heather to the Court! Don't tell me that no-one else knew! I wrote her a final letter saying that she had encouraged my daughter to hate, rather than to love, that she had increased Heather's natural prejudices and fears about me rather than try to alleviate them, and that it was disgraceful that she had been in such a rush to get me into Court that she had pushed Heather into it with no legal representation which was her right, and free. How did she square this with her role of CEO of a charity which was set up to reunite people with their families? I never received a reply to this, of course.

It was with a degree of satisfaction that I saw NORCAP's office in Wheatley empty and up for sale early in 2013. A quick look on the internet confirmed that it had 'ceased trading'. Trading in what? Misery? Children? Forgive my sarcasm.

I later learned that my local representative had left well before this as she could see the way things were heading, with la Hodgkins refusing to listen. No change there, then. Hodgkins moved (with her family, apparently - lucky her) to Canada not long after the demise of Norcap, so she's well out of it now. Like so many of her arrogant ilk, she supped her honey and then she moved on.

I don't like these 'professional' charities. They're not like the charities we used to know. They receive government grants and have legions of Directors and Chief Executive Officers all on fat salaries and acting in some cases like politicians. The RSPCA, NSPCC (have you seen their offices in London? They must cost a fortune to run), Save the Children. . . .all more like businesses or political institutions than charities. Save the Children recently awarded Tony Blair a prestigious award for his 'helping children' - NURSE!!

The RSPB (Royal Society for the Protection of Birds) is another one that acts more like a political business than a charity. Pigeons are sometimes the bane of our lives here at the Nursery but we rescued some chicks that had lost their mother to a cat. We went over to Sandy (where the RSPB headquarters are) to ask their advice on feeding the fledglings. They refused to give any as the birds are 'common pests'. So its only protection for 'approved' birds now, is it? Have they forgotten that a pigeon received the Dickin Medal in the last war, for service to humanity?

I would advise people give their money to small, local charities where volunteers run things and then you know your money will go to helping animals or children or whatever. And not to help line the pockets of people who are already so rich they cannot possibly know what to do with their money, and make them a little richer still. If you start receiving money from the Government, you're going to be tied-up with politics. You're not going to be truly independent anymore. Which is why I now regard the long-established charity 'Families Need Fathers' with some reservations despite their record of excellent pastoral work. They've taken Parliament's shilling. F4J would never have got a grant! But which organisation has more influenced public opinion and done the most to bring the issue of fatherlessness to the public's (and Government's) attention?   I view Government grants to charities as hostages to fortune, and no more.

Just one, quick example. An animal charity in Norfolk called Hillside Animal Sanctuary (Patron the excellent Martin Shaw) has often sent undercover camera teams into factory farms and even RSPCA-accredited 'Freedom Food' farms to show truly appalling examples of animal cruelty and neglect. The RSPCA don't like it - they usually let the farmer carry on as before. Yet the RSPCA get loads of Government money; Hillside gets none. I'll leave the reader to work it out.

HITTING THE ROOF

You've got the words to change a nation but you're biting your tongue
You've spent a lifetime stuck in silence afraid you'll say something wrong
If no-one ever hears it, how we gonna hear your song?
So come on, come on - come on, come on.. . . . .

At night we're waking up the neighbours while we sing away the blues
Making sure that we remember yeah, 'cos we all matter too
If the truth has been forbidden, then we're breaking all the rules
So come on, come on - come on, come on!

I want to sing, I want to shout,
I want to scream till the words dry out
So put it in all of the papers, I'm not afraid
You can read all about it, read all about it!

Excerpts from 'Read All About It' co-written and sung by Emile Sande,
from her album 'Our Version of Events'.

I can't remember how I heard that Fathers 4 Justice were re-forming.
Certainly Matt O'Connor didn't tell me. We were to have a meeting in a
Travelodge at Reading Services on the M.4 if I remember rightly. It was in
August 2007 and unfortunately I was on holiday with Rosa in our
ginormous old motorhome the week it was held. I had to get a train from
Taunton early one morning and give up a day of our week's break. I didn't
mind really, I was delighted that the group were going to be a force for
fathers again, but I was miffed that it turned out to be the only really fine
day that week!

To be honest I was disappointed with the meeting. Matt showed us all a
load of slides of past protests, of past glories, and I felt that we should be
concentrating on doing new stuff. A number of ideas were mooted but there
was nothing really new. However, I was offered a lift back to Taunton with
Richard Adams, a long-time member of F4J who was to play a crucial role
in some of my protests. We talked a lot on the journey and found
considerable rapport.

The next meeting was at the 'Slug and Lettuce' pub in Winchester. We
were to do a demo at Seend in Wiltshire, home to the then head honcho of
the Family Division in the High Court, Lord Justice Thorpe. He had

described Mark Harris' case as 'simply another contact dispute' and, like all the other 'top men' was in denial that anything might be wrong with the Family Court system. We were all to wear monkey suits, and for the life of me I can't remember why now!

A couple of weeks later I rolled down in the motorhome to Wiltshire, and joined around two dozen protestors in a good-humoured demonstration outside Thorpe's palatial residence. He'd got wind of our demo and predictably had 'left the building' the day before. There was a heavy police presence but a couple of chaps managed to get into Thorpe's garden and, I believe, peed on his lawn. 'Well', one of the lads said to me later 'he p****s all over dads in his f*****g Court, so why not?' I hated the monkey suit and put the head bit on wrongly so I couldn't see anything at all, then couldn't get the bloody thing off. Struggling with the damn thing, I walked slap bang into a police car, much to the driver's amusement. He kindly relieved me of my headgear.

Fathers 4 Justice Christmas demo in London, 2005

Next, was a trial at the Magistrates Court in Salisbury. Jolly Stanesby and another member, Richard West, had scaled one of the stones at Stonehenge and put up a banner saying 'Take Family Courts out of the Stone Age' and Natural England had pressed charges for trespass and damage to the Stones. The first charge was justified, the second was nonsense - they had gone to great lengths not to damage anything. We went to support the lads in Court and dressed appropriately in 'period costume' - I was Captain Caveman.

The barrister for Natural England was a pretty young woman with absolutely no sense of humour at all, and she looked daggers at me when I sat on a whoopee cushion just as the proceedings started (placed hurriedly by another observer who shall remain nameless). She was almost theatrically aggressive, pointing her finger at the two miscreants and feigning (I think) utter outrage at their misdemeanours. Jolly and Richard were found guilty and were fined.

Then (though I may not have got this in correct chronological order) Jolly and Jason Hatch were in Court again, this time in Manchester, after making a citizens arrest of the then Children's Minister Margaret Hodge, Jolly handcuffing himself to her with a pair of Ann Summers finest furry handcuffs. I could only attend the first day of the hearing, and initially we were not allowed into the Courtroom. In the afternoon, the Judge relented and we were allowed in.

Margaret Hodge had been leader of Camden Council in London when there was a lot of child abuse happening in children's homes there but she had been in denial about it. Now she is contrite and saying 'she didn't know' about it. When one lad who had been abused spoke out, she rubbished him in the press and had to pay him damages. She had also said in the past, along with Harriet Harman, that fathers were not necessary in the bringing-up of children. (Except, presumably, as cash-points). So it was felt that she was a legitimate target. She lost the action and Jason and Jolly walked free. This was, of course, trial by jury. If it had been in the secret Family Courts, they might well have gone to prison.

Next up, Jolly and Mark Harris scaled the roof of Harriet Harman's house, hanging a huge banner from the chimney 'A Father is for Life, not just Conception'. I thought this so good, I vowed to use it on my demos. I got an urgent call from Matt one glorious morning asking me to get down to South London as soon as I could, and I made it just as Harman decided to leave for another venue 'to spare my neighbours'. I spoke to one or two of her neighbours, who seemed very pleased to see her go! As I mentioned this demo earlier, I shall just refer to Jack Dromey's (Harriet's husband) comment that he felt threatened by the protesters. This way the man who played a large part in the ugly Grunwick dispute in the seventies, which I remember well, where a number of people including police got seriously knocked-about. Later, when our Harriet was campaigning for all-women shortlists in Labour constituencies, Jack Dromey was parachuted into a safe West Midlands constituency. Don't we just love a bit of hypocrisy.

A few days later, another couple of protesters got on her roof again, rather embarrassing the 'tightened security' in force at the time.

As far as I'm aware, no large-scale protest occurred between this and the next meeting, held in late autumn at the Reading venue. This was the last one I attended. To me, it seemed the 'same old, same old', but I was immensely lucky to meet George Standen at this meeting and agreed to support him in his own battle with Christ Church in Oxford. He has since helped me far more than I have been able to help him.

I think it was after this that a number of F4J protesters disrupted a National Lottery Show, leading to the suspension of transmission for a while. An effective demo, much more entertaining than the show itself! Certainly it was a lottery, going into the Family Courts.

That winter Matt disbanded F4J again, and I lost patience. Again, there was no notice to us members, we heard about it in the press. He would not entertain even letting others who wanted to keep the campaign going, keep the name. I asked to meet him when he was in London, and we did meet, at a café in Waterloo Station one soggy evening. I pleaded with him to let someone else take over and keep the name alive - it was so well-known. But though he said that someone should 'step up to the plate' he was taking the plate away! I couldn't fathom why he wanted to keep the name as 'personal property' yet was urging others to take up the cause. No-one else could use the name because he'd registered it at Companies House, I understand.

He seemed bitter and disillusioned and yet obstinate and defensive. I told him I would plead on bended knee if he would relent and the F4J name continue but he said 'it's dead - finished'. I left with nothing but an uneasy feeling that he wasn't being totally straight with me. My instincts are often correct, and they were on this occasion, though it took a while for this to become obvious. At least I got a large glass of wine out of him! I felt he loved having all the kudos of being top man of Fathers 4 Justice, even a defunct Fathers 4 Justice, rather more than continuing to try and help those trapped in the Family Court shambollocks.

Very quickly, like a phoenix rising from the ashes, two organisations formed - Real Fathers for Justice and New Fathers 4 Justice. I couldn't be enthusiastic about this development. 'Divide and Rule' and all that. Both these organisations were formed by ex-F4J members who were determined to carry on the fight. 'Real' was largely based in the North, and 'New' was largely based in the South of the Country. Despite my reservations I joined 'New', mainly because membership was free! Although we had the ideal that there was no committee, no rules, and no leader as such, the founder was Nigel Ace, who had been a prominent activist in F4J, and he effectively became a leader of the group, with Richard Adams doing the publicity. We also had Mark Harris amongst our number. 'Real' was a more formal organisation, with a committee and rather strict parameters, I have to admit it's probably easier to do things that way but personally I preferred our approach.

However, I did my first demo off my own bat, with one friend accompanying me. I was 'testing the water' a little, and the event was fairly low-key. We stationed ourselves outside the Court in Oxford and unfurled a few banners, including a huge one with 'A father is for life. . . .' etc. on it. The Oxford Mail came down and we got a little press and a nice photograph in it. We also were able to talk to anyone who wanted to find out why we were there, which you can't do so well bellowing from a rooftop! This happened in February 2009. I wore a Court Jester outfit. I felt uneasy about wearing a 'Superhero' get-up as I could not ever call myself a Superhero after so many years of being so blind and so stupid. A Court Jester seemed perfect.

The first new Fathers 4 Justice demo I attended was in Southampton, and I was amazed at the public support we received. The police just stood aside and let us do it, even when Mark Harris burned some of his court papers in the street. We seemed still to largely be carrying public opinion with us.

By now I was talking to Nigel Ace on a regular basis, discussing with him about a rooftop demo in Oxford. He wanted to see Oxford and the possible venues for himself, and around Easter-time we met up and took the opportunity to leaflet several churches along the lines of the 'crucifixion' of fathers in the Family Courts. We climbed the Carfax Tower, a significant landmark in the centre of the City from where you have magnificent views all around. We looked around and then looked at each other. 'This is the perfect place' Nigel said. Looking down the length of the High Street, with the open-topped tourist buses passing underneath and approaching up the High Street (or 'The High' as it's known) I agreed that it was a 'no-brainer'. We would just have to pay our admission (£2 if I remember rightly) and climb up the stairs, no ladder required!

We consulted with other members (one of whom came from the South Coast, and Nigel came from the other side of Bristol) and agreed a date for my first 'proper' demo - Thursday June 18th., 2009. I was sixty years of age.

The night before, I prepared my rucksack with the essentials - a megaphone, an umbrella, sandwiches, chocolate, leaflets, and my jester's hat. I didn't need the entire jester's costume as my torso would be hidden by the retaining wall; the Carfax Tower is the only remaining bit of a church still standing there. I confirmed the arrangements with everyone including George Standen, who was to notify the local press and T.V. as soon as we were in place. I went to bed praying for a fine day on the morrow; and my prayers were granted.

I rose early to a pristine dawn. I put several bottles of beer (and an opener!) and a freeze-pack in the rucksack, collected the rolled-up banners, and got into my 1988 Ford Orion Diesel, started her up, and thought - s**t, I've forgotten my mobile! Rather important, as I was to telephone George from the Tower. Then I was off, getting ever more nervous as I approached Oxford. Parking expensively in the Westgate Car Park, I met up with the other lads and went for a breakfast before the Tower opened to the public.

Then back to the cars, and Peter Smith, Nigel and I got our stuff ready. In an elementary misjudgement, I had failed to realise how much room the rolled-up banners would need and we had to leave one of them behind. I had done four - the big 'A Father is for Life. . . .' one, and three others which were to hang vertically. One said 'Heather' the next 'my love for you' and the third 'is unconditional'. I reluctantly had to leave the 'unconditional' one behind but as the photos show, it didn't matter too much. We rolled-up the other banners and secured them to the back of our rucksacks, so they looked rather like rolled-up sleeping bags. We could have been tourists on a round-Britain walk. We nonchalantly walked in to the entrance to purchase our tickets, and no-one batted an eyelid. I say 'we walked in nonchalantly' but I was shaking like a leaf. This demo was very low risk compared to others, but it was my first one and I didn't know what to expect.

It's quite a climb to the top! You ascend via a twisting staircase, and it goes up and up and up, very steeply. The rucksacks weighed heavy and it was very narrow in places and they were bulky, so we had to ascend carefully. It was quite a relief to emerge into the sunlight. Nigel wasn't going to stay with us, he was organising the ground support but he gave Peter and I instructions not to do anything but admire the view until the boys were ready down below. He would ring me when they were ready. It seemed an age before he rang, but there is no time-limit on the ticket and it gave me plenty of time to ring George and tell him we were up, and indeed to admire the view.

Eventually I got the call from Nigel. Peter and I dropped the largest banner over the railings and secured it with the rope already threaded through the eyelets. Then I donned my jester's hat and we dropped the other banners (actually carpet runners I'd bought from B&Q) each side of the main one. Thumbs-up from Nigel, and the ground crew erected their posters and banners right on the corner of the High Street and Cornmarket, where no-one could miss them. Shortly, the young guy who manned the ticket office below came up and simply asked how long did we intend to stay. I told him 'until the press and T.V. have covered the event', and apologised for being a pain in the backside but we didn't want to prevent people from visiting the Tower. 'I'll send the police up, then' he said. He was so relaxed about us being there, I think we enlivened his day a little.

High level, high profile protest on the Carfax Tower in Oxford June 2009.

Pete Smith and myself in defiant mood on the top of the Tower.

A very out-of-breath officer then appeared, followed by several others, saying 'bloody hell, it's a climb up here alright!' and proffered his hand. I was so relieved I shook his warmly. 'I'm a dad' he said 'There are times I wish I wasn't! But I do understand you guys. You seem a reasonable bloke, can we come to an agreement?' I said I'm sure we could, and we had no intention of keeping people off the Tower. 'I'm afraid we can't allow anyone up whilst you're here' he said 'And the owners are concerned that you're losing them money. I'm going to have to speak to my superiors, but I'll come back and tell you what we propose'. I had thought that we were going to be arrested and led down so I was absolutely delighted that we could stay, at least for the time being. The officer (and I'm sorry I have forgotten his name) was as good as his word. A while later, he reappeared and seemed pleased to inform us that as we'd paid for our ticket and therefore weren't trespassing, we could stay as long as we wished until the Tower closed. We weren't even cautioned. Furthermore, the Tower was run by the same people who ran the open-topped tourist buses, and by this time they had got so much custom from people wishing to get a closer look at us from those buses that it I understand they overcame the losses sustained by the Tower being closed!

There were certainly crowds of people gawping up at us, and the lads by the crossroads were kept busy handing out leaflets and explaining to people what was going on. You could see us and our banners from all the way down the High Street. People offered money, motorists and some of the buses sounded their horns. Nigel was   ace (sorry Nigel) at using the megaphone, and I was interviewed by the Oxford papers. We achieved everything and more than we expected, and I felt such a sense of liberation 'playing to the gallery'.

At around two o'clock our police officer came to see us again and said that there were a group of children who had booked a visit to the Tower and would we come down, as we'd achieved what we wanted. A quick conflab with Nigel and we agreed; we had no wish to stop kids having an afternoon out. I said to the officer 'give us five minutes to pack up, and we'll be down'. We again shook hands and he went down to relay the information to the rather anxious teacher waiting at the bottom. As we'd packed up rather hastily, the banner that I had attached to my rucksack wasn't as neatly folded as it had been in the morning, and as I descended the narrowest part of the stairs it got caught between the two walls either side and I was left dangling in mid-air, completely helpless. Peter dissolved into laughter, as did our police officer who appeared below me to ascertain the cause of the delay. Peter freed me and we emerged from the Tower to cheers, handshakes and congratulations. What a day! My first 'proper' demo was,

I think, the most successful and the most enjoyable. I couldn't wait to do another.

Acknowledging the crowds at the end of the demo

I called in to see George on my way home. He was almost totally disabled so he couldn't come to the demo and was disappointed to have missed it, but full of enthusiasm and encouragement and eager to hear the details. I'd promised Nigel the use of the Ford Orion (he was car-less) and he drove it back to Bristol whilst I got the bus to Aylesbury where Rosa met me and drove me home.

We made the front page of the Oxford Mail the next day - brilliant! However, the accompanying headline was 'New F4J, same old costumes'. No they weren't - no-one had worn a jester's outfit with F4J before! The Oxford Times, a weekly paper, also gave us generous coverage under the headline 'Fathers take their protest on high - using stairs!' I liked that.

Nigel, Peter and I were soon busy planning our next stunt. This was to be a little more ambitious, scaling one of the towers of Clifton Suspension Bridge near Bristol. I went down before the planned day and Nigel and I did a recce. He showed me where we could get up but it would need meticulous preparation and be a very slick operation. One day in the height of summer, I motored down to Nigel's home in Clevedon and that evening had a superb meal in a pub with him. Then we got an early night as we had to be out of the house before dawn next day.

Nigel drove in my old car. He'd wanted to change the numberplate as the Bridge has cameras everywhere, but I said it would be better if we did it immediately before the operation in case we got stopped on the way. We approached the bridge from the south side and I noticed the arc of a blue flashing light swirling around in the pre- dawn mist by the bridge, just below our eye-line. 'Nigel' I hissed 'turn the lights off! There's something going on at the bridge'. He did so and we stopped in a gateway, getting out to obtain a better view. There was a police car parked just in front of the bridge. 'We'll go round to the other side' said Nigel. We drove round, which necessitates going almost into Bristol itself, then climbing up through Clifton. We approached the bridge, and there was a bright white light near it plus a lot of revolving blue ones. 'Turn round, turn round' I shouted 'there's police everywhere. It's crawling'.

The bridge is, unfortunately, used as a jumping-off place for suicidal people, and we assumed that this was the problem. But as we reversed and did a U, a pair of headlights left the bridge and followed us. 'Shit, we've been rumbled' said Nigel. 'Just drive normally' I suggested, 'we haven't actually done anything wrong'. 'Yet' he grinned. The car didn't have its blue light on so we kept going. 'Thank God you didn't alter the numberplate' I said. I assumed they were checking it out, though I don't think they had ANPR then. Then the blue light came on. We pulled over. 'Sorry gentlemen' said the affable officer. 'We had to check you out, we are expecting an incident on the bridge, but I see you're from Bedford so you're obviously not who we're looking for'. ''What sort of incident' asked Nigel. 'I can't divulge that, and we have to get back' he said 'Sorry for the inconvenience'. And with that he roared off.

We looked at each other and both went 'phew!' The officer hadn't seemed to notice the coils of rope on the back seat, the rolled-up placards, the costumes. . . .thank God it was still dark! We had been due to pick up Peter, but he'd actually seen us being tailed and had returned to the pub he'd recently acquired, pronto. We met him there and calmed down whilst he got us a bite to eat and some coffee. Who had ratted on us? There was some rivalry between our groups and some characters put their own particular prejudices ahead of the larger picture and failed to see that we were stronger united than we were divided. It's sad, but Matt had had similar problems with F4J, even in its heyday. Then he went on to cause more.

We went back to Nigel's after, it was still early and we went via the bridge, which still had a police presence. I collected my car and decided to come back over it, I wanted a proper look. So I parked the car and walked over it. By now there was just one woman police officer stationed there. I telephoned Nigel and we did consider a second attempt, but we couldn't get hold of Peter. I said I'd do it on my own. 'Christ alive!' he said. 'No, it's too risky - the old bill will really be pissed-off that we've outwitted them, and it's daylight and the road's busy - forget it'. So I went home, but at least we'd given it our best shot.

I know that quite a number of people will think this sort of demonstration is reprehensible or pointless, or even pathetic. My view is that anything that brings the current system of the 'Family' Courts to the attention of the public is good, as long as the protest does not damage property or cause any other harm. Inconvenience to people is inevitable. Father's demos have most certainly highlighted the heartbreaking failures of these courts more than any other medium, so I reckon they can be considered a success. And we felt we had nowhere else to go - the 'official' routes and diplomatic approaches had all failed. They had yielded nothing. If it hadn't been for the publicity surrounding F4J I would have felt I had nowhere to go for support. I hadn't even heard of Families Need Fathers. And I did want to protest!

Matt O'Connor had originally prophesied that Fathers 4 Justice would change Family Law within three years. This was akin to John Reid saying that we would be in and out of Helmand Province 'without a shot being fired'. It was unwise to have said it as it instilled false hope in people and I'm sure contributed to Matt's own disillusionment. And he had a tendency to be a bit arrogant about it. When Pam Wilson approached him seeking support and co-operation with her Grandparents Action Group, he rather airily dismissed it as a 'piddling little group', saying they should join F4J as they were the only group who were strong enough to change things. I always find a kind and sympathetic approach works better than that. And we all shared a common goal. Matt thrived on confrontation, and that was so needed with the bovine complacency of officialdom, but he should have reserved his ire for that, not used it against people working in their own way for the same ends. Both New F4J and Real Fathers for Justice (RFFJ) had a dose of his approbation. Would you believe, around his time, Matt formed F4J all over again? No wonder he was so adamant that he wouldn't pass on the name. Had he planned this all the time?

Mark Harris commented that Matt's departure was 'The Long Goodbye', but he hadn't actually said goodbye! Here he was, popping up yet again.

Both New F4J and RFFJ continued to use very similar posters, stickers etc. so people knew exactly who we were and Matt (or it may even have been a solicitor) sent letters to the groups accusing them of plagiarism and of using registered logos. 'Divide and rule' again? He now titled his 'The official organisation for fathers'. 'Official'? Matt was certainly coming across as one! I think both groups simply ignored the letter, and we certainly ignored the warnings. As often with bully-boy tactics, it's the best way and the threats simply melted away.

I heard about this somewhat later, and I felt very angry about it. After all his insistencies that F4J was dead in the water, and his refusing our pleadings to keep and use the name, he starts it all up again and then accuses us of copying him! It seemed to us that he still wanted all the glory, and now disapproved of the actions that he'd previously trumpeted. I felt he was trying to destroy the movement and wrote to him 'Every movement has within it the seed of its own destruction. I never thought I would say it, but it seems to me that you are that seed'. It was a cruel thing to say, especially given Matt's previous dedication to the cause, but I felt it was true now and I was totally disillusioned with him. He made the father's movement a success, and then by saying he was walking away from it but then coming back, at least twice, he has done more to dilute the strength of it than anyone else. He has caused bitter division and intense disillusionment, with no real explanation, no apology, and threats of legal action. How sad.

I wanted to make a protest at Oxford Court again, and liaised with Nigel and a number of others, but we couldn't do it as a group until November 2009. In the meantime, one Saturday afternoon I went, armed with stickers, intent on covering the doors of the Court with them. The building seemed deserted, and I commenced my 'work'. Quite soon, there was a kerfuffle inside and, before I could sneak away the doors flew open and the security guard who'd taken my badge off me before, emerged red-faced and swearing. 'You f*****g idiot' he shouted at me 'You bloody lunatic!'. He looked and sounded rather preposterous, gesticulating wildly as he berated me in my jester's hat, and several people started to snigger. I said I'd go but he followed me, using the f word many times and getting ever more wound up, 'I've got to take all those f*****g things off now!' They were just small stickers saying 'trouble seeing your kids? Contact New Fathers 4 Justice' and gave the web address. They unpeeled easily. I think I interrupted his watching a football match on the telly. Later, I went back and stuck one in the middle of the centre doors, just because. Then I went off and stuck a few on a window of the Norcap office in Wheatley.

The demo at Oxford Court attracted quite a number of protesters, and we did it on the 9th November. The Court has a flat roof and we judged it OK for a demonstration and of course particularly for me. The problem was, getting up there. On each side of the main doors at the front are curved balconies, easy to get up on with a ladder, but the next level is much higher and really needed more room on the balcony to get an acceptable angle on the ladder. I'm not much good at heights but after a lot of deliberation, decided I would do it. What I hadn't reckoned on was how cumbersome a tall ladder was - how unstable it was when fully extended and how difficult it would be to extend it on a narrow ledge. And I was on my own. Sure, there were many supporters present but I was the only 'scaler' this time.

That morning, we again congregated in the Westgate car park very early and donned our costumes. A chap who lives near me, called Jim, who was with me on my very first demo outside the Court, put his Spiderman costume on inside-out and back-to-front, causing great hilarity and bemused looks from other people using the car park. Then he couldn't get out of it. I was told during this to 'get up there' anyway, and a chap called Christian who'd come all the way from South Wales helped carry the ladder and acted as look-out. As we reached the Court entrance we received word that Jim was still struggling with the costume - caught in a web of confusion, perhaps? I heard Nigel saying that 'we are dropping too many balls' and as I looked up at the sheer face of the building and across to the Police Station opposite I had to agree! It was about seven in the morning. Not many people were about, and I had donned a yellow jacket as a hasty 'disguise' as a workman. Christian and I got the ladder up against the balcony and I was up it like a rat up a drain. Then I pulled the ladder up onto the balcony and the banners I was going to use, with a rope thrown to me by Christian. I was surprised to see the 'floor' of the balcony covered with fag-ends. Where had they come from?

Now came the difficult bit. I couldn't extend the ladder, it had jammed and there was no room to put it down to un-jam it. As I wrestled with the thing I managed to extend it by several feet but it was the devil's job to keep it steady. I lost control of it and it crashed back onto the balustrade, protruding way over the edge. People were in the Court - I could see movement through the windows - but miraculously no-one heard the cacophony and no-one was looking out of the police station's widows either! It was a bit like a scene from 'Some Mothers do 'Av 'em'. I got the ladder upright again but then one of the windows opened and out stepped my old friend the security guard. 'You f*****g idiot! You barmpot!' he stormed. 'Get off here, now'. 'Yes, you've called me that before' I smiled 'and I'm not moving'. 'I'll call the police' he shouted. 'Please do' I said.

He got an attractive young lady to 'stand guard' who was very pleasant. 'We're worried that you'll fall off' she said. 'So am I! but I'm not that bothered. I've lost my only child through this Court and I don't much care'. 'We do' she said. 'It would be bad publicity'. The security man returned with an officer from just over the road, who was most pleasant. So was the security guard - quite obsequious in fact! I was amazed in his change of demeanour. 'You can't stay here' said the officer. 'If you don't come down, I'll have to arrest you and I really don't want to do that'. 'Do you insist?' I asked. 'Sorry, I do' he said. 'In that case, OK. I don't want to cause unnecessary trouble but we do want to make a protest'. 'Who's we' he said. I looked over the balcony - everyone had scarpered!

After having my ladder put into police custody for the rest of the day, along with the banners, I returned to the car park where all my colleagues were gathered. I received a loud cheer, which was very generous of them considering what a balls-up I'd made. We all decided to 'picket' the Court and there were enough of us to make an impressive noise. On our arrival, our friend came blustering out again but seemed a little intimidated by the numbers. He said we could do our protest outside the Court but we weren't to hang banners or anything on the walls, so we did.

We made the Oxford Mail again and we also made a lot of noise, so much so that the police sent out an officer to tell us that they enjoyed being entertained by us but the noise was a little excessive. We adjourned for lunch before going on to Witney to protest in the town centre. Witney of course is in David Cameron's constituency and his constituency office is there. There was quite a lot of interest in our demo here, and I was asked for an interview with a reporter from the local T.V. channel which duly appeared that evening. We quickly ran short of leaflets and a lady from the firm of Family Law Solicitors next to where we were loudly demonstrating offered to copy a load more for us, for free. I said to her that I thought we were on opposing sides, to which she replied that we weren't, not with her anyway. Sometimes you receive support from the most unlikely quarters and it is especially welcome then.

We all agreed that, despite my failure to get on the Court roof, it had been a worthwhile demonstration. I was amused to read in my own local paper the headline 'Drama as furious Dad is wrestled from Court roof', when I had gone very quietly!

As Christmas approached, we did a noisy but ground-based protest outside Canterbury Cathedral. The Church had turned its back on family breakdown under Rowan Williams, who seemed to be so anxious to be politically-correct but ignored the fracturing of society all around him. This too was a successful and noisy demo, and we got on the local T.V. there as well.

We had some extremely cold weather just before Christmas that year (2009). On the Saturday before Christmas Day, Rosa and I had arranged to start a petition for equal parenting outside the Carfax Tower. I had put a quarter-page advert in the Oxford Mail and into the Oxford Times saying I'd be there from ten o'clock. On the Friday evening it snowed heavily and the journey over to Oxford was pretty horrendous and we arrived late. I managed to park in a very narrow street close to the Tower to enable us to unload our gear - a folding table, leaflets and the petition. As we set up, several people approached including a family who had been treated with contempt by Judge Corrie in Oxford Family Court; I've mentioned Sam, who was allowed to see her eldest children for just the eighteen hours each year. Her extended family was with her, and they all signed. I think we got well over two hundred signatures that day, which I was well pleased with considering how bloody cold it was and people were racing around getting their Christmas shopping done. This petition, with hundreds more signatures, was duly presented to the Ministry of Justice in London at the time of the Family Justice Review.

Two events stand out especially from that day: the first is the young lad who was on duty the day we ascended the Tower, who kindly came out to us with hot coffee and biscuits and signed the petition; and a leader of one of Oxford's mosques who signed our petition because he detested the idea of Family Courts being held in secret. A cultured and amenable man, he spent some time chatting with Rosa and left me free to go and grab us something to eat. We didn't receive one negative comment throughout the day, even from one militant feminist who also signed the petition as it was for 'equality'. The weather may have been freezing, but we were heartened by the warmth of our reception in Oxford, again.

DON'T VOTE FOR ME!

Over the Christmas holiday period I was approached by Ray Barry, who had been an active participant in Fathers 4 Justice but had also, since then, helped form a political party, the 'Equal Parenting Alliance'. I thought that this was a fantastic way of spreading the word, particularly as, if you are a bona fide political candidate, you are entitled to get your leaflets delivered free through every door in the constituency you're campaigning in, courtesy of the Post Office. One chilly winter's day I motored up to Ray's house on the outskirts of Wolverhampton to meet him and the founder of the Party, Steve from Manchester. They outlined the principles of the Party and the procedures you had to go through, and sized me up at the same time. I was thrilled that they thought me a worthy candidate for the Party and I said I wanted to campaign in the Oxford East constituency, which was readily accepted. Now this was something else. I loved being the centre of attention, playing to the gallery on a roof, but I love even more talking with people and engaging in dialogue and argument, and as a political candidate I would be able to do this to my heart's content. Almost all forms of protest against injustice and of wrong are valid, but engaging with people directly is, for me, the very best.

I had no idea what running as a candidate entailed, but Ray and Steve quickly enlightened me as they had already done one campaign (in Scotland!) a year or so before. The General Election was due in May 2010 so we had, say, four months to prepare. And to save up - the deposit is £500 which you lose if you fail to receive at least 10% of the vote in your constituency. I had no illusions that I would retain my deposit! Also there were leaflets to design and pay for, and the campaign would need me to travel over to Oxford as many times as I could to attend the hustings; and I would have to go to Swindon to deliver the packaged leaflets for distribution well in advance of election day. I would have to do interviews, too, of course, so it meant a fair degree of commitment. Once Ray and Steve were satisfied that I could and would do the campaign, I was largely given a free reign to conduct 'my' campaign as I wanted and to design my own election pamphlets and posters. I relished the opportunity and will forever be grateful to Ray and to Steve for their encouragement and largesse.

There were to have been a number of other candidates in other constituencies but in the end, only Ray and myself campaigned. The others either had too many other commitments or couldn't afford the deposit or the costs of printing the leaflets. I was very lucky I still had a little money left from my mother's estate.

If you run a campaign such as this, there is a requirement that you engage an agent. George Standen was the obvious choice, and a role that he took on with alacrity. You also need several people to 'endorse' your candidature, who live in the constituency; George sorted these out for me.

I was interested in Ray Barry's story. Ray trained as a priest after leaving school, but decided that the priesthood was not for him and married and had three children. After his marriage dissolved, he had to fight in the Family Court in Walsall for access to his children. He found he had no support whatever from the Church, his priest merely saying 'these things happen'. He had no support from the Court, either. On 23rd. March 2001 Ray had the great misfortune to be landed with District Judge Hearne who, despite one of the children expressing the wish to live with his dad, took a coin from his pocket, tossed it, and asked the father to call. Ray lost the toss, so the children were sent to live with the mother. If there is one case that illustrates why the Family Courts should be made open, surely this is it. Something like this should never ever happen, and it would never have happened in open Court.

There was a period of limbo between agreeing to campaign and starting to campaign. I used the time to get some ideas together for the election leaflet and make sure I knew the procedure and liaise with George over his role. Ray had engaged the services of a printer he'd used for the Scottish campaign last time. We couldn't start campaigning until the election date was announced, but of course the major parties were gearing up for the fight. I think it was in the middle of March that Gordon Brown announced that the general election was to be held on the 10th. May 2010. We had about six weeks of campaigning.

First, I had to register as a bona fide candidate. One evening all the potential candidates were invited to Oxford City Hall to register and to hear the rules and regulations governing canvassing, etc. I was asked if 'my' party was really Fathers 4 Justice and I explained it was 'the political wing', which caused some amusement.

The first hustings I attended were at the Oxford East Community Centre in Cowley. There was a good attendance of a multi-cultural audience and lively debate. One of the advantages of campaigning for a single-issue party is that you can say 'sorry I haven't a clue' on, say, economic matters - and get away with it. I was introduced to the other candidates including Mr. Andrew Smith who was the sitting M.P. (Labour), the Liberal candidate, the Tory one, a far-left Socialist candidate, (I'm sorry, I am terrible at remembering names) the Green candidate Sushila Dahl and Julia Gasper who was representing UKIP. I was pleased that there was no animosity between any of the individuals and we all had a fair chance to speak with members of the audience. I instinctively knew I would enjoy campaigning in Oxford East. It's so diverse, including as it does most of the Universities, areas such as Headington, Shotover, Cowley and Rose Hill, Blackbird Leys and Risinghurst - and it was a Labour stronghold in a sea of blue. It was a privilege to campaign there.

FORBIDDEN TO SEE YOUR CHILDREN?
Vote for something that <u>REALLY</u> matters and <u>CROSS OUT</u> this madness
<u>VOTE Roger Crawford</u>
Your Equal Parenting Alliance Candidate For Oxford East

For more details visit
www.equalparentingalliance.com

During my election campaign in 2010 this was a handy card to give to interested passers-by or to put through letterboxes

The Conservative Party were majoring on the theme that Britain had become broken and seemed to be recognising that family breakdown was a big issue. Many were tipping the Conservatives to win the election (though not in Oxford East!). Certainly the Labour Party had ignored the effects of family breakdown on the wider society for years (simply and simplistically blaming 'feckless fathers' or 'deadbeat dads') and the Tories gave the impression at least of understanding there was a deeper problem, including the actions of the family courts.

Iain Duncan-Smith was a major force behind this thinking. I was invited to a meeting in London where he and a number of others spoke and there was little I could disagree with. Afterwards I introduced myself to Mr. Duncan-Smith, 'representing Fathers 4 Justice' I said. He looked a little startled, rather like a rabbit caught in the headlights, but I assured him I wasn't about to scale the walls and merely wanted to point out to him that many fathers couldn't have a relationship with their children through court orders, not because they were feckless or 'deadbeat'. 'I know' he said 'most absent fathers, in fact'. For a politician, even in opposition, to be so candid impressed me. I would like to say here, (and will again in my treatise on the planning system), how helpful my own M.P., Nadine Dorries, has been. Something of a renegade, she is disliked by many in her Party (Conservative) but largely loved by her constituents. When I asked her, years ago now, what her party's stance was on Family Law, she said 'I honestly don't know'. But she made it her business to find out, and then tell me. I believe that is an indication of an excellent M.P.

Naturally, New Fathers 4 Justice latched-on to the 'Broken Britain' theme and we concentrated our efforts on the Tory Party who we as good as lobbied for change. I personally wanted to use the theme and combine our efforts to mobilise a big rally (for us) in the period leading up to the election. Nigel suggested we try and find an open-topped bus, I thought it an excellent idea, and of course I had contacts in the business. I could borrow a very large double-decker coach from the firm I was working for, but hiring an open-top proved, unexpectedly, very difficult. We even thought of buying one. Despite the best efforts of George Standen and ourselves, I grew concerned that we weren't going to get one in time.

Heather would be turning eighteen in April and I particularly wanted to mark the occasion with a plea to her to 'vote to see your dad', emblazoned on the front of an open-topped bus.

Then Rosa found one on the internet. It didn't belong to a coach firm but to a group of people involved in theatricals and promotional work, and were based in Coleshill between Birmingham and Coventry. I rang them up - they were by far the most helpful and enthusiastic people I had contacted with regard to this, and they invited Nigel and I to come and look the bus over and discuss our requirements and our budget. This we did ASAP. It was as near perfect as we could hope to get, and included a P.A. system on the upper deck. Yes, we could affix banners to the sides and the front, in fact they could manufacture the banners if required! They had to supply a driver (for insurance purposes) but the rates were incredibly reasonable and it was great that they were so willing and enthusiastic about helping us. I would recommend them to anyone - the name is 'Commbus'. I suggested to Nigel that we did a joint demonstration for New Fathers 4 Justice and for the Equal Parenting Alliance, one which effectively launched my political career! He readily agreed.

We booked the bus for Saturday 10th. April, just a month before election day. We decided to tour round the Oxford East constituency and then go on to Witney and to David Cameron's country 'cottage' near Charlbury. Very quickly we attracted a large number of people to this event and it became apparent that we would need another bus to transport the participants back from Charlbury to Oxford, as the open-top would go direct from there back to Coleshill. So I was immensely thankful that the firm I worked for offered me their largest double-deck coach for the day. As long as I drove it, I could festoon it with banners and they would only charge me for fuel. Everything was falling into place.

'Battle bus' at Oxpens Coach Park in Oxford prior to departure in April 2010, taken from the upper deck of the open-top bus. The poster covering the rear has a picture of my step-grandson Ben, my little dog Pipsqueak, and me: the caption reads 'Roger says Vote for Me', Ben says 'Vote for Him', Pipsqueak says 'WOOF!'

If I remember correctly, we had about two weeks between seeing the open-topper and using it on the 10th. I left Nigel to organise the banners for the open-top bus whilst I did the ones for the coach I was going to drive. I did want at least one professional poster for mine, and asked Nigel if he would object to having another professionally-done one for the front of the open-top. He had no objection, so I asked Commbus to do that one, celebrating

Heather's eighteenth. For mine, I approached a local sign writer, Broome Signs, who did a magnificently large one which just about covered the back-end of 'my' bus. Meanwhile, the owner of the firm I was working for let me have the coach for two weeks for no charge. This incredibly generous act enabled me to campaign in Oxford with it long after the 10th. April, and made the outlay on the posters far more worthwhile.

We had challenged David Cameron to meet us outside his country home, but very shortly before the 10th April, we learned that he had asked the then shadow minister for the Department of Constitutional Affairs, Henry Bellingham, to meet with us on Witney Green. (We really didn't think that Cameron would actually meet us). This indicated that the Conservative Party were beginning to take us seriously. It was with a sense of hope and expectation that we looked forward to the day, all we needed now was enough people to actually turn up and for the sun to shine.

The forecast was brilliant - a cloudless day and temperatures up to 70 degrees F. I couldn't believe our luck. This would be the second time one of 'my' demos would be blessed with fine, warm weather.

Confirming the day's plans before departure in Oxford. We always found the Police to be cheerful, supportive and helpful.

I took the coach over to Oxford quite early in the morning, and was gratified to see the Commbus already in the coach park at Oxpens, being dressed with our banners. We were due to pick up the assembled multitude by the Carfax Tower at 10, and we liaised with the police about parking the two vehicles opposite Christ Church, where the road was wider. I was amazed then to see a forest of superheroes and purple flags making their way down the road from the Tower towards us. Nigel and Richard had done a brilliant job of publicising the event - this was going to be a good day. People came from everywhere - one had even made the journey from Dundee.

I wanted us to start by driving down the High Street but the Council had refused us permission (the road is restricted to service buses during the day). The always-helpful police in Oxford said 'Go down the High - we'll be escorting you, you'll be OK'. So we did. And we were OK. We had a police presence throughout our tour of Oxford East but at no time were they officious or restrictive. We had informed them of our future itinerary for the day and once we left Oxford for Witney, we had a police escort. This was much appreciated by the driver of the open-topped bus as he was limited to a top speed of 38 mph. On the A40 west of Oxford, that is pretty slow! As we toured Oxford, people waved, sounded their car horns, smiled at us - I don't think we had any negative reaction that morning.

We reached Witney at around lunchtime. I'd assumed that Witney Green was where the parish church is in Witney but I was wrong - the Green we were supposed to be at is on the Hanborough road out of the town, in the opposite direction! We had a bit of fun negotiating a U-turn and I was pleased to see the smiling faces of Mark Harris and his eldest daughter, Lisa, who had arranged to meet us here. The police arranged the parking of the buses close to the correct Green and we disembarked ready to meet with Mr. Bellingham.

On the road in Oxford

We appreciated his coming all the way here from his constituency in Norfolk, I'm sure he would have much rather been doing something else! He immediately impressed us with his knowledge of the Family Court system and he obviously knew exactly why we were protesting against it. He promised that the Conservative Party would address the issue as a priority should they win the election. I think it was a great mistake of Cameron to appoint the notoriously complacent Ken Clarke as Justice Minister in 2010 rather than Henry Bellingham. I believe we would have seen a much more robust shake-up of the system if Clarke had not got the job. Mr. Bellingham endured a question-and-answer session with considerable aplomb and Mark Harris gave him a copy of his book 'Family Court Hell'. I think most of us were pleased enough with our encounter, which had lasted for nearly one hour.

Discussing the needed changes to Family Law with Henry Bellingham, the then Shadow Minister for the Department of Constitutional Affairs, who had travelled all the way from his Norfolk constituency to Witney in order to meet us.

For the journey to Charlbury the open-topper was asked to follow a police car, and I followed the open-topper. The road from Witney to Charlbury twists and winds a lot and there are a number of places where the trees are quite low. I heard several calls of 'DUCK!' from Nigel, addressed to the occupants of the top deck, almost always followed by twigs raining down on the front of my vehicle. The sun continued to shine as we made our way slowly along; an idyllic Spring day. Newly-born lambs gambolled in the fields, the air was filled with bird-song, green shoots were appearing in the hedgerows - a day of hope and promise.

David Cameron's 'cottage' is in a hamlet beyond Charlbury and only approached by narrow lanes, but the police found us a place to safely park the two buses.

We delivered a letter and another copy of Mark's book through Cameron's letterbox, posed for photos, then the open-topper left and everyone boarded my coach for the journey back to Oxford. It had been a very successful day, both vehicles had run faultlessly and everyone, I think, enjoyed themselves. It was a great start for my electioneering.

The open-top bus at our stop at David Cameron's country home

Over the next couple of weeks I drove the 'battle bus' over to Oxford a few times. I once used it to attend a hustings, held at one of the Universities. On that occasion I drove it around the Oxford East constituency during the afternoon and it was then that I received the only unpleasant reaction to my campaign. I'd got halted by a set of traffic lights (in Cowley I think) and a cyclist pulled in ahead of me, turned round, and spat very obviously, in my direction. The lights changed and I got ahead of him, only to notice that there were another set of lights ahead, on red of course.

As I slowed, Mr. Spittle began to catch up but then the lights changed to green. On this coach there was a 'mixture enrichment device' which you operated to help start the thing on cold mornings: it simply enabled a bit more fuel to run through to the engine and you don't use it unless you have to because it causes a lot more smoke. 'I'll have him' I thought and waited a couple of seconds for him to get really close before pulling the cable and flooring the accelerator. I glanced in the mirror to see him disappear in a huge cloud of black smoke - and I never saw him again. Childish? Certainly. Satisfying? Oh yes.

It was with some reluctance that I returned the coach to the depot at the end of the two weeks. It took three of us over two hours to remove the posters

222

from one side of the bus - the sun had baked them on!

I enjoyed every one of the hustings I attended. I have to mention that it was notable that Julia Gasper representing UKIP was given a fairly hard time on occasion. She is a diminutive lady but makes up for her lack of size by her huge spirit and her pugnaciousness on occasion. We got on well, and I thought she talked a lot of sense, and if she had stood this time around (2015), I think she would command the respect she richly deserved in 2010. We kept in touch for a few years and I regret I've not been able to wish her well this time around. One person who was listened to was the LibDem candidate. I think he expected a higher proportion of the vote than he achieved, but if he stands this time I doubt whether he'll expect much. The dishonoured 'pledge' to scrap tuition fees will sink him in a place like Oxford. The Conservative candidate was known as the 'Invisible Man' because he didn't attend many hustings. I found him a very pleasant individual but he knew he didn't stand a chance in Oxford East. Andrew Smith, the Labour man and incumbent M.P. looked a bit worried on election night, but against the trend he actually increased his majority. The Green candidate, Sushila, did well, I thought, in the hustings but the result was disappointing for her I think. And I? I never received a negative comment. Not one. I wasn't there to garner votes, just to get my message across. I was listened to with respect and courtesy, every time.

Along with everyone else, I was asked to do interviews on local radio. One of these was done over the telephone from my house; the radio station ring up at an agreed time and you are put on hold until the DJ (in this case) is ready to interview you. I can't remember the station, but it was obvious the DJ regarded this part of his programme as an irrelevance. Far more important to be playing the next record. . 'You're not going to get any votes, are you?' he said. I tried to explain that I wasn't interested in obtaining votes but he'd already started playing the next track, not even thanking me for my 'contribution'; I was just expected to hang up. The next time I did an interview of this nature I was asked what would I do if I won the seat? Laughing, I said that I would probably have a severe bowel movement, which at least raised a chuckle. I was much happier actually sat in a studio where you can inter-act with the interviewer and have a little more time to state your case properly. Again I was treated with unfailing courtesy in these situations.

As election day drew closer, it became imperative to get the leaflets delivered. Only I hadn't received mine from the printers. A couple of days before the deadline set by the Post Office I made a frantic phone call and the print shop owner drove all the way from Kilmarnock to deliver them to me personally. That was very good of him, but he hadn't sorted them into two separate lots, as required by the Post Office; one lot to be delivered to the main post office in Oxford and the other to Cowley. I had to deliver the whole consignment to a huge depot near Swindon, on the very last day possible, where the staff there kindly said they would sort it into the two lots required. So, every constituent in Oxford East received my election pamphlet, but it was a close-run thing. George Standen had been an immense help in designing the leaflet, and we were both very happy with the result. The leaflet was attractive and the message was clear and upbeat.

Just before election day I put a half-page advert in the Oxford Mail which read something like 'Now for Something Completely Different - Don't Vote for Me (if you want a Politician)'. And that was it, my campaign was over. All I had to do now was attend the Count, held in the City Hall.

Friends came to support me, including Sam and her dad; I wore my jester's hat so that anyone who wished to talk with me would recognise me immediately. The counting seemed interminable, but it became obvious by the piles of votes on the tables who was in the running and who wasn't. I was disappointed that Julia decided to leave before the result was announced and I pleaded with her to stay, but she herself was most disappointed and upset with her proportion of the vote and after staying a little longer than she originally intended, quietly slipped off when I wasn't looking. I talked with the far-left man, noting that our piles - if we could call them that! - were very similar. 'It's neck and neck!' I laughed.

The count finished in the early hours. I think I received 73 votes (I'm amazed I got that many!) and the far left candidate received a few more than me. Andrew Smith was duly returned as M.P. to huge applause. The Lib-Dem candidate put on a brave face but he was obviously disappointed. He said 'watch us because we're not going anywhere' which was true, if a rather unfortunate way of saying it. We all were invited to make a short speech and I am told that, after Mr. Smith, I received the biggest cheer of the evening. For some reason I hadn't expected to be asked to speak and I don't think I did very well, but I meant it when I said I had enjoyed every minute of my campaigning in Oxford East. I truly had. I'd never in a million years expected to stand in a General Election, it was probably last on my list of things I wanted to do ever, yet everyone had received me so warmly that I looked forward every time to taking part in the hustings. It was a brilliant experience. My eternal gratitude to everyone I met on the campaign trail.

After the result, we were invited for drinks but by now I felt exhausted and still had the long drive home. It was beginning to get light as I climbed into the car.

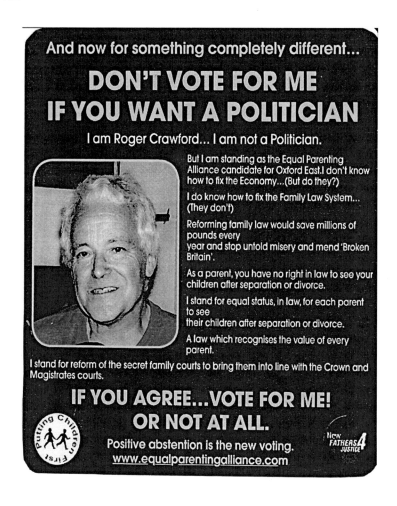

My election poster that appeared in the Oxford papers just before the General Election in May 2010.

Postscript: Ray Barry campaigned in Wolverhampton West and polled more votes than me, despite not using an open-topped bus in his campaign! He also received some hostility from some quarters. In retrospect, perhaps we should have occasionally campaigned together in each other's constituencies, which would have broadened our experience further. I think we would have made a good double-act.

THE SNOREGROVE REPORT

I was pleased that we were going to have a change in Government. My parents had both been socialists but I had been pretty a-political. Shirley had proudly asserted her socialist credentials initially but by now I saw them as hollow as a roll of toilet-paper. Blair ditto. I'd always regarded Gordon Brown as at least sincere, but he had not impressed as Leader of the Labour Government. Most people craved for change.

No-one expected immediate change in Family Law, but we expected more from the Norgrove Report than what we eventually got. What report? Quite. The Norgrove report had actually been commissioned by Labour to look into changing Family Law and the coalition allowed it to continue. I don't know why they felt it necessary to commission a report - everyone knew the changes needed. I call it 'Snoregrove' because they seemed asleep to most of the real issues.

I wrote the following piece for a book 'Direct Action Dads' shortly after attending one of Norgrove's 'consultations'.

There is, as I write, a review going on into the Family Justice system, at great cost to the taxpayer. We don't really need one. Anyone who has even a basic knowledge of the present system knows what is required and everyone acknowledges that the present system isn't working. As I understand it, none of the Panel are what could be called 'end users' of the system. No disenfranchised parents were asked to sit on the panel. This Family Justice Review Panel has produced an interim report and invited those who submitted comments to attend a 'consultation' with them at various points around the country. I attended the London one, with my fellow-campaigner Mrs. Maggie Tuttle. The Chairman, Mr. David Norgrove, introduced the panel to us but stated he could only stay for half-an-hour as he had to dash off to another of his many enterprises. Excuse me, isn't this one of the most important issues of our time? Affecting, as it does, countless families? Sorry, gotta dash.

Ah well, better make the best of it. . .only to find that they are really going to tinker about with the system to make it more 'efficient', rather than implement the fundamental changes that are needed. Many of the most important issues were not even mentioned by the Panel. No right in law for either parent to see their children (didn't know that? If you go to the Family Court you'll find out). No mention of parental alienation (where one parent alienates a child from the other parent) despite this being one of the main

causes of children not seeing a parent. No burden of proof needed for allegations made by one parent against another - just the 'balance of probability'.
No mention at all of opening-up the Family Courts. In other words, the same old, same old. . ..

The Norgrove report was quickly forgotten by the coalition and by the public alike, with good reason. What infuriates me (and many others of course) is that God-knows how much tax-payer's money was wasted on all this palaver. The report took around three years to compile and it produced very little that we did not already know, and it did not address any of our main concerns. It simply reiterated the fact that the Family Courts were 'inefficient'. If only that was the only thing wrong with them! 'Inhuman' would have been a better description. Norgrove said that his report would be 'child-centric', which was total bullshit. I do hate these trendy, meaningless phrases. How could anything be 'child-centric' if it were not 'parent-centric' at the same time? The 'public consultation' was a mere public relations exercise. There were some very knowledgeable people, highly qualified to comment on the system, present at the London meeting, including a number of Magistrates, but not one of their suggestions was even considered, never mind mentioned in the final report. My colleague Jeremy Pogue walked out of the Cardiff 'consultation' in disgust. The whole thing was an utter farce, a waste of taxpayer's money, a sham. Fortunately the coalition quickly buried it, or at least large parts of it.

We felt we needed to keep the pressure on during the time the Norgrove report was being compiled. None of us felt we could rely on it to suggest a fairer and less corrupt system.

CAMPING AND CLIMBING

I believe the first demonstration we did after the election was at the M.P. Jonathon Djanogly's house near Huntingdon. He was certainly involved with changing the Family Law system. He knew we were coming and arranged to be out, but nevertheless we had a well-attended demo there. Someone had brought a 'batboat' along to float past the other side of his house; a small brook wended its way on the edge of his garden. However it had dried up for the summer, so it was never launched! After photos etc., we moved on to demonstrate in the centre of Peterborough and raised a bit of cash there. Some of this was used to reimburse me for the cost of hiring the open-topped bus we'd used in Oxford. We did a 'chug' through some of the pubs. Nigel or I would go up to the barkeeper or manager to distract him or her and ask if we could go round the tables with a bucket for loose change, knowing we'd be refused, whilst the other lads were doing it anyway and raising a fair bit. By the time the barkeeper or manager realised what was going on, they'd more-or-less covered the entire bar. None of the customers seemed to mind; it was all done very light-heartedly.

A few weeks after this, one of Mr. Djanogly's election team described Djanogly as a 'wet blanket' for some reason. I used this to do an amusing little piece outside his home again, just to keep the press interested. Djanogly was relieved of his position in dealing with Family Law some time after this, and I've never heard his name mentioned again, anywhere. The curse of New F4J?

Many of us quickly began to feel uneasy at the lack of progress made by Cameron after all his promises. Yes, there were lots of issues he had to deal with but he had made 'family breakdown' a big issue in his plans before the election. We felt he needed to be reminded and this feeling was shared by many Grandparents too. We'd already made a presence in Witney and it was decided we'd camp on Witney Green over a weekend in August. 'Nothing like stirring up the locals in Dave's constituency to get results' said one. The Town Council said there were by-laws preventing anyone from camping on the green at anytime. Much to our surprise, the 'Witney Gazette' took our part and suggested that as the issue was such a serious one, the Council should relax their rules on this occasion. The police were supportive too. We went ahead. Now, I hate camping! I love sleeping in my motorhome in remote locations, but camping on wet grass with bugs crawling all around? - not for me, thank you. Nigel kindly agreed that I could park alongside the campers and sleep in the 'camper' - as long as I offered to provide breakfast in the morning! (I could only stay one night).

Fair enough, I thought.

I had to leave after breakfast but everyone else did a noisy demonstration in Witney town centre that day. Apparently they sought refreshment in one of David Cameron's favourite pubs in the town, and one guy climbed on to a lavatory roof there for a bit. Just a bog-standard protest, really. Mark Harris had a snoop round, coming back to tell the boys that Cameron's constituency office roof would be a doddle. . . . and this information was quickly relayed to me.

A couple of other guys, Archi Ssan and Jem Pogue were up for it. I did a recce and thought, indeed, it would be easy to get up there. There was a steep roof facing the road over which we could drape a banner or two, but the ascent from a side entrance was as easy as pie. We would be up there in a trice. Only a step-stool required! And when I looked, there was no police presence. Very early in the morning of 2nd. August 2010, I met Archi near the Carfax Tower in Oxford in my camper, and we motored down to Witney to meet Jem (who was driving from South Wales) at The Green. After a breakfast in the 'van, we strolled down to Witney town centre and sauntered past Cameron's constituency office. No-one was about. 'Let's do it' said Jem. We quickly made our way over several low roofs up to a safe spot where we could unload our banners, and no-one had spotted us. Yet again we were blessed with fine weather. The main banner, simply stating 'Give Dads Equal Rights' was secured with rope lashed round a chimney and the banner thrown down over the front of the roof.

At this stage we had no ground support, they were appearing later, so we kept quiet as Witney slowly woke up to a beautiful sunny day. I believe it was a person living next-door to Cameron's office who first espied us. It probably was a little unnerving to look out of the window first-thing and have Superman, The Jolly Green Giant, and a Court Jester prancing about on the roof next-door. We were shortly hailed from the footpath below by two uniformed officers. 'How long are you going to be up there then?' said one. 'As long as it takes!' said Jem. One then had a conversation on the phone whilst the other kept watch on us. We assured him we were not intending to do any damage. 'I'm handing this over to the Special Operations Unit, they're on their way' said the one who'd used the phone. 'OK' we said. Special Operations Unit? What did they do? Would they air-lift us off the roof? Abseil up the front of the building? We phoned Nigel, who was on his way to us from Bristol. 'Don't talk to them' he said. 'Don't give them any information at all - just 'no comment'. I'll be there in an hour.'

It's not in my nature not to talk to people, whoever they may be. Three (if I remember rightly) officers from the S.O.U. turned up within half-an-hour. They were most friendly, and by the time Nigel arrived we were engaged in light-hearted banter with them. 'You're talking to them!' he exclaimed 'I said. . . .' 'Nigel it's OK' said Jem. 'The local bobbies wanted us arrested, but we're not going to be now they're here. They just need to agree a time with us when we're coming down'. Nigel then had a conversation with them and we agreed that when the papers had arrived and got our photos, we'd come down. 'Christ alive!' said Nigel 'I don't know how you get away with it!' 'It's my natural charm' I told him.

No-one, except me, flinched when Jem boomed into his megaphone 'GOOD MORNING WITNEY! JUST LETTING YOU KNOW THAT NEW FATHERS 4 JUSTICE ARE IN TOWN. WE'RE ON CAMERON'S OFFICE ROOF AND WE'RE STAYING ALL DAY!'

Nigel and a number of others set up a sort of stall on the other side of the road, and waved placards and gave out leaflets to the increasing number of passers-by. Cars tooted, Lorries blasted their air horns, people waved. At one time, all the people on the top deck of a double-decker stood up and cheered as they went past. In some ways, being on the roof is easier than being ground-crew. You receive all the attention simply by being there, whereas those on the ground have to talk with the police, deal with inconvenienced people and those who don't like noise. We made quite a lot of noise. Then the Press arrived, first the local papers and then a photographer from the Sun. We always have to pose for photographs, very few were used that weren't. By the time they were done it was around mid-afternoon and we decided it was time to honour our agreement and come down.

The police wanted to chat with us for a bit. 'Next time you do anything like this in Oxfordshire, ring us. [The S.O.U.]. I don't expect you to tell us where you're going to be in advance, but ring us when you're up. It may stop you getting arrested!' We were amazed at their tolerance. 'Look mate' said one 'we know what you guys go through because quite a few of us are having to go through it. This job's not really very compatible with a full home life. As long as you do no damage and keep to any agreements we come to, you'll be OK. Besides, you don't hate us, not like that lot from Animal Liberation. They hate our guts. It's so much better for everyone if we can get on'. We all shook hands and we went for a pint, hardly able to believe our good fortune. 'Not even a caution! - that's a result, isn't it! Cheers!'

I must say that throughout my campaigning, wherever it has been, I have always been treated fairly and with respect by the Police, but especially in Oxfordshire. From being escorted through the rural roads between Witney and Charlbury or down Oxford's High Street, to the heights of the Carfax Tower or the court balcony or David Cameron's Constituency Office roof, to the many ground-level demonstrations or camps in Oxford and Witney, I think all of us who attended found the Oxfordshire Police unfailingly pleasant, helpful and understanding. I would like to put on record here, my appreciation of the consideration we received.

The demonstrations continued, with another one outside Djanogly's house, outside the Ministry of Justice, and an attempt to infiltrate the 'Big Brother' studios in Elstree.

My birthday is at the end of September and I spent the day in 2010 with others outside the Ministry of Justice in London. It was the last day for evidence and representations to be submitted to the Family Justice Review Panel and we were there to deliver a joint statement from New Fathers 4 Justice, The Equal Parenting Alliance, Real Fathers for Justice, Grandparents Apart, and the Grandparent's Action Group, plus letters from Sam in Oxford and from Lisa Harris, Mark Harris' eldest daughter. And my petition. The day before, Archi had scaled the wall which runs on one side of and away from the Ministry of Justice building and did a one-man protest on the top of it. As a result, we had an 'enhanced' police presence for our demo! Archi had also scaled the 'iconic' Transporter Bridge in Newport (Monmouthshire) earlier in the month and had been arrested for that; he had been detained after the wall protest but was able to join us on this day. The security guard at the MoJ and he shook hands and I don't think the issue was pursued any further. At this demo, I met Maggie Tuttle for the first time who later went on to form the charity 'Children Screaming to be Heard'.

Our joint letter to the Review Panel read thus:

"FOR THE ATTENTION OF THE FAMILY LAW REVIEW PANEL

We are very concerned that there is no disenfranchised parent or grandparent on the Family Law review panel, or anyone affected by forced adoption. Some of our number here today are deeply sceptical of yet another review body looking into Family Law, and have mentioned that there may be some on the panel who may feel that their own interests are best served by keeping the 'status quo'.

However, we do earnestly hope that this review will take into account the views of people like these and others who feel wronged, damaged, and disenfranchised by the current Family Court system in this country.

We, as representatives of these people, believe it is in the best interests of families and therefore of society as a whole that the following two changes are made without any further delay.

These changes will go a long way to meet the financial reductions required of the Ministry of Justice, and free-up time and the staff to deal with serious child-care cases.

(i) Give each parent an automatic presumption, a right in law, to see their children after divorce or separation. This alone would stop up to 100,000 cases going to Court in the first place, and would in almost all cases enable grandparents to have a meaningful part in the lives of their grandchildren.

(ii) Make the Family Courts open and accountable, bringing them into line with the Crown and Magistrates Courts. Concerns over anonymity and privacy are unfounded as there are already measures to protect privacy in open court. This measure would stop the bias and corruption so many have experienced in the secret Family Courts.

As a 'rider' to this, we would recommend that agreements made in mediation should be recognised in the Courts if one party fails to keep to the agreements made.

We urge you to make these changes for the sake of countless children, parents and grandparents, and help therefore to make a fairer and happier society for everyone."

.I think it is also worth printing Lisa's letter to the Panel. Intelligent and articulate, Lisa states very clearly her own and her sister's experiences of the Family Court system. She also gives an excellent account in her own chapter in Mark Harris' book 'Family Court Hell'. I believe she was about twenty when she wrote this;

"My name is Lisa Harris.

I'm responding to the 'call for evidence' questionnaire attached to the family justice review for myself and on behalf of my two sisters.

When we were children our parents separated, and because of how the family court system operates, we lost contact with our loving and dedicated father. For years we grew up without his essential input in our lives despite every humanly perceivable effort on his part to father us.

Those lost years and contact are too precious to quantify, but we want to say emphatically, that it clearly harmed our childhood and quality of upbringing.

Our dad constantly fought against the intransigent family court system that continuously dismissed his claims, and evidence, of how your court procedures harmed our upbringing. There was absolutely no justification whatsoever in our father being excluded from our childhood. He spent years exhausting his money, time and nerves trying gain justice for us whilst the court system spent the same years and wasted almost £1 million of public money maintaining their biased procedures against our interests.

During this period of estrangement the family courts endeavoured to keep secret the fact that our mother's boyfriend abused us while ignoring all of our wishes to see our dad. They also ignored us when we tried to tell them our mother's boyfriend was hurting us all and making our lives a misery. It was only when we were old enough to run away to our father did the abuse stop and we got our dad back.

You never listened to him; so now in your 'call for evidence' in this latest inquiry, we want you to listen to us and take our testimony AS EVIDENCE. But, before any of that, for the sake of a little human decency, stop saying the corruption and prejudice your institution practices is in our best interest. It's breathtakingly callous to hear that jingo, and it's so untrue; you behave with the narcissism of holocaust deniers when you pronounce your prejudice as in the child's best interest.

We take exceptional offence to any public official who sustains this anti-father bias by falsely claiming that it is in the best interests of the children. You should be deeply ashamed of yourselves for constantly fobbing off the public with that highly offensive jingo. In our experience, you appear to be callously indignant in the way you bully silence from those who try to plead reason with you. You abuse the power of your office, and facilitate harm to countless children all over the country, by what is clearly prejudice against good fathers and say it's in the children's best interest.

As young adults we have had time and mind to examine the huge collection of legal documents our father has collected from your procedures. We can see for ourselves how prejudiced and falsely condemning your institution is. There is also more than enough evidence, statistical and anecdotal, from various groups and sources detailing the bias through which you operate, and we want you to regard it seriously.

'Arbeit macht frei'; those were the German words found on the signs above the entrances of Nazi concentration camps. The meaning approximately translates to 'work sets you free'. We relate to the insincerity and insult of 'work sets you free' in a similar way to how your officials say "in the child's best interests".

Stop the destruction of the lives of multitudes of British children which has led to the creation of today's broken Britain!

Stop rationalising your prejudice!

Stop issuing your insulting arrogant spin!

Stop wasting vast amounts of public money facilitating anti-father bias!'

Lisa Harris

Sam's letter was another outstanding contribution and I regret not being able to contact her in time to obtain a copy for publication here.

The Norgrove Report - the Family Justice Review - was published on April 3rd. in 2011. We weren't surprised that it was such a miserable, duff publication which seemed to ignore almost all the recommendations made by so very many people who had been through the system. We'd got a taste of it from the 'consultation'. Mr. Norgrove probably has no idea how near he came to having several of us appear on his roof in North London. But as David Cameron was making noises about ignoring substantial parts of this report, we decided Norgrove was best ignored by us as well for the time being. We'd see what would happen.

It was around this time I paid a visit to Oxford again and noticed there was scaffolding being erected on the building next to the Court. Some of the scaffolding had easily-accessible platforms very close indeed to the Court's roof. I told Archi about this and he and I, and A.N. Other, went to have a further look.

We agreed that it was immensely 'do-able' and I was gratified I was being given another opportunity to get up there. At the same time, we were planning a much more ambitious demonstration up in Scotland in support of Dave from Dundee, who had made the journey down to be with us on the open-top bus demo. He'd been imprisoned for celebrating his estranged son's birthday by putting up balloons. . . .the Courts are just as vindictive in Scotland, if not more so.

Our plans had reached an advanced stage when, for no reason known to me, Archi ceased any further communication with me. He'd always said that the cause was greater than any individual, but seemed unable to put this philosophy into practice. I had no prior warning, and was mystified as to why this had happened. I had gone with him to meet his step-mother (whom he liked) and we all had attempted to effect a reconciliation between him and his estranged son. This was at no small cost to me, financially and in time and effort. I had also (at his request) spoken with his natural mother, who Archi did not like - perhaps he thought I had been 'tainted'. I'd even talked to his brother, who he detested - again at his request. I couldn't try to put things right if I did not know what it was I had got wrong!
Archi would heap any failings of his own onto the fact he had Asperger's Syndrome but I'm afraid that I don't really buy that. What he did scuppered my own plans for Oxford but more importantly scuppered that important demo for our friend in the North. Nevertheless, I was pleased to hear that he was reconciled with his son. I got this info. from another member of New F4J of course - not from him.

It's normal for people to disagree, and sometimes fall out. But when it affects an entire campaign, it really is hopeless. And if the person who feels wronged or whatever refuses to tell the 'guilty' one what the problem is, it is impossible. How childish. And how damaging to the movement.

On Father's Day 2011 David Cameron made one of the more crass remarks of his Premiership. He stated that Deadbeat Dads were worse than drunk drivers. No matter how strong the evidence was that most 'Deadbeat Dads' were only thus because of the rulings of Family Court judges, no matter what he'd pledged or promised during the election campaign, he comes out with this populist but cheap and highly inaccurate guff. Father's Day is one of the worst days for dads who cannot see their kids. Would he have said this about 'Muppet Mums' on Mother's Day? You can bet your cotton socks he wouldn't. He must have known - he MUST - that this was an utterly stupid, brainless remark.

I cannot comprehend how he and Gordon Brown, who have both lost children and related how they have been profoundly affected by their loss, continue to this day to ignore the suffering of parents who have lost their children through the Family Court system for no just cause. David

Cameron went as far as to say that he almost gave up politics due to the overwhelming grief over losing his son.

Is it somehow different for us? I think it's probably even worse for us. To be denied access to our own children - to not be able to see them, to reach out and comfort them, knowing they are still out there - they are in fact dead to us, yet still alive. I tell you, Cameron, Brown et al - it's hell. Many describe it as a 'living bereavement'. As I write this, two of our protesters have been handed 'harassment notices' for campaigning outside Cameron's country 'cottage' over Christmas (2014). Apparently Cameron has been reported as saying 'Oh no, not you again. You're spoiling my Christmas'. Do you think, Sir, that they WANT to be there? Do you think that you maybe, by your inaction and your broken promises, have 'spoiled' their Christmas this year and every year? Think on!!

As I write, a report shows that 'non-resident' parents - usually fathers - are three times more likely to die early than resident parents. Since 2003, 8,515 non-resident parents have died compared to 3,090 resident parents.

Matt O'Connor wrote an article in the Sunday Express January 11th. 2015, revealing that the death rate is nearly nineteen times the number of British forces killed in Afghanistan. Despite a freedom of information request, no causes of death were given by the Department of Work and Pensions, but I think we can be pretty certain that the majority were suicides. I do wish the Government would heed this, and fulfil the election pledge of 2010 on shared parenting.

We couldn't let Cameron's remark about deadbeat dads go unpunished! On July 7th. 2011 three of us again scaled his constituency office roof in Witney. We - Jem, Archi (yep, Archi) and me again met up at The Green early in the morning. I bade Archi a loud 'Good morning Archi' to which I received a muffled reply, probably 'sod off', and we took a stroll down to the Town Centre. Passing the archway beside the office we espied a panda car parked there. 'Uh-oh' said Jem 'have they rumbled us?'. I doubted it - this probably was routine now that Cameron was P.M. and we'd already done this roof.

'We'll go for breakfast' I suggested, an idea that was taken up with enthusiasm. We were joined by some members of our ground support team. After a leisurely breakfast we thought we'd convene in a car park at the rear of Cameron's office, but out of sight of it. One of the ground support team went to have a look at the situation and came back quickly to tell us the police had gone to get a coffee. 'Let's go!' I said, and we bundled ourselves and our gear over various walls, up to and on to the now-familiar roof. We'd made it! Within minutes, the police returned but it was a fait accompli. Jem had already rung the Special Operations Unit and they were on their way. The local guys I think were not best pleased, (they may have got into trouble with their superiors for leaving their post) and assumed we'd been watching them, but we hadn't, we'd got up there by sheer luck really. Once again Jem boomed out the message 'GOOD MORNING WITNEY! WELL, HERE WE ARE AGAIN! JUST AS WE PROMISED. IT'S A PITY DAVID CAMERON HASN'T KEPT HIS. . . .' etc.

Just before our demo, Cameron had made a remark about 'too many tweets make a twat', so we did a quick banner saying he was one anyway for spouting such rubbish about deadbeat Dads. The atmosphere was lightened as soon as the S.O.U. arrived. We descended to shake hands with the two officers sent this time. 'Same agreement?' they asked 'you get the publicity, you do no damage, you come down?' 'Absolutely' we said. 'Done'. It was agreeable that the police could keep their word even if the Prime Minister wouldn't.

The day was a good one for us, but I didn't really want to do this venue again. We weren't that visible from the High Street and it wasn't that busy. And it was bloody uncomfortable on that rooftop! At least it didn't rain. We came down at around the same time in the afternoon as before, and again had a chat with the officers. 'We're surprised you didn't do Oxford Court earlier - it was surrounded by scaffolding, it would have been easy-peasy!' one of them said. 'I was going to do it, but I was very badly let down by others' I told him, shooting a meaningful glance at Archi, who looked suitably sheepish. 'A missed opportunity' the officer said 'You'd probably had at least one of us up there supporting you!'. We, as a group, had most certainly been badly let down. I've not talked to Archi since. But it was very heartening to know we had this support from the S.O.U.

This demo was followed in August by a further camp at Witney Green. When we were packing up, a lady resident approached us and we were expecting a dressing-down for disturbing the gentility of this area. Instead we received from her a cheque for £1,000 'to cover your expenses' she said. We were gobsmacked. Gary Roe and a few others were in tears. 'What you're doing is right' she smiled 'I fully support you'. What could we say? This lady insists on remaining anonymous, but on behalf of us all I would like to thank her so much for this most generous gesture. We left uplifted and wondering again at the kindness of strangers.

Not only had Cameron reneged on his promises to us, so had Nick Clegg. It was time to give him a bit of attention. In October, I took the trusty camper up to Sheffield and met up with a number of activists who were to support Gary Roe and myself in our bid to climb Nick Clegg's constituency office roof. Mr. Clegg is now well-known for making rather implausible promises but at that time he'd had to renege on a <u>pledge</u> he'd made to scrap tuition fees, and was extremely unpopular with students country-wide (and their parents!). The day dawned grey and wet and it only got worse. We got to the constituency office in the district of Hallam, Clegg's constituency, in pouring rain and a howling gale. I usually do a recce of the 'target' but hadn't been able to on this one - Sheffield was just too far away. It didn't look too difficult and Gary and I said 'let's do it'.

We got up there only to find the flat roof quite 'soft' in places, and we had to tread very carefully. 'The LibDems must be short of funds if they can't even look after their leader's office roof properly!' Gary joked. The wind was terrific. We unfurled a large banner to stretch between us only for the wind to catch it and it was the devil's own job to stop being launched into the air. Water was being picked-up from the gutter below and blown directly into our faces. We endured it for about an hour and a half before conceding defeat. By this time a very friendly copper was keeping an eye on things and we did get some local press coverage. Clegg was so unpopular in Hallam, any demo would get publicity. One of the staff came out to talk with us once we were down, but he seemed completely unfamiliar with the cause and seemed bemused by our actions. He also couldn't remember the address of the Deputy Prime Minister! By this time, we'd had enough, and gratefully accepted a lift back for some hot soup and a change of clothing. On the way back, a watery sun broke through and a rainbow appeared ahead of us. That was nice.

Protest outside the notoriously complacent Ken Clarke's home in Nottingham.

My last rooftop demo was in January 2012 on what we thought was the local Conservative Association's roof, opposite Ken Clarke's constituency office in Nottingham. We were all very angry with the apathetic Ken, who'd refused to budge on Family Law at all and seemed in total denial that there was anything wrong. Gary Roe had instigated many demonstrations outside his home and I'd attended one of them, but it was Jem once again and myself who did this one, assisted of course by Gary and by a number of guys from Real Fathers for Justice. Although the building had been the local Conservative Association's venue I understand now that it wasn't and belonged to a fitness club! Nevertheless, it still sported Conservative Association lettering and the roof was flat, unlike Ken Clarke's office roof which we deemed 'unscaleable'.

Jem and I got up there without any problem and there were substantial areas to hang banners. They were thrown up at us by the ground support team and we largely covered the sides of the building with them. This was an excellent site on a very busy main road, where we were very visible but did not obstruct people or traffic in any way. It was also a brilliantly sunny January day but my, it was freezing! The roof was like an ice-rink in places so we had to be careful. As usual, the police arrived, but allowed us to carry on as long as we informed them when we were coming down. We stayed up for a few hours and only came down when both of us began to get seriously cold. The chief police officer introduced himself to us and said he wasn't going to arrest us but did warn us that they'd received a number of objections and complaints about our actions and to please now disperse peacefully. Which we did. Several went to the pub, but I drove home in my nice warm campervan.

Twenty-twelve of course was the year of the Olympic Games. Word got around that Matt and the 'official' organisation of F4J were to hold a peaceful demo in Trafalgar Square with the theme of the 'Fatherless Games'. We had been invited to attend, perhaps as a goodwill gesture of reconciliation. Whilst vowing never to trust Matt himself again, we had no argument with those who supported F4J and quite a number of us attended. We were at least united in our sadness and disappointment that the Government were letting the issue of 'Breakdown Britain' slip down the agenda, together with Cameron's 'Big Society'. To echo Ghandi, we marched from Trafalgar Square to Downing Street and back, barefoot. Matt gave me one of his famous bear-hugs and as far as we could in the circumstances, we ceased to be at war.

At the F4J rally in London in 2012. Richard Adams and   myself hold a banner before walking barefoot down Whitehall to Downing Street.

CRIME OF THE CENTURY

Now they're planning the Crime of the Century
Well, what will it be?
Read all about their schemes and adventurings
Yes it's well worth the fee

Well, roll up and see; How they raped the Universe
How they've gone from bad to worse. . . ..

Who are these men of lust, greed and glory?
Rip off the masks and let's see!
But that's not right, oh no! What's the story?
Well there's you and there's me.. . . .
(That can't be right. . . . .)

Rick Davies and Roger Hodgson (from the 1974 Supertramp album 'Crime
of the Century').

The State, despite all its protestations, really doesn't care for children. In
many ways, nor should it. It's the parent's job, society's job, to see that our
kids are well and safely brought up. This was largely so in the fifties and
early sixties, when I was a kid. It is now no longer this way; the State feels
it has the right to interfere more and more in our lives, and in our children's
lives. To do this it has to convince people it works 'in the child's best
interests'. An increasing number of us know that it does not - it cannot, it is
not equipped to do so.

Since 2012 we have learned more and more of the shocking treatment of
hundreds (and it will become thousands and thousands) of children in State
'Care', and the blind eye turned to the abuse of our children by both the
State and by paedophiles, with the two collaborating on occasion. I'm
writing this in January 2015 and I am quite sure that there will now
become an overwhelming surge in reported cases of State-sponsored child
abuse in all its forms. I shall link it now to the abuse of vulnerable adults
and will return to this. I have pilloried the Family Court system, with its
secrecy, bias and corruption, and it is no coincidence that the notorious
Court of Protection comes under the same auspices. The Court of
Protection first and foremost protects itself, and it does this in the same
manner of the Family Courts - through secrecy and on pain of
imprisonment should anyone wish to describe their treatment within it or

their case. The two Courts are inextricably linked, like Siamese twins.

The present revelations, emerging since the Jimmy Savile scandal, are, in my opinion, all linked with the abusive treatment of decent parents and their children in the Family Courts. They all come under the umbrella of State family abuse, which is why I have entitled this chapter 'Crime of the Century', because it is, and has flourished by surrounding itself with secrecy and threats. Many within the system will be at one with ordinary folk in hating Jimmy Savile - but for different reasons. Those within the system will hate Savile because the scandal surrounding his activities with kids has opened, just a little, the whole foetid can of maggots which will, this year I hope, engulf the entire State system and the way that it has treated families over the last fifty years. Cameron wasn't referring to any of this when he mentioned 'Broken Britain' five years ago. The State is not good at looking in the mirror when making accusations.

I was not particularly surprised when the claims of child abuse in State care suddenly emerged. I'd been working with Maggie Tuttle who had founded the charity 'Children Screaming to be Heard' and we had spent several nights talking with young (and not-so-young) homeless people in London. Many had been shunted around from home to home and been abused whilst in care. We also learned that they were never listened to, let alone believed. 'No-one cared' was the overwhelming theme.

Senior social workers, chief executives, Care Home managers, etc. get huge salaries compared to many of us. We pay for them out of our taxes, but we don't of course have a say. It is stated that 'we have to offer large salaries in order to attract the best people'. It doesn't seem to be working very well, does it? May I suggest that we return to the idea of a vocation rather than a highly-paid job? Then perhaps those who are found out would stop hanging on for so long afterwards until their position becomes untenable. If we had modest salaries, would we have had these people at the 'top' of our social services? Or better, more dedicated, humanitarian people? I cannot answer this, but feel the question should be asked. And answered.

This unravelling of our child-care system is present and ongoing as I write, so I will leave Natasha Phillips to make an apposite comment from her 'Researching Reform' website. We're all hoping for something better as 2015 opens.

"Whatever The Timpsons and Loughtons of this world have to say about progress for children in care, the reality is that not much has

changed since light was first shed onto the dire conditions most children experiencing social care face, almost a decade ago now.

Jackie Long is social affairs editor over at Channel 4, and her recent blog on outcomes for children in care is a stark reminder that whilst adults seem to be talking about change, virtually nothing is happening on the ground. And no one is actually listening to our children.

Her post highlights several things ministers tend to forget whilst they're busy patting themselves on the back for jobs seemingly well done. It costs more to see a child through the care system, than it does to send a child to Eton. Despite this, whilst children at Eton get the Rolls Royce of education and pastoral care, children in care most often face the prospect of illiteracy and physical and emotional abuse. Here are some stats from Jackie's piece:

- *Almost one third of children in care leave school with no GCSEs at all.*

- *Only 6 per cent of care leavers go onto university – as opposed to 38 per cent of all young people.*

- *Almost 40 per cent of prisoners under 21 had been in care while they were growing up.*

- *Children in care have a higher chance of developing mental health problems or ending up homeless.*

All this we know, but we tend to forget amidst the clarion calls for reform and the loud trumpeting for more children to be taken into care, taken from 'abhorrent monster parents' to be placed in the arms of loving foster carers and residential staff.

But that's bollocks, and we know it.

We can have as many voice of the child conferences and seminars as we like, but until we get staff on the ground to understand what it means to listen to children and to show them love and affection at the same time, these children will continue to go unseen and unheard.

Time and again we hear social workers saying they can't show love and affection to children because it might cause emotional trauma once they're moved on, but that is to suggest that children's emotional development can be frozen in time once they land in care and reignited at a later date once they are 'safely housed' with foster carers or adoptive parents. The merits of that sentiment about safety too are questionable as children continue to be bounced around from carer to carer, let down by people who are either unable to cope with vulnerable children or are simply looking for a quick way to make cash (the debate raging around 'salaries' for foster carers is a big issue as well)

Playing to the gallery on David Cameron's constituency office roof in Witney.

Along with vulnerable children, vulnerable adults and sometimes those who try to help them are also routinely abused by the State, through the Court of Protection, the Family Courts' even uglier siamesed sister. Almost everyone I have spoken to about this Court has not heard of it. Lucky them. This is the most secret court of all, and is imbued with draconian powers. It merely needs to rule that someone 'lacks mental capacity' and social workers or other court-appointed officials can take control of their whole lives (including their property and finances) and can and has jailed people without those people attending a hearing or their names being made public. There is a Judge Cardinal who rules in these courts, who as I write this has committed a seventy-two year old grandmother to three months clink for hugging her grandchild, who Social Services did not want hugged. [The grandmother has since been released - Roger.] This is the same judge who jailed Wanda Maddox for her efforts in trying to remove her father from a care home, against social services wishes, because she thought his care was inadequate, without making her jailing public knowledge, and without her being present at the sentencing. These two are cases that have become public knowledge. How many others, do you think? We can but guess, but the Court of Protection controls over <u>two billion pounds</u> of people's assets......

There's just one more aspect of all this I'd like to raise, and this involves not the Courts but ourselves, and our own behaviour.

Well into the sixties and probably the seventies, too, there was a popular mantra with couples that went 'We're really only staying together for the sake of the children'. From the late sixties and into the seventies this was increasingly derided and laughed at and thought wrong, by my generation. The generation who had been brought up, mainly, by both parents and had the security and stability that this bestowed. If my parents had split up whilst I was a child, would I have joined with those who laughed at our parent's moral stance? No, I wouldn't, I'd not have joined in with anything - I'd have been broken. Lost. Baffled and hurting. It is only into my own late sixties that I have begun to wonder whether my generation's ideas were actually right-on, man. Were we actually being 'liberated' or merely being selfish?

In 2014 a well-known left-wing child psychologist, Penelope Leach, wrote a book called 'Family Breakdown' which rather disturbed some people, particularly some men in the 'Father's movement'. Her first book, published in 1977, was entitled 'Your baby and child: from birth to age 5' and sold over two million copies. Ms. Leach is very well respected in her field, being a world-renowned expert on child development.

In her 2014 book Ms. Leach explored the affects that parent's splitting-up had on children. She wrote 'No matter how well-intentioned parents are, no matter how civilised they feel they are being, their divorce or separation always makes children unhappy. Always'.

She follows this by detailing some of the affects that acute stress, such as parents separating, has on the brains of children: neuroscientific research from various countries, including Britain, shows that the ill-effects can last a lifetime. Her book is very much worth reading, for it majors on facts, rather than what may be politically-correct dogma. It appears under my 'recommended reading' at the end of this book.

Penelope Leach doesn't recommend that parents stay together for the sake of the children, and I'm wondering whether she should: perhaps she may yet get there. And she angered many separated fathers by saying that sleepovers with them for children under four were not a good idea, if as is usually the case, they were the non-resident parent. Some of my male contemporaries described her remarks as 'evil' without reading the book, which went on to mention how important a father's role is. She writes 'I believe it is absolutely vital that fathers spend time with their children and keep in regular contact with them at all times. . . . .there is a mass of new research that shows the crucial importance of fathers to children, from infancy through to adult life'. Ms. Leach explained her stance on 'overnighting' very well, and basically it's about stability for the child in the earliest years, where the principal care-giver (usually Mum) is vitally important to the child's development. If the resident parent was the father, then overnight stays with Mum should be out. You may not agree with her, but she is really one of the 'good guys' and you would need to read all her arguments, and the facts. In the end, all that matters is the truth. No matter what our philosophy, no matter what we believe, no matter what we may wish for; all that matters is the truth. If that is established beyond all reasonable doubt, we have to accept it. And if that truth reveals that previous generations were generally right, after all, and not nearly so stupid as some of us like to think. .. . .well, we may have to accept that, too.

And here I must also mention ex-High Court (Family Division) Judge Sir Paul Coleridge. Judge Coleridge was forced to step down by the Lord Chief Justice, Lord Thomas, and pressure from Chris Grayling, the Justice Secretary. His crime? Championing marriage! You couldn't make it up. Judge Coleridge had witnessed the effects of the breakdown of relationships on parents and children over many years and in 2012 set up a think-tank called the Marriage Foundation. He supported marriage because parents who are married are considerably less likely to split up than parents who are not, and if they do split, on average it comes later than those who cohabit. And, as we have already learned from Penelope Leach, children whose parents split up always suffer. Judge Coleridge qualified his remarks by saying 'I am not saying that every broken family produces dysfunctional children, but almost every dysfunctional child is the product of a broken family. Separation may be good for the parents. It is never, never, never good for the children'.

Despite this echoing almost every word of Ms. Leach, (because it's an indisputable truth even if sometimes an inconvenient one), he was pilloried and forced to step down. In my opinion, a reflection on the way that the State views children, and those who tell the truth. I say again - no matter what stance we may take, we have to recognise the truth. If I sound like a zealous newly-converted believer, so be it, but I hope not. It's just that, for most of us, our children matter the most, and the mere believing in something because it suits our book is not good enough.

I would totally accept that children are always hurt and damaged by parents separating. I have witnessed it within my own family, where a young boy has radically changed his personality - for the worse - since his parents split. There's absolutely no doubt that this change was as a result of the split, in this case the mother becoming the non-resident parent. Although the parents did avoid the Family Courts, and the split was as amicable as it could be in the circumstances, seven years on from it that boy is still troubled. He's now a teenager. As it was the mother who left the family home, he finds it difficult to relate to women in the same way he can relate to men, and this affects his schooling as well as his home and social life. When we rail against the Family Courts for not working in children's best interests, we should always question: Are we? Before you split - think! Think twice.

However, it's unlikely that in the foreseeable future most parents will start talking about staying together for the sake of the children. In 2014, 42% of all marriages ended in divorce and this does not include the countless separations of parents who never married. So how can I advise? My first advice is that you must stay out of the family court. Do try and work out an agreement, and keep to it. If you feel you need mediation, do that, but try to honour the agreements reached there. Avoid the Court at almost all costs. No-one except lawyers and judges and CAFCASS officers, win there. You never will, and neither will your children. And the rest, I can do no better than quote Matt O'Connor in his book 'Fathers 4 Justice - the Inside Story'.

Don't listen to your solicitor. Best rule of thumb is to do the opposite of what they advise. If you don't avail yourself of this advice, I can assure you that within twelve months your pockets will be several thousand pounds lighter. Your savings, the children's inheritance, pensions, the lot, will be spunked and the Legal Services Commission will slam a charge on the family home so that, whatever you've spent, you'll end up paying back when you next move house.

Don't go to court - [we've covered this].

Go for shared parenting. Kids are not there to be carved up like material possessions - they are your flesh and blood and deserve the best of BOTH parents. Draw up a parenting plan and stick to it.

Don't leave the family home. Whatever anyone says and no matter how much you think you are doing this in the children's best interests, leaving the family home is a big no-no. You'll find moving back in nigh on impossible. Set out demarcation lines with your partner and, whatever else you do, try, try, try to find a way of resolving your problems without using solicitors. If you think things are bad now, multiply that by a thousand, because that's how it will be once these vermin get their noses stuck in the family trough.

Do mediate. It's not big and it's not clever to think that mediation sucks. Unless you and your partner are hell-bent on inflicting a lifetime of conflict on your family, sooner or later you will have to sit down and talk. Try and deal with the difficult personal issues in your relationship first, so that these can be set aside. This will allow you to then concentrate on making arrangements for the children. One day your children will thank you. They won't thank you if you fuck up their childhoods just because you can't learn the 'F' word: forgiveness.

Do provide support for your kids. No matter how much you hate your ex, you should always provide both emotional and financial support for your children. However, if you are being denied access for no good reason and being fleeced for the privilege, I'd recommend paying this money into a savings account or trust fund for your children to draw on when they are older. But whatever you do, keep paying it!

Don't denigrate the other parent. Denigration can lead to the alienation of a child from the other parent. Remember half your child is your partner; hate them, and you hate half your child.

Finally, NEVER hate your ex more than you love your kids.

I could not possibly have put this better myself, and am pleased that, many moons ago, Matt gave me carte blanche to quote from his book, as long as I credited him. I am more than happy to do that.

A quick word about that f-word - forgiveness. I'm afraid I have to confess that I fail on this one. I have tried, I genuinely have tried very hard, to forgive Shirley because I know that it would help me 'move on' as they say. I don't think Shirley would give a toss whether I forgive her or not. But I do, and I can't do it. How can you forgive someone who feels they've done no wrong, and would never dream of saying 'sorry'? I'm no Ghandi. I believe in the power of forgiveness, and I'm able to forgive a great deal, but I struggle on this.

I think my generation, in general, were naïve and idealistic rather than totally selfish or evil. We had this great idea of enjoying personal freedoms, unshackled by the constraints of the past. It sounded wonderful. I don't think many of us gave a thought to how this may affect the bringing-up of our children and their security and happiness. I don't give the same latitude to social workers or judges, because we know so much more: THEY know so much more, today.

To snatch babies from the womb and sell them for adoption; to keep one parent from seeing the other for no good reason; to alienate children from one or both parents; and to send children to live with an abuser, or into care for spurious reasons when there is family available and willing to look after them, all are despicable crimes, crimes against humanity, and, collectively THE crime of the century. The damage done (and indeed, cost) to our families and to our society is incalculable; this is not a small issue.

How many times have we heard 'lessons will be learned' when yet another care order has resulted in a tragedy? If lessons were going to be ever learned by these people, they would have been learned very well by now. It's yet another little mantra designed to placate an increasingly-suspicious public. Just occasionally, you get the measure of some of these people when they slip. Quite recently (in 2014) one 'senior social worker' in Essex (notorious for its authorising a caesarean birth on a mother without her knowledge) put a gleeful message on her Facebook page about her breaking up a family. Siobhan Condon gloated over it; 'It's powerful to know that children's lives have been massively changed for the better'. Yeah, yeah. Going into care really 'massively' improves kids lives, doesn't it? I've one question for her. How would she feel if she were the parent whose child's life was going to be 'massively changed for the better' by some unfeeling, brainless bimbo masquerading as a caring senior social worker?

Throughout the twentieth century, the Catholic Church in Ireland (and presumably elsewhere where they were the dominant orthodoxy) ran what became known as the 'Magdalene Laundries'. Young girls who became pregnant out of wedlock, sometimes by members of their own families, were sent to these places to have their babies 'in secret', away from the nosy tittle-tattle of their friends and neighbours. The families were terrified of the stigma attached to a daughter having an illegitimate child. Most people know about these places now; they were run by nuns aided by priests and the inmates had to work bloody hard doing menial work (usually washing) to justify their keep. They were treated like serfs and often sexually molested by their 'betters'.

When the babies were born, the mothers were allowed to bond with them before they were forced to give them up for adoption. There is some evidence emerging that some children who couldn't be found adoptive parents were murdered. Some of these places existed into the nineteen-nineties; this is very recent history. We can only imagine the excruciating anguish felt by most of these mothers, and the system is now regarded as barbaric and wrong, even by the Catholic Church itself. But the principle is not history at all. Much the same happens today, here in Britain, in our Family Courts. The nuns have been replaced by Social workers and CAFCASS officers, and the priest signing-off the papers has been replaced by a Family Court Judge. The secrecy of the Laundries has been replaced by the secrecy of the Family Courts. There's no real difference, and no difference at all to the anguish felt by parents who lose their children. There's no difference between the barbarity of sanctimonious nuns and the barbarity of smirking social workers. Each are equally as evil. Believe me, it happens every day, in this country, now. You can't even say 'Lord forgive them, for they know not what they do'. They bloody well do know the effects it has on parents and children, they do know the risks that children face going into 'care', yet they do it still. Still, they do it.

A plague on all their houses.

HOW I BELIEVE WE SHOULD CHANGE

'We must be the change we want to see in the world'

Mahatma Ghandi

I'm not talking about couples staying together now; I'm talking about how the Father's Movement should change. And the Mother's movement. And those campaigning against forced adoption and the State removing children from families, 'dysfunctional' or not. (Nothing more dysfunctional than State 'care'). Each group are campaigning on their own fronts, which is perfectly natural. However, I feel we should all unite under a 'Family' banner, for we all want and fundamentally believe in the same thing. I last suggested this a few years ago in a Father's rights column and received such ridiculous abuse (I can take criticism but not abuse) that I just held up my hands in submission. Some dads wrote as if they were the idiot's idiot. Silence from the mums.

There is, understandably, considerable hostility between the respective movements, but what many seem to fail to see is that there is far more that unites us than divides us. We all believe that what we are campaigning for will improve our lives and our children's lives and benefit society as a whole. We tend to fight thinking only of our own bad experiences, which almost always involves a previous partner of the opposite sex. This tends to blind us to the wider issues, and to the fact that the Family Courts dole out random cruelty, particularly to non-resident parents. It is usually the father who is the non-resident parent, hence the popular conception amongst father's groups and the wider public that it is only fathers who are treated appallingly. That is why I wanted to publish the articles from grandparents, mothers and children in this book, to show that it is not just us fathers who suffer from the Court system.

So I would plead again, here, that each movement should hold a meeting together, first to air our differences and then to discuss what unites us and how we should proceed. If parents and families tackled the current system together, if we could manage to present a united front, my God that would be a strong movement! The present system is in a feeding frenzy at present, gorging on the dismembered corpses of families riven even further apart by the Court system. Let all mothers and fathers, grandparents and relatives of good faith, unite as one, and then watch the system try and get their 'expert witnesses' and other bottom-feeders around that. They would genuinely fear a united movement of families.

251

For all our words, and theirs, for all our protesting, very little has changed in the Family Courts. I believe dads came close just at the time Matt disbanded F4J for the first time - I think we were in touching distance - which is why I for one feel angry with him. The best we have achieved is a greater public and political awareness of the issues. My friend George said to me he thought that politicians were afraid of families. I couldn't agree with him at the time, but, you know, I think he was at least partly right. Families united are the biggest force you can have. I personally believe that unless we do tackle the current Court and State systems united as families, we will continue to fail to fundamentally change the system. We do want that, don't we? All of us?

FAMILY (MIS)FORTUNES

My birth mother died in 2008. She'd come close to death in hospital some months before but had recovered enough to be sent home. My youngest sister Brenda and Les, her husband, found it very difficult to cope looking after Mum, and she was found a nice care home not far from them. I think she was quite happy there, with the company of others and gentle non-intrusive care and her own private room which she could retire to at any time: and good food.

One Saturday morning fairly soon after Mum had moved I was sitting on the apex of a roof (not protesting this time. I was mending one of the greenhouses) when Rosa said I was needed on the phone. 'I can't come, I'm on the greenhouse roof!' I shouted. 'You have to come' she said. It was Les, telling me Mum had suddenly died that morning. She'd been so ill previously that I wasn't taken by surprise, but apparently Brenda was and had been affected very badly.

The funeral took place in Loughborough. I'd met all my siblings, but my two brothers and the eldest sister Lynne had not kept in touch. As far as I was aware, they bore me no animosity, we just didn't bother! We didn't have an awful lot in common. Pamela and Brenda kept in regular contact, and I regarded Pam as a soul-mate really. It felt good to meet up as a family again, despite the circumstances.

I'd visited Pam at her home in Brighton, as regularly as I could, over several years previously. When I stopped paying Shirley, I switched to paying Pam as she was the least well-off of us all and she had three children, all, fortunately, beginning to make their own way in the world. Pam had been stricken with meningitis as a teenager and had struggled at times since. Her children were all just fine. I loved them all but had a particular rapport with Sade. She wrote a lovely letter to Heather, via Heather's solicitor, which I print at the end of this book.

My mum's sister, Olwen, and her son and his wife were also at the funeral of course. Both they and we left after what we considered to be a decent interval; we had a fair way to go (Olwen lives in north London). As we left, Brenda's husband Les took me aside and said 'Mum wanted me to tell you that she's sorry'. I said she had nothing whatever to be sorry about, and I was surprised that she'd said anything like this. This seemed, somehow, to be wrong. I was surprised and somewhat shocked to hear that after we had left, my brothers and sisters had more-or-less stripped Mum's house bare.

I was even more shocked when, during a routine call to Brenda, she said that 'someone' had accused Rosa of saying 'inappropriate' things to my younger brother. A quick call to John confirmed he had no idea what she (or we) were talking about. I wrote to Brenda asking for more information and received a hostile reply saying I was 'shooting the messenger'. I wasn't - I hadn't accused her of anything. This was distressing enough, but I then found that Pam wouldn't talk to me either.

We had had to curtail the payments to her shortly before the funeral, we were running out of money, and it seemed just too much of a coincidence; so I wrote quite a strongly-worded letter asking if this was the reason. I knew - or thought I did - that it wasn't but I wanted to provoke a reaction at least. It worked. She was 'insulted'. Yes, you were meant to be, Pam, because I knew you'd respond to it. You weren't responding to anything else. After receiving so much support from my sisters, and having felt I had been accepted (see the letters at the end of the book), and having visited Mum with Brenda when Mum was in Hospital, this was devastating, particularly as it came shortly after I'd lost in the Family Court.

I still haven't a clue why this happened, and my aunt Olwen is equally baffled. Thank God she was apart from all this, not a part of it. I wasn't offered a single memento of Mum's life. I had already told Les that I didn't want any money from Mum's estate, and I didn't, but some small memento would have been nice. Olwen kindly gave me one of hers. I now have lost my child, my adopted parents, my adopted brother, and most of my birth family. Families, eh? Makes you value your friends.

An amusing aside to this is that I'd undertaken to discover the family history. I'm not computer –savvy at all, so I took up my sister-in-law's offer of doing it. Fran did the most brilliant job and put the story into a proper glossy book with many photographs. It took her ages. I was going to do copies and send them to Brenda and to Pam, but then the sudden estrangement happened. They had said they'd be really interested in knowing more, so I gave them the option of receiving the book but they didn't reply, so they didn't get it. Apparently Pamela at least did not like some of the facts that had emerged (I'd let slip a few). Much of our history is not very honourable! Fran is now something of an authority on family history, and appears on various 'ancestry' websites. Last year Brenda inadvertently contacted her as she was doing some research of her own and had come across Fran's name. Brenda was told that I had all the details if she wanted them. Neither of us have heard any more.

THE GREAT BRITISH BLANDSCAPE

'He who sacrifices freedom for security, deserves neither'.

(Attributed to Benjamin Franklin).

Family and home: the two most basic things for any 'normal' human being, and I have fought for, and come into conflict with, both. What is the matter with me? Friends are also of great importance. Two of my closest friends - Clive and Douglas - became an Orthodox Jew and a born-again Christian, respectively. What do I do to these people?

I'll just concentrate on the home bit now. I have long thought that the planning rules are all wrong, at least in rural areas. I am incredibly lucky to live where I do and in a way that suits me. I am well aware that most people cannot do what I have done, though many would like to. People ask me how I've done it - and I honestly have to reply that really I haven't a clue. Much of it is through sheer luck and having enough 'neck'. It's been at a price, not so much in financial terms but in the amount of hassle we've had to endure in order to get where we are today. Or, rather, to keep where we are today.

It's not illegal to build your own home on your own land, or to put a caravan on it. Many think that it is. It's not. It becomes illegal if the local planning authority subsequently deem it so, after they've found you've done it and you submit a 'retrospective' planning application. A lot more people think it <u>is</u> OK to build your own home on your own land, that somehow it is an inalienable right. That's not correct, either. I think it should be.

I can imagine the legions of 'country lovers' (mostly urban dwellers) throwing their hands up in horror at my impertinence. So I think it's time for a proper, grown-up discussion about this. How do we want to live? How would we like our children to live? How much do we value our countryside? What do we think of sky-high property prices? How important is the individual as opposed to the State? How important is personal freedom as opposed to State control of our lives?

My biggest objection to the Planning System is that it doesn't work. And, yet again, costs us all a huge amount of money. In that, it's like the Family Court system. It is supposed to stop 'urban blight' and ribbon development but, at least here in Central Bedfordshire, there is more suburban sprawl being created than at any time since the thirties. There's all this mantra about 'sustainable housing' but I can't see it. What's 'sustainable' about having houses where there is little or no work and people have to travel by car to get to work?

Our nearest little town of Shefford has been completely ruined courtesy of Central Beds. Council. When I came here it was a 'one horse town', a 'one-eyed, blinking sort of place', almost unique in the Home Counties for those very reasons. It was, truly, a modest, self-sufficient little town, tainted neither with 'executive homes' or on anyone's tourist trail, either. It did have a traffic problem, and had been under consideration for a by-pass since the nineteen-thirties! Five years after I'd moved here, its new by-pass opened. People in the town were grateful, but surely it must be a case of 'be careful what you wish for'. Firstly, a huge (proportionate to the town) estate of modern houses started to be built, inbetween the existing environs of the town and the by-pass. If anyone had suggested to the Council that this happen a couple of years earlier, they would have had an apoplectic fit. Then a large service station/local supermarket was placed by one of the roundabouts. A new road was constructed to link two existing ones in order to service a new light industrial estate, the new housing estates, and the supermarket. This 'major' supermarket was extended, a bit. Since then, many more houses have been built on all sides of the town.

Shefford has been changed from a rather unremarkable little town into a totally unremarkable suburban satellite. And, far from improving the local services and shops, the town still has just the one major supermarket (thank God) and has lost many smaller businesses such as the Family Butchers and the Steam Hand Laundry. Not only this, but the neighbouring villages are being submerged under a tide of new housing, getting ever closer to each other in what is the equivalent of ribbon development and suburbanisation. The result is that not only is the town centre just as choked with traffic now as it ever was before the by-pass was opened, but the by-pass itself is virtually at full capacity at busy times. No-one was told that this was going to happen, of course. The final nail in the coffin was the new Council offices, which of course meant that the road needed further 'upgrading' complete with suburban lighting, roundabout, a huge car park, traffic lights, etc. It was if the planners were putting two fingers up to Shefford.

Most of the many houses going up around here are sold as 'exclusive' or 'executive' homes. They shouldn't be 'exclusive' - they should be inclusive! And why should only 'executives' be allowed to live here? And why have all the estates got such ridiculous, twee names; 'Orchard View',

'Bellcote Meadow', 'St. Gregory's Heights', 'Priory Mill'? If they have names like these, you can bet there's no orchard and certainly no view; no bellcote and no meadow; that St. Gregory, if ever he was here, has long fled and there are certainly no 'heights' to look out from; and there's no Priory and no Mill either, as they were more sensible in the old days and did not build on the flood-plain.

The Council insists that they include 'affordable housing' in the developments, to which I would ask 'what's the point of having any unaffordable ones?'

I've no wish here to go into the protracted arguments we had with the Council, for it would make tedious reading. I have mentioned that Mr. Hill, made 'Enforcement Officer Team Leader', was a fair and reasonable man, but he seemed overwhelmed by the pressure from other characters on the Council. When Mid-Beds. became Central Beds. (how much did that change of name cost all of us?) and moved to a swanky new building just down the road from here (opened by the Queen!), he disappeared and any further dialogue with the Planning Department ceased.

We had a new 'team', led by a Mrs. Cawthra, who seemed totally indifferent to anyone's personal circumstances and was determined to get us out. When this happened, we had been here for fifteen years, with no local objections to our being here. In fact, a petition set up in our support was launched locally, and received nearly three hundred signatures, with minimal publicity. Meanwhile, a few miles away in a village called Arlesey, a group of 'travellers' (who didn't travel) had set up an illegal site on the edge of the village which had received numerous local objections and the objection of the local town council, yet Central Beds. approved it. Political correctness ruled above commonsense or even basic humanity in typical Orwellian style. They took us to the Magistrate's Court in Bedford. The Magistrates seemed out of their depth on this issue, and simply fined us £500 plus 'victim surcharge'. Who were the victims?

We were not helped through this time by Dora. She still used a half of the existing land for keeping chickens and the odd goat, sheep, and pig or two. As Albert had become older and less able, she struck up a friendship with someone else and he proved (for us) to be a most unpleasant and malign individual. Dora was thinking of selling her bit but was asking from us £80,000 when the valuation was less than a tenth of that. We finally came to an agreement with our neighbours to share the cost, at £20,000. Before this, Mick, her new man, tried to get a friend of his to buy it. Dora and I had a 'tenants in common' agreement so she could not sell it to anyone without my agreement. Instead of introducing himself in the conventional way, this man's first words were 'I'll be charging you rent'. There was no way I was going to let it go to someone like that. But this infuriated Mick, who physically attacked Rosa (I wasn't around when he appeared) so we had to take out an injunction to prevent him entering our property again.

Nevertheless he appeared at our final appeal under a different name, telling the inspector that we were 'the sperm of the devil' or something similar and actually making himself look an aggressive fool. We were obliged to tell the inspector that this man was not able to enter our property under the terms of an injunction, which the inspector readily accepted. We lost that appeal too, by the way! But we stayed on. . . .I should add that since then Dora has distanced herself a little from Mick and we are on good terms once again. As Dora is nearly eighty-five as I write, I am glad of this. It seemed totally pointless and damaging to all of us that we were at loggerheads.

When I moved here nearly thirty years ago, the area was a predominantly horticultural and agricultural one. Next to us was a pig farm. When this was closed down for economic reasons, the local coach firm that had been operating for many years in the centre of the village applied to relocate their business to the site. This would have benefitted everyone - especially me! (The firm, Taylors, had an excellent reputation). The road through the village was becoming busier and the coach operator had to reverse coaches out into it from their existing yard. Given approval, the business could have expanded, employed more people, and the coach operation would have been made safer. No more reversing out into the road. Planning permission was refused.

Instead, it was granted for a huge new nursing home which still dominates the whole area and is extremely visible for miles around. (Years later, it was forced to close because of abominable standards of 'care' but I suppose that's irrelevant). The increase in traffic that this business caused was phenomenal. The place looked like a giant out-of-town superstore. We, on the other hand, were completely invisible from the road, and working a business that was traditional with the area, yet for twenty years we had to fight to the last ditch in order to live our traditional 'green' ('sustainable') lifestyle.

The council said we could still run the business but would have to live away from it. How 'green' is that? They were advocating we live in one of the poky little houses on one of their numerous estates and get here by car (there's still no bus). We paid our council tax. What? You ask. You pay council tax whilst they try to evict you? Oh yes, they accept that. Their argument is that you are accepting their services so you have to pay. We didn't ask for those 'services' (in our case only a diminishing rubbish-collection) but there you go. . . .

I'm not saying we don't need homes, of course we do. But do they all have to be on soulless estates, all looking more-or-less the same, all with gardens so small you can't grow very much in them? With people paying what I think is a fortune for this, saddling themselves with soul-destroying mortgages for twenty five years, necessitating a lifetime of commuting? How green is that?

Little boxes on the hillside
Little boxes made of ticky-tacky,
Little boxes on the hillside
Little boxes all the same.
There's a green one and a pink one
And a blue one and a yellow one
And they're all made out of ticky-tacky
And they all look just the same.

Malvina Reynolds, 1962

I really feel for any young person who simply wants to live a sustainable, independent lifestyle on their own land and in their own home. I don't think it will be possible for any one of average means, unless they inherit such a place. But there is an alternative which, given what I know now, could prove a worthwhile thing to do.

My suggestion, should you wish to live a 'simpler' or more sustainable life, is to buy the cheapest property you can find (such as a terrace house) as near as possible to some allotments. Allotments can still be rented for fairly modest sums and if several plots are vacant, you may be lucky enough to rent two. I think allotments are great. You can swop stuff with your neighbours, you can take time out with similarly-minded people, you can get healthy exercise without paying for sessions at the gym, and produce delicious produce that you _know_ hasn't been sprayed with some noxious substance. You can swap tips on growing stuff and you can agree with your neighbouring plot-holders to grow stuff they can't for any reason, or vice-versa. If you want to go on holiday, you can often entrust a fellow plot-holder to keep an eye on your plot. If you're really lucky, you may find a house with a back garden that backs onto the allotments, and have your

259

own private gate! On some allotments you are allowed to keep hens, too. Don't dismiss it out-of-hand.

Everyone should be able to live quietly on their own land if no one locally objects, which is the right of the robin or wren. To those that say it would 'ruin the countryside' I would say that it would bring the countryside to life, with happy and healthy smallholders instead of one or two disgruntled and defensive big landowners. What is the point of the countryside if it is simply an empty shell?

The countryside of my boyhood was a heaven on earth (well, it was for me). Green, well-layered hedges surrounded the small fields, the farms were alive with the sound of animals, with ducks on the horse-pond and horses in the stable. By the time I left school, it was all changing very rapidly. Agribusiness was to replace agriculture, hedges were to be ripped up to make larger fields to accommodate ever-larger machinery, and chicken Belsens, pig sweat-boxes, and veal crates were becoming the rage. Monoculture was the way forward.

In East Anglia, the former varied landscape was replaced with vast prairies of barley. Barley, barley, barley, until you began to think that no crop other than barley was of any use to mankind at all. And, after the barley was harvested, the fields blackened and burning as if the Visigoths were there. In a manner of speaking they were - but these Goths rode swivel chairs, not horses - these were the Goths with the large bellies and the double-chins, living in their vulgar new gin-palaces, the old farmhouses having been tarted up and sold to commuters. It is better now, but it could still be so much more varied and beautiful if we had more people living on the land, particularly young people. Not in vast estates of 'little boxes' but independently, on their own plots. It's an experiment I should like to see tried, anyway; but I doubt I'll see that. In my lifetime I have witnessed what I regard as the Lowland Clearances.

At least young people could be encouraged rather than dissuaded to lead a greener, more self-sufficient lifestyle. Sixty-odd years ago, George Henderson, author of the famous and inspiring book 'The Farming Ladder', wrote 'Farming in small units, with diversified production, which is essential to make the best use of the land, requires management in addition to the performance of labour. It therefore presupposes a certain degree of initiative, skill and intelligence, as well as a willingness to work, to take a risk, and stand on one's own merits. All good human qualities which we should seek to foster in our race. . . . .the greatest security any nation can have is a property-owning community.' He also expressed the wish that he would see many young people living in their own homes on the new small farms he sincerely hoped would become a feature of the English countryside. Well, alas for that dream. It is a huge pity that such a relatively modest, natural ambition should now be so enormously difficult to achieve.

Part of the problem is that most planning officers come from urban or suburban backgrounds, are academics, and have no conception of a vibrant rural economy. They see people living in the countryside as necessarily detrimental to it, unless they live in picturesque cottages in old-fashioned villages. Any divergence from this, such as a small group living in 'roundhouses' or tepees is anathema to them.

Not very long ago, a community living in Pembrokeshire were spotted by a planning officer in a spy-plane (they've always got the money to do this sort of thing; very environmentally-friendly). This group were living in roundhouses built very similarly to those built in that area thousands of years ago, and were virtually self-sufficient in food and clothing. Enforcement proceedings were initiated, whilst at the same time the same Council were importing round-houses built in Estonia as a visitor attraction in the Preseli Hills! After a lengthy and very expensive battle, I am glad to report that the round-house dwellers won. But why on earth couldn't the planners see the contradiction in their policies when everyone else could? Can they not ever see the bleedin' obvious? They have tunnel vision, only seeing things in black-and-white, no wonder our countryside has become in many areas so bland and boring for those who live there as well as those passing through.

Like social workers, many planning officials think they are the law. And therefore they can be as petty and vindictive as they bloody well like. I wrote an article about this for our local village magazine. Here is the last half of it.

'...*The most ridiculous example of this that I have heard of concerns an elderly lady doctor who lived in the canal-side hamlet of Thrupp, in Oxfordshire. She was unfortunate enough to live in a 'listed' ex-canal-workers cottage (now euphemistically described as 'artisan's dwellings') and she suffered badly with arthritis. Her front door, being wooden, swelled in damp weather and she found it increasingly difficult to open it - sometimes having to call a neighbour to help. So she replaced it with one made of a composite material which did not swell, making sure it looked identical and was the same colour. She even kept the original door. She was taken to Court at least twice by Oxford CC for fitting an 'inappropriate door'. What is more important? The composition of someone's door or the quality of life of the person living behind it? What 'elf'n'safety would have made of a sticking door we can only conjecture. Sheer, blinkered stupidity and arrogance.*

A word now on these 'listed buildings'. Almost all of them were built without planning permission or building regulations, and would not be allowed to be built today. Yet the owners of them are told they have to be preserved in aspic and they are not allowed to do anything at all to them without permission, and permission is seldom granted. Notwithstanding that many of these buildings have been added to in a mix of styles over the hundreds of years they've been standing which gives such joy to so many people because of their quirkiness and diversity of style.. Now they have to be preserved 'just so'. Except of course when the Government wants to build a high-speed railway line or another motorway; then they must be demolished, pronto - preferably no questions asked. Hypocrisy is the word that comes to mind. Or 'official vandalism...'.

Finally, our own case. For as long as people have lived on this planet, they have built homes wherever they thought it best. This is how communities have grown over the centuries and why so many of them look 'right' or at least they did so before the planners came and dumped new houses all round the edges, often with no extra facilities for all the new residents. It is natural and 'environmentally-friendly' for people to live on, or very close to, their place of work, particularly when that work is agriculture, horticulture or forestry. What I did here is what thousands of people have done over hundreds of years; make a home on my own land. Now it is 'inappropriate development in the open countryside'. If mine really is, then how is a giant Nursing Home right next door 'appropriate'?

After nearly twenty years, and we are now in our sixties, we are facing the very real threat of eviction. Not only that, but they are going to put a charge on our land (in effect, compulsory purchase) so we will be landless as well as homeless and totally reliant on the State. The plan is that they will 'remove and 'safely store' our home and our possessions. The cost is estimated at £100,000. We have offered to settle for 'private permission' to stay which means that when both of us are dead, the home will be removed and the land returned to horticulture or amenity use. More than that, we have said that we are willing after our demise for the land to be given to our local community, for use as allotments, or a nature reserve, or whatever the community want, but not for speculative building. For us, this means no financial advantage at all, in fact it means our heirs will be financially disadvantaged. And we can't move, because the place is financially worthless. We don't mind that, but we do mind being evicted

262

after all these years with no compensation and having to take 'social housing' when there are so many young people in dire need of a home.

In Central Bedfordshire alone, there are around 12,000 registered for 'social housing' and last year just 3,000 properties were offered. The Council themselves state 'It is simply not possible to offer everyone a rented council or housing association property'. Why, then, exacerbate the situation at a time of financial constraint? Particularly when no-one locally objects to us being here? It pains me to say this, but I agree with our MP Nadine Dorries when she says that this issue has become 'personal and vindictive'. There should be no place for this when it comes to someone's home. And these issues should not be allowed to go on for such an inordinately long time. I can tell everyone that it is enormously stressful. If the Council haven't removed you from your own land within, say, five years, they should not be permitted to continue enforcement after that time. As it is, they are under no legal obligation to do this. There has to be a balance between enforcement and all the other considerations; we feel there is no balance at all in this case.

Perhaps the council should read the Human Rights Act where it states; Article 8: Right to privacy

1.   Everyone has the right for his private and family life, <u>his home</u> and his correspondence.

2.   There shall be no interference by a public authority with the exercise of this right except such as in accordance with the law and is necessary in a democratic society in the interests of national security, public safety or the economic well-being of the country, for the prevention of disorder or crime, for the protection of health or morals, or for the protection of the rights and freedoms of others

Are we really such a threat to others?

Needless to say, 'answer came there none'. However, at the eleventh hour, I did what my friend George had suggested I do, ages before, and contacted one of my local councillors.

I was, as I so often am, immensely lucky in my choice. Mr. Lewis Birt had been on the Council for many years and is one of those rare people who do it because they want to serve the community rather than for financial gain or enhanced social standing. He believes in compromise and in fair dealing, acting with sensitivity and humanity rather than with the finesse of a bulldozer. Virtually single-handedly he turned everything around for us. The deal was that the Council took our land but we were able to stay here as long as we lived, and work the land as we had previously. The mobile home remains ours but the land belongs to the Council. We pay a peppercorn rent of £1 a year. I'm quite pleased with this: we have security of tenure and if the Council want our land before we go, they will have to pay us for it. It means our place is worth practically nothing - and I'm quite pleased with that, too. No way are we a part of the housing racket. Yes, if we had the choice, we would like to move to somewhere truly rural - Herefordshire perhaps or Shropshire or maybe West Somerset - but we can't have everything. My one worry is that this area will cease to even look rural and we'll be surrounded by suburbia, but again, there's a risk in everything.

I must pay tribute, too, to our M.P. Nadine Dorries who again had the courage and integrity to stand a little apart from the bureaucrats and tell them what they were doing was disproportionate and rather vindictive. I understand it got her into some trouble but she's the sort not to care overmuch if she's standing on principle, which she often is. She's been in a lot more trouble over other things, and although we do not always agree totally with what she says or does we do admire her. She's an excellent M.P.

I can't advise anyone to do what I did, but if you do, then the best of luck to you - you'll need it!

JESTER MINUTE!

Like a bird on the wire
Like a drunk in a midnight choir
I have tried, in my way, to be free.. . .

If I have been unkind
I hope you can just let it go by
I have been untrue
I hope you know it was never to you. . . . .

I saw a beggar leaning on his wooden crutch
He said to me, "You must not ask for so much."
And a pretty woman leaning in her darkened door,
She cried to me, "Hey, why not ask for more?"

Like a bird on the wire
Like a drunk in a midnight choir
I have tried, in my way, to be free.

Excerpt from 'Bird on the Wire', by Leonard Cohen

Well, we're up-to-date and nearly done (well I am). During my time writing this, I have been approached by a number of people who say to me 'why don't you include this' or 'why haven't you mentioned that?'. Well, you can't include everything, unless perhaps you're Stephen Hawking. . . and I'm certainly not him!

So here are one or two of the philosophies that I have tried to live by, or at least keep in mind. And the longer I live, it seems the more relevant they are (at least to me).

Food for Thought

I described earlier in this book how much John Seymour, author, self-sufficiency guru and philosopher, influenced my early thinking. When he wrote 'The Fat of the Land' in 1961 he really was a one-off. He'd lived in all sorts of places, including in a trolleybus and a small boat before managing to rent a cottage in Suffolk with some land, and writing the book about it. He'd fought in Burma in World War II and in Italy, had been a cowboy (in all but name) in Africa, gone mining, and had farmed in many

265

places. His book 'One Man's Africa' became a classic. In 1974 he wrote 'Practical Self-Sufficiency: a guide to producing and preserving your own food'. At that time many people had become interested in doing it; many craved for a simpler way of life, and John and his wife Sally tapped into this burgeoning feeling and the book was a huge success. He knew what he was talking about; he'd done it all for years.

I think this rather short-lived 'simpler life' movement was partly down to people of my generation having become very materialistic only to find that they craved the uncomplicated life that their upbringing had been. This combined with the hippy movement and a far greater awareness of 'green' issues, and care for the planet.
The Government of the day was far less interested in 'green' issues than it purportedly is now. By 1974 I was into taking children on country holidays rather than living a more self-sufficient lifestyle but the philosophies of John Seymour and of George Henderson never left me.

Considering how important politicians and many other people now think the environment is, it may be interesting to just briefly quote some of their works that have influenced my thinking along these lines. If they get you to pause and think, reflect and consider, even if you then reject their ideas or find them impossible to implement, then that would please me (and them, if they're looking down on us now). I think they were far more 'green' than we are today, despite all the present-day hype.

As a thirteen or fourteen-year-old, reading 'The Fat of the Land' for the first time (and thinking it was a bit flippant, after reading serious farming and countryside books before it) I'd got about two-thirds of the way through when I got to the chapter entitled 'The Raft-Loads'. At the end of this chapter I was spell-bound as John was putting into words thoughts that had been loosely circulating in my head for some time, usually when I was supposed to be concentrating on my maths. lesson.

He wrote: *'So we are not altogether bereft of beauty. But natural beauty is not enough. There must also be plenty of that different sort of beauty which is created, consciously, by man.*

I have no doubt that if we had a week or two to prepare for it we could live here at the Broom [the name of his cottage] on our five acres and with the wild food from the surrounding woods, estuaries and marshes, for the rest of our lives without any contact with the rest of the world at all. That is if the world would leave us alone, which it would not. But by doing so we would lose a great deal. Society is good as well as bad, and we have no objection to trading in a controlled way with the rest of the world.

But living here, so far away from society, has altered our sense of values. We find that we no longer place the same importance on artefacts and gadgets as other people do. Also - every time we buy some factory-made article - we wonder what sort of people made it - if they enjoyed making it or if it was just a bore - what sort of life the maker, or makers, lead. Every time I have to travel to other places - to London or Birmingham - I wonder where all the activity I see in those places is leading. Is it really leading to a better or richer or simpler life for people? Or not? Whenever the Yankee planes roar over my head, as they do many times a day because we have an airbase near here, I wonder about the nature of 'progress'. One can progress in so many different directions. Up a gum-tree for example.

I know that the modern Birmingham factory-worker is supposed to lead an 'easier' life than, say, a French peasant. But I wonder if this supposition is correct. And I wonder if, whether 'easier' or not, it is a better life? Simpler? Healthier? More spiritually satisfying? Or not?'

None of my contemporaries were thinking like this, and none of my teachers or family or adult friends were either (except Aunt Ellen), but this truly struck a chord within me. Today, he probably would have sacrificed the term 'Birmingham factory worker' with 'computer operator' or such, but I think the meaning holds fast. It does for me, anyway. I was avid to read more along these lines and I was not disappointed. Later in the book came this…
'It is through listening always to the financial argument that so many people in the world lead such boring lives…

I used to think that an old petrol tin was as good for carrying water in as an earthenware pot. One day I read something by Tagore, in which he touched on this very comparison. He said - yes - an old petrol tin is as good for carrying water as a chatti, or one of the beautiful pots that Indian women carry on their heads, except for one thing: the petrol tin is mean. It is grudging. Because it just serves the utilitarian purpose - and no more. It carries the water all right. So does the chatti. But the chatti is delightful to look at, delightful to feel and to touch, pleasant to have around. Every time you look at it you think of the love and care with which it was made, by the hands of a human being. Every time you look at the petrol tin you think of a huge, ugly clanking machine, mindlessly slamming out ugly objects….

But we have to buy, occasionally, the grudging things. The only way to treat the twentieth century [and the twenty-first! - Roger] *is, not to ignore it, but not to let oneself be overruled by it. ... '*

No other book influenced me as much. It made me reject the contemporary wisdom that you should try and make as much money as possible at almost any other cost (that was pretty general thinking in the early sixties, and much the same today) and kick-started me into thinking laterally. That has served me well all my life.

I'd like to end this tome on a gentle note. George Henderson became a very well-known author in farming circles during the War in 1943, when he published his first book 'The Farming Ladder'. He and his brother had bought a run-down farm near Enstone in Oxfordshire in the depression years of the mid nineteen-twenties and despite the continuing depression of the thirties, and it being a relatively small farm, had built it up to be astoundingly successful. They applied the sound farming principles of an earlier age and improved on them, always though keeping to age-old and largely organic principles and the humane treatment of their stock. Ten years after publishing the book, he wrote a postscript, parts of it were quite lyrical and echoed Ruskin. These lines still move me today, and I hope you enjoy reading them too.

"We in farming have so much to be thankful for, and to share with others, when all real and wholesome pleasures are available to those who work in contentment and in peace. To watch the corn grow and the blossom set, to learn the skill of spade and scythe; to work, to think, to plan; to love, to hope, to pray; those are the things in which we must strive to make more clear the way.

When we ponder on these things, and working farmers like myself have always had ample opportunity for reflection, we realise that the most important factor in the relationship between work and human happiness is the creative instinct. The industrial age has denied it to millions, the lack of it may be responsible for the general apathy and neurosis of our times, but in farming we have something which is truly creative and for its own sake worthwhile; for farming is not only a means of earning a living, it is a way of life, a calling, a craft, a science, a business, and above all, an art.

I think it was Ruskin who defined art as a creative imitation of Nature. If that is so, then farming must be the most truly creative of all the arts, for the farmer imposes a dynamic, if fractional, influence upon the processes of nature in which like begets like and new forms are evolved. The musician and the dancer thrill us with their interpretation of fleeting movements; the sculptor and the painter express in various inanimate mediums colour, light and form; but the farmer has all the resources of Nature with which to mirror that which he loves best in an art which has for its basis order, its essence unity, and for its soul the very spirit of creation".

I have finished by quoting others, which is perfectly correct. They were far more gifted than I will ever be, and it's a pleasure and a privilege to pass on their words of kindness and wisdom. May I wish you the peace that they found. You don't need to farm to achieve it, but if you till your little piece of earth on sound principles and live right, you will have every chance. And if you've managed to read thus far, you will have certainly deserved it.

As for the future; what? I hope to be spared to spend a few years more travelling and working my little acre, and I'm not intending to stop trying to change Family Law in this country. I really hope to be able to live long enough to see a fundamental change in this. And I do hope that my daughter and I might be reconciled. Other than those, I haven't a clue. But I hope whatever happens, it'll provide as much love, interest, amusement and challenges as I've enjoyed (or not) in previous years. Onward and upward!

'So strongly is the desire implanted in many men to work as they like and not in accordance with instructions, and so great is their love of farming, that they quite cheerfully take up smallholdings and produce more food per acre than the average large farmer. . . .This spirit is entirely commendable and it never fails to excite the sympathy of the British public'.

Sir John Russell in 'The Farm and the Nation', 1933

We believe that the roots of justice, freedom, social security and democracy lie not so much in access to money, or to the ballot box, as in access to land and its resources.

Demands to 'make poverty history', and responses from those in power, revolve around money; less debt, freer and fairer trade, more aid. Rarely will you hear someone with access to a microphone mouth the word 'land'.

That is because economists define wealth and justice in terms of access to the market. Politicians echo the economists because the more dependent that people become on the market, the more securely they can be roped into the fiscal and political hierarchy. Access to land is not simply a threat to landowning elites - it is a threat to the religion of unlimited economic growth and the power structure that depends upon it.

The market (however attractive it may appear) is built on promises; the only source of wealth is the earth. Anyone who has land has access to energy, water, nourishment, shelter, healing, wisdom, ancestors and a grave.

The first and inevitable effect of the global market is to uproot and destroy land-based human cultures. The final and inevitable achievement of a rootless global market will be to destroy itself.

Rome fell; the Soviet Empire collapsed; the stars and stripes are fading in the west. Nothing is forever in history, except geography. Capitalism is a confidence trick, a dazzling edifice built on paper promises. It may stand longer than some of us anticipate, but when it crumbles, the land will remain.

From the manifesto of 'The Land' incorporating Chapter 7.

CONCERNED AT THE BREAKING
OF MODERN BRITAIN ?

**YOUR JESTER
NEEDS YOU !**

**THE JESTER NEEDS YOU TO SIGN A PUBLIC PETITION :
EQUAL RIGHTS FOR DADS &
OPEN FAMILY COURTS**

WHERE?
The recruitment stall
Cornmarket Street (by the Carfax Tower), Oxford

WHEN?
Saturday 19th December 2009, 10 am To 5 pm

REPORT TO : Recruiting officer ROGER CRAWFORD
(alias the Court Jester)
AND SIGN UP FOR A FAIRER, MODERN BRITAIN !

APPENDIX 1

I would like you to ponder on the comments of five very articulate ladies, ranging from a child to a grandparent. All have had experiences of our wonderful Family Court system and it is a great honour for me that they have given me permission to put in print their experiences.

1 <u>ROSY STANESBY</u>.

I am totally indebted to Rosy Stanesby and her father, Jonathan, always known as 'Jolly', for the following piece. Jolly has been a very high-profile campaigner for Fathers 4 Justice, climbing all manner of buildings and objects, and was sent to prison for scaling, along with fellow member Mark Harris (who wasn't jailed), Harriet Harman's house in 2008. I was one of the 'ground crew' that day and noted how delighted some local children were to see 'Batman' up on the roof! I also attended Jolly's 'trial' at Westminster Magistrates Court, where the lady Judge, a Judge Wickham, commented on how 'scared' the children would have been so see this going on. What a total farce and deliberate distortion of the situation. Judge Wickham seemed to take a delight in denigrating anything Jolly had to say, and she was confirmation to me of everything wrong with the system. Those kids were not 'scared' at all, quite the opposite, and she would have not considered for one moment the anguish the Family Courts cause to parents and children every working day of the year, every year.

There's another new Government booklet out especially for children involved in family break-up. It's called 'My Turn to Talk', giving the impression of course that those who decide the fate of these kids it's their time to listen. And that not only will they listen, they may actually act. I cannot think of a more cynical publication, except perhaps the one put out in the eighties called 'Protect and Survive' which detailed how you might survive a nuclear attack. (They may just as well have said 'Put your head between your legs and kiss your arse goodbye'). This one might as well be called 'It's Your Turn to Talk but shut up anyway'.

So you think your schooling's phoney?
Guess it's hard not to agree.
You say it all depends on money
And who is in your family tree.

Right, right, you're bloody well right,
You've got a bloody right to say.
Right, right, you're bloody well right

You know you have a right to say
But me, I don't care anyway.

Write your problems down in detail,
Take them to a higher place;
You've had your cry, I shouldn't say wail;
In the meantime, hush your face.

Right, right, you're bloody well right
You've got a bloody right to say,
Right, right, you're bloody well right,
You know you have a right to say
Ha-Ha, you're bloody well right,
You've got a right to say. . . . .

'Bloody well right', from the album 'Crime of the Century' by Supertramp, 1974

Rosy, was a speaker at the 'Children Screaming to be Heard' Conference in 2014 when she was just fifteen. She has also given evidence to yet another Parliamentary body. This is her story, exactly as she gave it. So it really is, now, 'Her Time to Talk'.

<u>Rosy Stanesby:</u>

'These authorities who are meant to be professionals, taught me to trust no-one. Why did the Family Court turn everything into such a war?'

What did I do wrong?

My parents separated in 2000 when I was 2 years old and for the next 9 years, I struggled through the heart-wrenching family court battle my parents were geared to defeat each other in, whilst I was ripped apart between them........ The 'contact order' allocated me four days a month to see my Dad. This was no relationship. He knew nothing of my friends or school life. I knew nothing of my absent family. He was my Dad. Could he not just pop round and ask me how my day was? ... No... It was not his time. When I was at my mums it was like I was not his daughter anymore because he wasn't allowed to see my Dad. It was all on paper, in writing, in court orders – my life being controlled like some kind of computer game.

At my Dads when I was young I couldn't sleep without holding his thumb. I was scared that people were going to come in the night and take me away.

This links back to the vague memory of when police visited us whilst my mum was on holiday in America. They told my Dad that I was on the missing persons' list and needed to be taken away. When he refused, they insisted to get me out of the bath and check me for bruises or any signs of abuse. They treated him like he was some kind of criminal. They left, but my mum's solicitor later said that the police should have 'forcibly removed' me from our house.

I loved him, so much, and I couldn't make sense of it all. I knew he was not bad. Or was there something wrong with the way I felt? I was so confused, but I couldn't talk about it. Everyone was against my Dad, everyone but me.

I remember talking about him at my mums once and her crying and crying. I did not want to upset her so I tried never to speak of him. I felt really lonely and that I had to be careful about everything I said in case it was used against either of my parents in court. I was used to hurt them, to break my own family, and the courts did it oblivious of my feelings.

The damage of the family courts was clear. I hardly saw any family on my Dad's side because there was simply not the time. It was not fair or right that I missed out on the relationships of my cousins, grandparents, aunts and uncles. None of it was right. At Dads, our door had always been open and kids from our street would come over and play with me. But, things changed. Soon, our door was always locked. Our curtains out the front were always closed and any knock at the door sent our house to silence. Police…bailiffs… They were constantly out to get my Dad…and why? Because he was fighting their corrupt system? Because he would not let them separate us? Because he loved his daughter?
When I was at my mums one time, the police raided our house at Dads. I returned to a home where the computer, pictures and poems I'd drawn for Dad and his fancy dress costumes he wore for protests had been taken. They had no right to take what I had done for him. I could not believe they could invade our lives like that…and why? Were they scared? My Dad was determined. My Dad was not giving up. He was not scared of being arrested, of going to prison, or of telling the whole world what heartbreak we were suffering. They picked on the wrong man!

My mum had the police drive us to Dads every time because she needed 'protection' from my 'dangerous' father. However, before this , my Uncle on my mum's side drove me between houses to help out. One day, my Uncle came to collect me. I worried that every goodbye could be the last for a while, and I couldn't face that anymore. I hated missing him.

It all hurt too much and I couldn't see why I couldn't just stay... I can see it now – my Dad and I stood on the pavement outside our house. I won't accept that I have to go and I start crying and crying in his arms. I know he doesn't want me to go either. I'm clinging to him but my Uncle's trying to pull me away. I was screaming and crying in our street but, eventually, my hand left my Dad's as I was put into the car. As my Uncle drives down our road, I took off my seatbelt and clambered onto the back seats, screaming for my Dad through my tears, banging on the windows as I watched him disappear as we turned the corner. I kept trying to open the doors and kept hitting the car window, crying my heart out...that stupid court order. My mum had to meet us half way as my Uncle couldn't calm me down.

For years, even now sometimes, that memory visits me, forcing me to feel that desperate, that heartache, that helplessness, all over again.

A lot had changed. My Dad met many people in the same situation as him- caught in an unjust system that denies parents their own children for no good reason. He realised that the inequality of the family courts was a massive problem all across the UK, and further. He began campaigning on a huge scale, to bring light of the secret family courts to the public.

I remember thinking how funny my Dad was climbing buildings. I must have been very small, but I was very proud of him. I encouraged him to wear his Robin suit because I thought the R stood for Rosy, and every time there was a protest or march, I loved the excitement and wanted to go.

At primary school, there were awards which were celebrated in assembly where your parents could come and see you. For me, this had to be done over two assemblies so my mum could come separately to my Dad and I found this really embarrassing. However, in school, I felt I could talk about my Dad. Every other Friday, I was due to see him that weekend, and I called it Daddy Day at school. I would get so excited and my friends would all get excited with me.

CAFCASS, the children and family court advisory and support service, is a government organisation that is meant to advise the court by talking to the family and children. During my childhood, I had quite a few meetings with them. At age 5, they asked me my views. I told them that I wanted to spend half the time with my Dad but I was ignored because my feelings were wrong in their eyes. They rejected me by saying that I was too young to know what I wanted. Yet I know if I'd have asked to stay with my mum in that meeting that day that they would have used it in court.

In another meeting when I was a little older, about 8 years old, I spoke to two Plymouth CAFCASS officers. Again, I told them that I wanted to see more of my Dad. He replied, "But how would this make your mum feel?" I should not have been asked anything to do with my mother's feelings, it was meant to be about how I felt – not her. I replied honestly and said that "I expect it would upset her." He answered, "And how do you feel about upsetting your mum?" By this point I didn't know what to say. No child wants to hurt their parents, but this wasn't about that. It was about what was right, how I should have been brought up, and from the beginning, it should have been equally, with both parents. They made me feel bad for feeling the way I felt. There were two sides, and I just wanted to be on both.

I finished speaking to them and sat out in the waiting area, whilst my mum spoke to them. From where I was I could hear her crying. I thought they must have told her what I had said and I felt really guilty. They'd tried to trick me into saying that I wanted to stay with my mum. But, they didn't even need me to say it. They twisted my words and lied in court, saying that I didn't want to see more of my Dad.

In 2006, after my Dad and I were allowed 10minutes to talk to each other over the phone between 5.30 and 6 on a Wednesday evening, he bought me a mobile. A short time later, it came up in court that he sent 'too many kisses' on texts to me; that he was obsessive and wanted to see me too much.

Just to make life harder, the CSA took my Dad's driving licence away making it difficult to get to school, visit friends and family and confined us to the house. My mum's parents had to pick me up from Dads and drive me to school. This was uncomfortable for me as even speaking of my Dads name caused awkwardness. One day, I got upset when my Grandparents came. I did not want to go with them because I was sick of all the problems, the over complications and the hate. Before long, the police were on the phone to my Dad wondering why I was not at school yet. This annoyed me – they were always on his case. So I told my Dad that I wanted to go and speak to the police. I was determined to tell them what was going on and I believed that they could help. How many times have I trusted people I should trust, just to have it thrown back in my face?

In the police station, I completely emptied my feelings out to a police officer where everything I said, she managed to twist around and always make my Dad look bad. "You only want to see your Dad more because you have lots of fun weekends with him." I felt so small, humiliated, completely knocked back and eventually, I burst into tears in the police station. "Why won't anybody just listen to me" I cried at her. She reassured me she would get me a counsellor who I could talk to, but she never did this. Instead, she broke my confidence even more by telling my mum everything I had said.

These authorities who are meant to be professionals, taught me to trust no one. The lies they made up made life that so much harder on top of having separate parents. That alone is difficult. But no, they obviously felt I deserved more punishment. For what again? What DID I do wrong? Why did the family courts turn everything into such a war? They sent my parents into a courtroom, basically to rip each other to pieces, to choose the best parent. I was caught in the middle every time and I hated this. I felt like I had to choose a side to be on, but I needed both of my parents, like every child does, and people broke my heart denying me that. Quite often I wanted to die. As much as I loved my brothers, my mum, my Dad, I felt like I was the one hurting them and if I wasn't there anymore they would have no reason to go to court. I couldn't see any other way out. I wanted to be with my Dad. I needed to be. It wasn't a feeling I could control. He was my Dad. What was so wrong with that?

In 2008, he got sent to prison for campaigning with Fathers 4 Justice, for loving me, his own daughter. His involvement with Fathers 4 Justice caused him to do extreme things. But you have got to understand that they were in extreme circumstances and in the hell of the family courts, you are not heard unless you make it impossible to be ignored. Did they really think sending him to prison would make him give up fighting for me? This is clearly what they wanted. He was just a father desperate to see his daughter, not the criminal he was labelled as. But this is the sacrifice my Dad had to make, and I am so proud of him for doing this for me. If he hadn't, I doubt we'd be together now.

I remember being told the news. I was at my mums, and I cried and cried. How could those sick, twisted people possibly have the reason to lock my Dad away? All my life, I had been invisible through their pay cheques and business cards, and now it had come to this -my Dad in prison. I spent the rest of my evening on our sofa crying, in a very awkward situation as I hardly even spoke of my Dad, so this was a big thing to be crying in front of my mum over him.

I have two older brothers, Ben and David. We all have different Dads. I never spoke to them about it; after all, they were in my mum's side of my

276

life, so my Dad wasn't. That evening, they both came home from work to find me crying on the sofa.

After finding out why, Ben swore a couple of times, marched into the kitchen and slammed the door. David came home, gave me a hug, said nothing, and went to his room. Because of all our childhood complications, I knew it was awkward and I could understand that it was difficult for my brothers to comfort me in the situation, but it really opened my eyes to how divided my family was. I knew we all loved each other very much, but our relationships were complicated.

Whilst in prison, my Dad missed my 10th birthday, my piano exam, and our weekends together. This broke me that little bit more, stole another bit of hope that this could all just be over. I couldn't believe it was happening, still! How dare they deny me my father? How dare they not listen to me when they all say they work in "the child's best interests"!

Months later, after my Dad was out of prison and more court hearings were going on, another CAFCASS officer came from London to look into my family. I stressed for ages over my room at my Dads. I was so worried how he would judge it. I just wanted it to be perfect, so he could find no reason to separate us anymore. I tidied a shelf of pencils, books and teddies; neat, ordered and straight. I'd stare at it then worry that he'd think that my belongings were too neat, so that I wasn't comfortable at our house. I knew their tricks, and as a child, I should not have had the stress of this. I knew they all had ulterior motives behind their kind words and sympathetic smiles… Suddenly, I'd panic and mess it up to try and make it look more natural. That stupid shelf niggled away at me for days. I was so nervous when he came. Just that mere hour or so would mean so much. He would decide what was to be done with my life – again, MY LIFE, in the hands of some alien person.

In our interview at school, I made sure I made my feelings extremely clear. If he didn't listen, I would run away. I couldn't take it anymore. At age 5, they ignored me. But now, age 10, I would show him that I was not a child to be manipulated into their controlling, unjust and damaging games. I had a Dad, and I deserved to be with him. For the first time, I would force them to listen.

However, it should not have taken this. I should not have needed to threaten to run away to get a voice.

In the following months, days at court began to have positive outcomes.

277

Things were finally changing, and slowly, it finished. In the summer of 2009, I was granted shared care and shared residency with my Dad. EQUAL.

It was amazing. I almost couldn't believe it was over. It was how it should have been from the start.

But 9 years?! It took 9 years to win my Dad. They robbed 9 years of my life.

After, my parents seemed to get on almost as if nothing had happened which confirmed how much of a set up the whole thing had been. The lies and other excuses had been only as a kind of ammunition to defeat my Dad and make him look bad – not fit to be my parent. It was what my mum's solicitors told her to do. My parents were encouraged to make cases against each other – the courts made the fight.

What a waste of time. What unnecessary pain. At home my Dad has about 3 suitcases of paperwork. Was that in the interest of me?... or were people just making money out of me?

Nine years of precious time, I will never get back with my Dad. Government has lost its humanity: everything is about money and power and they'll abuse our human rights until they have this. Abusers like CAFCASS, who say they work in the 'child's best interests'; yet have no evidence to support this claim. Ofsted reports have repeatedly found the service to be inadequate.

An agency such as the CSA is meant to financially support children, but had no concern for me when they took my Dad's driving licence away. This is even people such as the police who left me hurt and ignored, like everyone else.

Their aims are united: government services are breaking families in order to destroy society to gain control and build the economy. Family breakdown costs the taxpayer £44billion every year. Dividing families results in two cars, two houses and two sets of bills. The government does this because 'happy families' make no money for them. Imagine the mass money made from the gruelling process of the family courts: counsellors, social workers, barristers, solicitors… All fuelling the cycle to weaken the people, creating higher demand for such professions.

Did you know that one in three children is without their father? Across the western world, families are being broken by government and family courts. Laws have been continually made to remove fathers legally, emotionally and biologically. We are left with a generation of fatherless families.

After separation, 93% of the time, children live with their mother by reason of gender. Domestic abuse is a major weapon used. In my case, my Dad buying the bigger packet of cornflakes rather than the smaller, more expensive one my mum wanted, was used against him as abuse. Petty, insignificant things like this separate good, loving fathers from their families every day. If a mother turns up to court crying, she has been emotionally abused. Alternatively, if a father brings proof of depression in counselling reports, doctor's notes; his plea is twisted as a weakness and is deemed unable to cope. I cannot emphasise enough, how biased our so called 'justice system' is.

Family courts are corrupt. They fill our societies with a generation damaged and hurt, unveiling crime, and chaos onto our streets. Prisons are swelling with young offenders, 70% of which come from lone-parents families. Fathers develop children's confidence, self-control and self-esteem. Without this, how do you expect them to behave? Fatherless boys are twice as likely to be excluded from school and girls 2.5 times more likely to become pregnant as teenagers. And government pushes 200 children a day through court battles where they are torn between their parents, just like I was.

I would cry myself to sleep, sometimes even unaware of why I was feeling so broken. There is so much I can't remember, as a child, which I blocked out, but the feelings and the emotions stay.

I was told that I was important yet nobody listened to me. I was told that my feelings mattered yet my screaming voice was silent. I loved my Dad and wanted to be with him yet I was treated as though I did not deserve a father. Their lies have gutted me.

I have written letters asking those responsible why they broke my family: CAFCASS, CSA, and to judge David Tyzack but nobody cares. I have even been threatened with harassment by my own police service for writing to the judge and even after all the trouble he caused my family. Even the NSPCC are protecting the corrupt government that is abusing so many children.

So, this is why I started Children 4 Justice, and is why I'm not giving up. I want to end the abuse on children in the family courts. I have decided to use my experience. Fight back. Give children the voice I never had. Thank you."

R.S.

The cynical amongst you will say that words have been put into Rosy's mouth. Indeed she has gained some of her facts from others, but she asked for those facts so that she could speak with wider knowledge. I have met Rosy and she is a most determined, intelligent and erudite young lady. Not only did the system pick on the wrong man in her father, it picked on the wrong child!

I met Rosy when we demonstrated outside Judge Tyzak's house in Devon in May 2013. Talking of him, I regard him as a bully (like many Family Court judges) and like all bullies, he is a coward as well. Fancy, threatening a child with claims of 'harassment' for simply seeking answers! Of course, he has no answers. He splits up families simply because that's what he does, and because he can, like so many Family Court judges. He actually told Jolly that if he wore a suit in court (rather than the informal attire Jolly feels most comfortable in), he would have regarded Jolly as a better father and he'd grant more generous access!!

As for CAFCASS and the CSA, as with social services - they never 'comment on individual cases'. Much easier not to, of course. Rosy has never had a reply to her letters to CAFCASS or to the NSPCC, they simply cannot reply to a child seeking answers. I give my word - this is the TRUE voice of the child. It's unfamiliar simply because, in the Family Courts, you've never heard it before, unless it happens to coincide with what CAFCASS officers want to hear. Rosy mentioned showing emotion in Court. I certainly found that if I didn't show emotion, I obviously didn't care. If I showed emotion, then I was unstable. Catch 22 in the Family Courts.

2 NATASHA PHILIPS

There is another current atrocity, the well-known case (well-known because of the nation-wide outrage it caused), of little Ashya King, who was desperately ill with a form of cancer and whose parents 'abducted' him from Southampton Hospital because the treatment they considered he needed was not available in England on the NHS; but it was in Poland. They fled with him to Spain, where they owned an apartment, and were arrested there, Ashya going into a Hospital there. Eventually the authorities relented (only, I believe, because of the outrage here and in Spain) and Ashya and his parents flew to Prague.

I'll let Natasha Phillips, from the Researching Reform website, take up the story. This piece appeared on the site and I repeat it here with her enthusiastic permission. Natasha is a single mother of one son. She trained as a barrister, but still was appalled at the adversarial nature of the Family Courts when it came to her own divorce and the unnecessary conflict it engendered and distress it caused all who were involved, including her child. She has served on the All Party Parliamentary Group on Family Law and The Court of Protection and still works with them as a consultant as well as doing pro-bono work for mothers and fathers, collaborating with Charities and organisations and organising events on Family Law and the Justice system. The piece below was written at the end of September 2014.

Natasha Phillips:

'....*poor communication, hostility to new ideas, a defensive response to the family. . .stems from a system that behaves more like a vulnerable person than a professional service provider'.*

The moment we thought would come, has done so. During the time that the Kings were reunited with their son, who was diagnosed with a form of cancer in need of urgent treatment, and who subsequently went without the love and support of his parents for three days, in a foreign hospital on his own, because authorities deemed it necessary to arrest and detain his parents without just cause, we spoke to the BBC about why we felt the story was far from over. And we spoke of why the actions of the professionals involved carried all the hallmarks of something rather less palatable than genuine concern for a little boy's wellbeing.

Ashya King cried like a wounded animal, we are told, until his parents were returned to his bedside. We now know that the Kings were threatened with the removal of their child, off the back of them wishing to explore other alternatives to the treatment on offer. Treatment which would leave their son with disabilities for the rest of his life.

The Kings detailed how one doctor told them that if they did not allow the hospital to treat Ashya, they would seek to remove their parental rights and go ahead with the treatment anyway.

The case will sound eerily familiar to anyone who works inside the child welfare sector. It carries all the hallmarks of a system gone rogue, unmanageable due to its sheer lumbering size, disjointed arms and resource-strapped quarters, not to mention an ever-falling standard of care.

In the interviews in which we spoke about the case, we explained (despite some scepticism by interviewers), that the King's ordeal sounded very much like the situations many of the families we assist find themselves in - desperate to do the best for their children, but constantly thwarted at every turn by an ultra defensive system which seems to breed a stronger strain of God-Complex, every day. Professional arrogance in this case, of which it has become apparent was a feature, is simply a symptom of a system manned by people under pressure, who often also happen to be not terribly good at the service they are supposed to be providing.

The hallmarks we identified were poor communication, hostility to new ideas and a defensive response to the family, which stems from a system that behaves more like a vulnerable person than a professional service provider. This is when families begin to take matters into their own hands, with many choosing to leave the country, looking for protection and better care, elsewhere. And who can blame them?

None of this excuses, of course, putting a child's welfare on the line. The system needs to regroup and remember why it is there in the first place. It can no longer run roughshod over families and children, the stakes are too high.

As for Ashya King's current treatment that the hospital in England wished to deny him, it has so far been very successful, and the Kings are delighted with Ashya's progress.

N.P.

Since this was written, Ashya is out of hospital and doing very well. The NHS has also agreed to fund the treatment.

Notwithstanding this, I am hoping the Kings sue for wrongful arrest. If any justice remains in this country, they should win. The conduct of Social Services make them certainly deserve the initials 'SS'.

3 <u>VICKY HAIGH</u>:

Vicky is fairly high-profile, having been mentioned in Parliament after she lost custody of her daughter, hers was a very controversial case. She is now in hiding after threats were made by the Social Services to take her second child away. Both mother and child are very well, of course. Vicky is currently investigating the culture of state-sanctioned child abuse and is probing into some very dark corners.

Vicky wrote this as a speech to be given at a Conference held by the charity 'Children Screaming to be Heard' in 2014. She dared not set foot in Britain for fear of being arrested, so this was read out for her by the campaigning journalist Sue Reid from the Daily Mail.

<u>Vicky Haigh:</u>

'Would you disagree with me that this country has a serious child protection malfunction? No child is safe in the U.K. and the biggest predator of our children is the State itself'.

I often wonder how successive governments have managed for many years to keep secret what many of us know is happening and what some journalists are now reporting on a regular basis - despite the threat of being gagged and imprisoned for doing so.

Parents and children are left devastated when the State steal their children for no good reason. I had no idea what was happening - and would not have believed such a thing - until it happened to me, and my child was stolen.

I have lost count of the times that I have been in a family court, a criminal court, a police cell, a prison cell or the times that I have been arrested by the police.

I am not a criminal - I am a mother trying to protect my child from the hands of someone whom I believe - because of what my child has told me as well as social workers and the police - is a sexual predator.

Now I realise that that child not only needed to be protected from that predator but from the Government and its many agencies which claim to protect children, but in fact are part of a hugely corrupt money-making industry.

Would you disagree with me that this country has a serious child protection malfunction? No child is safe in the U.K. and the biggest predator of our children is the State itself. [No-one could honestly think otherwise after Rotherham and Oxford. Roger].

While the police, the media, lawyers, the NSPCC, and other so-called child protection charities rake up historical paedophilia cases with links right to the heart of the establishment in the seventies and eighties, no-one is admitting the truth: that there is a strong link between today's paedophiles and the systematic snatching of children for forced adoption, forced fostering, and into the shamefully bad care system.

There have also been many cases of child sexual abuse in foster and adoption families, meanwhile one in five adoptions break down (only for the unwanted child to be thrown into the care system where sex abuse is rife too).

We know that the care system has already been infiltrated by paedophiles. Look at the south Asian sex gangs of our northern towns: who do you think these men were targeting? Yes, under-age girls, taken forcibly from their families, and put in the care system.

You cannot make the police prosecute a crime of paedophilia if they do not want to. Look at the cases of Cyril Smith and Jimmy Savile, they escaped prosecution for years. The police had an abundance of intelligence on these criminals yet did nothing.

We are seeing that the prison sentences given for paedophiles in our courts are laughable, that is when they are actually prosecuted by the police. Why?

I can speak about prison sentences as I have experience of these. I am a woman, a mother of two young and beautiful daughters.

After the secret family courts stole my eldest daughter in cold blood from me (claiming I had brainwashed her into making up stories about sex attacks on her) I investigated the big picture.

After campaigning to highlight our plight, I thought someone from the government would soon step in and overturn illogical injustice. I was sure about that.

What actually happened was the opposite. It was me they put injunctions on to silence me, it was me they bullied and blackmailed and it was ME

285

they put in prison. I realised I had made a very powerful enemy and I was intrigued to find out more.

The UK child care system is riddled with corruption. If you report the sexual abuse of your child or support your child who tells the authorities that he or she has been sexually abused by a family member, if you allow your child to have medical examinations at the request of the authorities, IT IS YOU THAT IS ACCUSED OF EMOTIONALLY HARMING THAT CHILD.

Corrupt as it may sound, the UK Government seem to have an allegiance with child sex abusers and not the parent trying to protect the child. Why?

You will all be hearing this in disbelief, apart from the parents who have blown the whistle on child abusers and found, as a result, that it is their own children who have been taken away, some given to an abuser, and others put into the care system.

The judges are allowing draconian removal orders that are against the Human Rights of parents and that are against the U.N. Convention Rights of a Child and they are getting away with it.

Our Government is not interested in our cries for help. How can it be that I have not been allowed to see or contact my own child for almost four years? What is my wrongdoing?

Can anyone imagine what this must feel like for a mother and her child? This is happening to many others in the U.K. today.

Why are many Family Court judges the patrons and directors of adoption and foster agencies? Why are so-called medical and social work 'experts' who get thousands of pounds for producing 'independent' reports on removal of children for the Family Courts, on the adoption and foster agency payrolls too? This is corruption.

So many working in the so-called child protection industry are responsible for taking away and trafficking our children through the U.K. care system. Some former social workers have set up companies to adopt and foster children. To make money from this they must have children; lots of them.

Is this why so many children are being stolen from their families? Is this why the courts are secret - with parents and journalists being told they will go to prison for contempt if they publicise what is going on there?

These are questions we need answering and answering quickly.

Mothers and fathers are being inhumanely separated from their children through no fault of their own, but because of the greed and corruption of individuals in the so-called child protection industry from judges to social workers, the court experts to adoption agency bosses.

When I protested about what was happening, I was told by my barrister from a chambers in Leeds after she lost my case (which I now realise was fixed) 'That is the system, what are you going to do about it? Start a revolution?'

I was actually being told that the system worked on the basis that if you report abuse of your child, your child could be taken into care or given to the alleged abuser.

Serious crimes against children are being hidden and covered-up in these courts.

I struggled to believe my barrister was actually informing me that it was no mistake that I lost my daughter, but it was by design even though she knew I was innocent.

Surely this barrister needs arresting and charged with extortion. She is using public money to assist case-fixing in a U.K. court. She knew that I would be gagged by Doncaster Council and that she would get away with her crimes. If the police are interested in interviewing her I can give them her name, in fact I can give them a whole list of names of the people who are corrupting further an already cruel, callous and broken system.

Which leads me to the question of who is actually protecting the child? Certainly not the State, as we are seeing more and more evidence that the State is damaging the young children of this country and blocking the parents from protecting them, using legal means and the threat of prison if necessary.

So my barrister's advice on starting a revolution was probably the only good bit of advice she gave to me.

I see that CAFCASS, the organisation that is costing the taxpayer billions of pounds a year, had a conference recently when it was stated it was the 'voice of the child' in these secret courts.

It is not the voice of the child at all and their officials routinely go against the wishes of the child, pushing that child into care, or assisting the Local Authority in obtaining the care order. This would be called child trafficking in any other country.

Let the public see all the complaints regarding CAFCASS, let them see my complaints. There are some very unsavoury CAFCASS officers out there with powers they are using corruptly.

I an give an example of what my daughter's CAFCASS officer wrote in his statement for the secret court. I quote: 'If X says she has been sexually abused in the future, we have to tell her that she has not'.

Can you imagine anything worse for my child who was screaming to be heard? How dangerous is this CAFCASS officer and how can he be the voice of a child? He needs striking off, not the prospect of retiring with a healthy pension paid for by us. Again if the police are interested in this man covering up crimes against a child I can pass his name on.

Why are local authorities being encouraged to take away children who are happy with their loving families?

Are innocent parents like me being used to create more business?

And who are looking after these hundreds and thousands of children, even babies, when they are removed without reason?

Would it be any surprise if paedophile rings are operating within this secretive system?

I have smelt a rat for a long time and I want the Government to tell us what the hell is going on here. Why, in particular, are children snatched and then put to live with paedophiles who they say have abused them?

The secret family court and social service system is a child-sex predator's playground. How many paedophiles are involved in this racket? How they must laugh when they watch yet another child being stolen from an innocent parent and put in the care or fostering system. Paedophiles have been known to wait years to get on the adoption list so they can get hold of a child, yet nothing is done.

Apart from the fears about paedophilia, you will see that it is routine for a mother (like me) who raises the alarm to be castigated and the person accused of sexual abuse to get the prize - the child.

Babies are being stolen at birth from innocent mothers who are accused of having the potential to 'emotionally harm' the child when they are older, even by shouting at them as a teenager in some distant future. By widening the pit, so many fall into it, and more children are removed. There is not a child caught up in the UK care system that is not being emotionally abused by the state.

Sir James Munby [head of the Family Court Division in the High Court] is making plans to open up the Family Court to the public. Well, I am asking Sir James not to just make noises, but to remove ALL the reporting restriction orders and super-injunctions that have been placed on parents in these family courts.

I want to see Sir James not only talk about opening up the courts, but doing so - so that what happens there can be reported, with names of the parents published if those parents wish (as many do).

Let the public see exactly what is happening to innocent parents and children under the spurious mantra of the 'best interests' of the child - a term first used by Hitler in Nazi Germany.

If I can get a message across to you all, it is this:

WE HAVE TO CHANGE THIS SYSTEM TODAY, WE CANNOT LET THIS CARRY ON INTO THE NEXT GENERATION WHERE OUR OWN CHILDREN WILL LIVE IN FEAR OF HAVING THEIR CHILDREN TAKEN BY A CORRUPT AND INHUMANE GOVERNMENT.

Insider trading is illegal but I have serious concerns that the same is going on in the adoption and fostering industries.

I always say that when there is corruption, you only need to follow the money to find the perpetrators of the corruption.

I AM, THEREFORE, ASKING THESE TEN QUESTIONS OF THE GOVERNMENT;

1)We need a public enquiry and disclosure from our government on how many state workers hold conflicting directorships. When will this happen?

2) Why are family courts holding child sex abuse cases behind a wall of secrecy where family evidence means nothing and every child taken means payments to lawyers, social workers, adoption agencies, and foster carers?

3). This is a criminal matter and why does the Government not take action to stop it?

4). MOSAC which stands for Mothers of Sexually Abused Children, is a government-funded organisation. Yet we are not allowed to know the horrendous statistics that it has collected on incest and abuse within the care system. Why are they secret?

5). Why are we being punished by having our children taken from us when we have committed no crime against them?

6). We want non-molestation orders used correctly and not placed on innocent parents when the councils have stolen their children. How many orders of this nature are there?

7). Why is perjury and case-fixing by social workers, lawyers and judges happening every day in those secret courts? And why is the Government ignoring it and not prosecuting them?

8). Why are our children who are screaming to be heard not being listened to in line with the UN convention 'Rights of a Child'?

9). We want the gagging orders on all parents lifted and we demand our right to protest re-instated without sending us to prison. Why are parents who have been wronged by the State then gagged to stop them revealing the ghastly truth?

10). I am a mother with a duty to protect my child who says she has been abused and I want this Government to tell me why it is not letting me do this?

These are legitimate questions and we have a right to know the answers.

V.H.

4 HILARY LAWSON

My next contributor is my long-time friend Hilary, I can't believe I've known her for fifty years. She is the youngest daughter of Mr. Bocking who was Minister at Harrow Congregational Church and his wife, and we've always kept in touch. Hilary has three children of her own by her former husband, and has a new partner now who she supported in Court in 2014 at Truro, Cornwall. I'll let her take up the story.

Hilary Lawson

'Why was the resident parent completely believed without the blink of an eye, but the non-resident parent almost needed to have every witness to every action lined-up outside the court just to prove he was telling the truth?'

Parental Alienation or 'my parents are aliens' was the closest I had got to this subject before 2013! A Dictionary definition clarifies that Parental alienation is when 'a child expresses unjustified hatred or an unreasonably strong dislike of one parent making access by the rejected parent virtually impossible' (on line dictionary Farlex 2014)

I have to honestly say that I did not know until the end of 2013, when my partner decided to seek legal advice to gain the already ordered contact with his daughters, that there was such a thing as parental alienation, and that it is written about and researched so widely. Unfortunately to our disadvantage this is not recognised by some judges who believe it is their right to ignore obvious actions of parental alienation in one parent to the detriment of the child losing the other parent, due to the child's developed fear of upsetting the resident one.

Having been a divorced parent of three myself I can see how 'easy' it is to force your ideas about the non-resident parent on your children, but then hopefully sanity ensues and the realisation that the child is the innocent party here, and they need to be supported and cherished to ensure that they are able to make up their own minds about either parent, whether they be resident or non-resident, in their own time. Remembering that a parent's divorce is enough to upset a child, regardless of the reasons behind it, surely we then owe it to that child, if there are no legal reasons why not, to support them to see the non-resident parent as much as possible, nurturing those relationships so they grow emotionally and physically with support from both parents. Also remembering that children can be manipulative when they see that parents are warring and wish to score points with the children, almost forcing those children to take sides to endure the changes to their home life.

Parental alienation or its 'syndrome' as some prefer to call it, has numerous signs. The first question that anyone, especially a judge if it goes to court, should ask is: "Why should children who were initially close to both parents, suddenly seek to reject one of them?" **(Lowenstein 2005).**Also when the non-resident parent has made concerted efforts to see his or her children, following their requests to visit, outings, gifts, help with homework and visits to school trips, that this should suddenly be thrown back in their face, for no valid reason when looked at objectively. For a Judge to immediately take the side of the resident parent and refer back to evidence which was thrown out as 'lies' by a previous Judge; when evidence of parental alienation is staring him in the face, is beyond my belief! But that is what happened to my partner in Truro Court. For the evidence to be laid before him, you would have thought that children are not always clear in their thoughts. Suddenly for a child to state that they don't want to see the non-resident parent because it suits on that day, and supports what the resident parent wants!

How many times were we told to do something we did not 'like' when we were younger, that did not hurt us, should we also just let children make the rules and not give them boundaries? Surely as a parent we should be guiding them to respect elders that have not hurt them, and protect them from those that can harm them. With this in mind surely the parent causing the alienation is causing harm, psychologically and emotionally to their children? Something the judge who my partner had to face was clearly not considering, or even had thought to enter it into his 'legal' brain.

When a child repeats events that happened when they clearly could not have remembered them without input from the parent or their family, why does that not ring alarm bells to those supporting decisions that will affect a child long term, and the parent who wishes to support them? Where is the duty of care by the social workers and Judge to not question why the child is repeating things that they could not possibly have remembered without being told again and again and implied to be important? Why do Judges not ask positive factors from the children 'what did you enjoy about being with your Dad? How about the outings and trips, walks, help with school work and projects, having fun on the beach?' to make this an even 'playing field' for both parents.

We all fall out with our parents and family members but this is a part of growing up. Parental Alienation forces these normal events to become actions that get taken to court for a judge and social worker to preside over, deciding what is apparently in the best interests of the child. But when the Judge says that Sir James Munby may well be 'advising' but he can make his own decisions regardless, what hope has one parent against the other who is clearly showing signs of parental alienation syndrome, to the detriment of the children stuck in the middle?

When in court my partner was asked by the judge to show examples of parental alienation. Being naive we believed that the Judge would have had the foresight to have read all the evidence we had put forward, of blocked letters, stalled visits, children being late at collection times, unkempt children, refusing to contact their paternal grandmother on her 80th birthday. How cruel is it to stop grandchildren from seeing or keeping in contact with their grandmother who does not live nearby and is only able to see them if they come to her? Why did he have to prove it any further when it was staring the judge in the face? Why was the resident parent completely believed without a blink of an eye, but the non-resident parent almost needed to have had every witness for every action lined up outside the court doors just to prove he was telling the truth?

All his evidence was factual and clearly not embellished yet the Judge seemed to be more comfortable with 'evidence' from ten years ago, that had been proved to be mainly fantasy by his colleague of the time, a Judge who proved that he had looked at all sides and had worked in the best interests of the children, so that they had enjoyed a good relationship with their father since that time. But this judge seemed to be looking for an easy life, perhaps he knows the resident parent well....? My partner was having to come to a different county to prove that he was a trustworthy parent, where life seemed to us to be a closed shop in professional circles.

At the initial court hearing the judge advised my partner to gain an enforcement order of the original ruling to ensure he could use this at the final hearing, but then this Judge chose to ignore it totally in favour of the resident parent. If we had known that the truth would not be seen as evidence perhaps we should have had every neighbour, friend and family member who had witnessed the positive relationship between their father and the children, away from their mother's influence, to turn up to court to prove that parental alienation was occurring? The judge also believed the mother when she mentioned that she thought that my partner was having an affair with a member of her family who had chaperoned him early on with the children.

There was no evidence of this but this judge sided with the resident parent (mother) stating that the witness would have come to support her statement if this was not the case!! I at this point really doubted his sanity and legal standing.

By allowing children to alienate a parent, they not only stop the child having emotional and psychological support from that parent but also from that parent's family, cousins, grandparents etc, missing events and occasions that can never be repeated especially as grandparents age.

Parental alienation needs to be recognised in court and also specifically by the social workers who are given the role of providing those biased reports that can affect the lives of those children for life, without giving a second thought to the heartache it also causes to the non-resident parent. Social workers who are not independent and therefore are not objective give reports that are totally biased.

We discovered that they did not even ask the children about the positive times with their dad, but were 'hoodwinked' through parental alienation to believe all the negative factors and angst that the resident parent was putting on the children through her beliefs. Where is the duty of care by social workers to recognise parental alienation, by looking at facts from all sides to protect the emotional and psychological well-being of children? If they do not recognise parental alienation and the harm it does, they are failing in their duty to safeguard the children and are responsible for supporting the alienation causing irreparable damage to family relationships and the emotional development of the children they have been put there to protect.

Ten years ago my partner had had a brilliant social worker from CAFCASS who did safeguard the interests of the children and saw through the alienation and embellishments made by the mother, it is a scandal there are not more of these.

The area in which the children now live and where my partner had to attend court in 2014 is in an area where it is not clear who the children's safeguarding lead for health and social care is. This puts in doubt as to where the safeguarding boards to support children from emotional and psychological harm are, where professionals are making up their own rules and not recognising the national calls for changes to Children's courts and the recognition of parental alienation. Is it easier not to see what is front of your nose? Yes, if it means facing the demon and questioning practice. Is Cornwall to remain in the dark ages where family courts are concerned?

Surely a caring mother would only being doing what is right for her children?? Until this is questioned and not presumed, fathers or non-resident parents will always be the 'poor relation' with regard to being believed, and parental alienation will be the winner, not the child.

H.L.

I'd like to think that things had changed even a little since my ordeal in Oxford, but obviously they have not. Though the way the Family Courts operate is so blatantly wrong, even obvious to Government, they are so insular, so secretive, and so defensive, it has been almost impossible to get even modest reforms through. Sir James Munby, now head of the Family Division in the High Court, has pressed for the Family Courts to become 'open' - but in reality he hasn't achieved much yet, and in fact he doesn't have any power to - he can only advise. And, indeed, Sir James was the Judge who sent my friend Mark Harris to prison in March 2001 for waving to his kids.

He must have had a Damascene conversion since then, with the bright light of humanity and commonsense shifting the dark gloom of secrecy and injustice.

Miracles do happen. Only he hasn't the power to make the courts 'open'. (It's Parliament that has to do this). Gives him good publicity, though, and what he is saying is so patently right that only certain Family Court Judges would ignore it. Like that one in Truro.

5. PAM WILSON

When couples split up and cannot agree over the children, the Grandparents are seldom considered, even if they have had an active role in the children's lives. In law, they continue to have no rights at all and have to seek leave of the Court for any access or involvement. This has caused many grandparents (and, no doubt, children) great hurt and distress, as leave is not automatically granted. I am privileged to have known Pam Wilson, the chair and founder of the Grandparents Action Group, for some years now. This group has campaigned for over twelve years for a right in law for Grandparents to see their grandchildren. I am very pleased that she has agreed to contribute her thoughts in this chapter.

Pamela Wilson:

'Grandparents are a link to the past and a bridge to the future. . . . .children need all their family to form bonds with them which promotes stability, security, protection and love. . . .'

The family should be a vital foundation, raising children in a loving, caring environment. A foundation that this country has always been proud of through the generations. However, many families today are fragmented as a direct result of the separation of parents: families are breaking up and the power struggles that often ensue are damaging to all of us. The biggest casualties are the children; when parents separate, the balance of power lies in the majority of cases with the mother; fathers are very often denied contact and this then impacts on the paternal grandparents. Whether paternal or maternal, grandparents have NO automatic rights to contact with their grandchildren: they have to ask for 'leave to apply' for a contact order at Court. This can be very expensive and time consuming. If the resident parent refuses to allow contact, the child or children will be denied contact with grandparents and the extended family, losing their right to a family life. How does this benefit children? To be deprived of the love, care and support that is the purpose and function of the family? Many non-resident parents - usually fathers - lose all contact within two years.

Grandparents are a link to the past and a bridge to the future, for family history and for medical details. Children need all their family to form bonds with them which promotes stability, security, protection and love, this in turn helps children to grow and develop into confident and responsible adults. It has long been the role of grandparents to provide the values which help achieve the latter. Children ALWAYS suffer when parents separate, even if the relationship has been a stormy one. This is made worse if the children are made a weapon (again, mainly for mothers) to 'punish' the non-resident parent. If a new partner arrives on the scene, the situation is often made worse for the non-resident parent and often for the children as well.

Courts and relevant agencies accept and uphold this awesome imbalance of power and say they are acting in the 'best interests of the child'. Upholding lies and false allegations (with no proof needed - just 'the balance of probabilities')? Perjury, it seems, is acceptable in these circumstances. Why should we allow children to be used in this way when throughout their formative years until the age of seven they are not allowed a voice unless the resident parent agrees? Again, the resident parent can wield the power. If there is a risk to a child a proper investigation would point to it, however, new partners are almost never vetted. Who poses the greater risk? All the reports show a child is at greater risk from boyfriends and live-in lovers than they are from their natural parents.

Grandparents (classed as non-relative!) have to prove themselves worthy, to have contact with their grandchildren. There has to be a fundamental change in this system that allows families to be destroyed by a lack of proper and much-needed legislation. Our children are our future. They live what they learn from us. Is this why we have the highest level of teenage pregnancies in Europe, a growing culture of single-parent families with fathers often sidelined and not encouraged to be part of the family unit? And why children in the UK are the unhappiest children in Europe according to UNICEF? Is this to be the way forward for the next generation? Shared parental responsibility should be the norm, incorporating grandparents and the extended family. Giving equality and fairness in law to this issue would help ensure children grow up with the best chance of being well-adjusted, achieve in education, develop good social skills and benefit all aspects of their lives to help them cope with an ever-changing society.

It seems to me that too many children have to undergo counselling for psychiatric and other emotional problems very often brought on by parents separating, and subsequently being alienated from one parent that they have loved by the resident parent (usually the mother). The conflict can cause continuing difficulties way into adulthood.

As for the Grandparents, being forbidden to see the grandchildren by someone you had welcomed into your family as your son or daughter's partner, and who you have treated with kindness, and tried to help in many ways, the sense of desperate anguish can be overwhelming. The terrible realisation that your grandchildren are being brainwashed, alienated against you with lies and false allegations (Grandma has done, Grandad said), the sense of disbelief that someone you felt was close to you is doing this - you feel you are being punished for loving them and that they are being punished for loving you. Sleepless nights, worrying about the harm this is doing to those children and being powerless to do anything about it. You know this is emotional abuse but no-one seems to care, Social Services will often flatly refuse to accept what you say and all doors are shut in your face. You have no right in law to see them, end of story.

It wasn't the end of the story for me, though. I felt I had to try and challenge this system and I formed the Grandparents Action Group. Before the general election in 2010 I wrote to David Cameron and received assurances that the issue of Grandparents having no right in law to see their Grandchildren would be addressed. I still have the letters from Mr. Cameron and from Tim Loughton who was then shadow Minister for Children, who kindly allowed me to give evidence to their Social Workers Commission.

P.W.

It is now nearly five years since the election and since David Cameron became Prime Minister. There is still no right in law for Grandparents to see their Grandchildren.

APPENDIX 2

LETTERS SENT TO OXFORD COURT IN MY SUPPORT

A selection of letters sent by friends and relatives, which were completely ignored by Judge Payne and not referred to even once. Presented to show that if CAFCASS have made up their mind, nothing will change it and the Judge will act like CAFCASS' poodle.

To whom it may concern.

I have known Roger Crawford for 30 years.

For thirteen of them we lived together very happily.

Since then we have continued to see each other on an almost daily basis and remain on good terms.

The Roger I know is a friendly, upbeat person with an almost childlike enjoyment and appreciation of life.

Since Heather was born he has been steadfast in his love, interest and commitment to her and has always wanted and hoped for a relationship with her.

Dora

(13-03-06)

To whom it may concern,

My Name is SADE ▓▓▓▓▓▓.
AND I WANT everyone to know that
My uncle ROGER is A DiAmond, he has
Bought So much Joy AND happyness
into my FAmily with such genuine love
AND Affection, He's A good role model FOR
my Browthers AND I and we have the
ut most respect FOR him, Heather can
only benefit FRom having him in heR life.
As my FAmily hAve, If only he would Be
given the chance to prove this. Henther
does not Just have a doting fAtheR But Also
hAS A lARGe family who would All love
to be ApArt of heR life, I feel pRivelaged
to hAve him As my uncle AnD wished
I'D OF hAD A DAD like him.

SADE ▓▓▓▓▓.

(niece)

300

6·2·06

To Whom it may concern,
I have known Roger for approx.
six or seven years, he was
adopted at birth so we were not
raised together. Roger took it upon
himself to trace his Birth Parents
and in turn found out that he
had two brothers and three sisters
of which I am one, I myself
have four children. In the time
that I have known him I have
found him to be a very genuine
man, he has a great sense of humour
totally honest and reliable and
he has such a good understanding
of other peoples emotions, since
Roger came into our lives he has
bought us such joy and happiness.

301

I have the greatest respect for the moon. My children do not have their Father in their lives and Roger has become the best male role for them, he is great with all four, always has time for them and takes a genuine interest in each and everyone of them.

I believe that Roger should have the right to have contact with his daughter Heather as he has so much to give to a child, he is a man of good values and morales, also Heather has a large family who would love to be in her life, uncles, aunties, cousins and an elderly grandmother. If only there were more Fathers in this world as determined and driven by the love for a child as Roger is, please allow this man to see his child as I know that given the chance that he deserves

he will benefit Heathers
life and make her a
very happy child. My
daughter who is 16 years old
has made her feelings clear
by stating that she wishes that
she could have a dad like Roger.
I hope that my brother is given
the oppurtunity to be a Daddy and
not just a Father.
                    Pamela Banting.

Dear Heather,

I'm writing this letter because
I feel that family is important and
would love you to be apart of it as I
am your cousin, Because we have never
meet I would like to tell you a bit
About myself, My name is Sade I'm
seventeen the only girl with three
Brouthers, I'm a vegetarian and love
all animals my hobbies are?
horse riding, going to the gym as my
Aim is to be a personal trainer,
cooking, music, fashion, Hair and
Beautey and writing a joornal
what are your hobbies I would love
to know? I have hoped and prayed
that you might consider making
contact with me and yoursipe of
the family though Roger, as he's
such a thoughtful kind caring man
with a lot of love to offer,

he's been a great role modle for
me and my brouthers we all
have the ut most Respect for him
and think you would only benefit
from having him in your life,
And wish I'd of had a dad like
him, you have a large family who
would love to be apart of your
life if you would just give us
the chance, I dont want you
to feel uncomfotable or feel
that I'm trying to tell you what
to do, just want you to know
you can write or call when ever
you like coz were cousins this
is my number and address

All my love sade.

29th November 2005

To whom it may concern

Re: Mr Roger Crawford

My family and I have known Roger since 1963 when my father moved to Harrow to be the minister at the local church.

My memories of Roger are approximately from the age of 8 (1968). Roger was the founder of a youth club, which he instigated as he was aware that there was no focus for young people in the area and by bringing them together in a safe environment he was able to provide guidance and leadership to them. From this involvement with young people, Roger showed his concern for the more disadvantaged amongst them, especially those from the inner cities, who did not have the advantages that we had. Roger founded the charity 'Earthshine' and used a lot of his time, money and energy to convert a coach to take disadvantaged teenagers on holidays to the country, which they had never had before. Throughout this time Rogers's concern for the welfare and well being of these young people was clearly shown to be at the forefront of any projects he was involved in. I have always been aware that Roger was adopted and the importance he put in his family and the openness with which he discussed this with others. In finding his birth mother and the positive affect this has had to his relationship with his birth family, on his recent life, has shown how clearly Roger acknowledges the importance of the support of family in these matters.

I am a nurse, having worked as a Gynaecological ward sister for many years, working with all ages from the teenage years and more recently as a Clinical Governance manager within a Primary Care Trust. I am very aware of the emotional upheaval that is caused in life and the importance of family support, even though birth parents may not be together. I have 3 children aged 15, 13 and 8 years who are very fond of Roger and his wife. I encourage the friendship they have with Roger and would have no hesitation in Roger caring for them at any time, as I know the respect they have for him and him for them.

In all the time I have known Roger he has been a very caring person who always puts his own interests last, especially where young people are concerned, due to his ability to empathise with them, but he will also always stand up for what is right.

Hilary C Lawson

Hilary C Lawson

RECOMMENDED FURTHER READING

Family Court Hell	Mark Harris	Pen Press 2007
Denied Access	David Chick	Pen Press 2006
I want to see my kids!	Tina Rayburn/ Tim Forder	Fusion Press 2007
Fathers 4 Justice - The Inside Story	Matt O'Connor	Weidenfeld & Nicolson 2007
Family Breakdown	Penelope Leach	Unbound 2014
Mummy Where Are You?	Jeanne D'Olivier	Endeavour Press 2015
The Fat of the Land (if you can get a copy)	John Seymour	Faber & Faber 1961 and 1974
The New Complete Book of Self-Sufficiency	John Seymour	Dorling Kindersley 2003
The Farming Ladder	George Henderson	Faber & Faber 1955

And any edition of 'The Land' magazine, an occasional publication about land rights available on subscription from Monkton Wyld Court, Charmouth, Bridport, Dorset DT6 6DQ.

Lightning Source UK Ltd.
Milton Keynes UK
UKOW04f1541200715

255505UK00001B/4/P